"Engaging, substantial, and helpful."

"In this smart rumination . . . for those wres_____
or their church culture that they don't agre_____
sive argument for doubt as a means to save _____ ___rituality and rescue
religion at large . . . will appeal to questioning Christians."

—*Publishers Weekly* (starred review)

"McLaren argues that doubt may be painful, but it's good for us. He then
lays out a developmental process detailing how doubt can drive growth
and, in the end, bring an experience of spiritual harmony. Even better,
his model applies to both religious and nonreligious spirituality."

—*Psychology Today*

"Wait until you see where doubt can lead you and what doubt can teach
you. . . . Personal and gently convincing."

—Kim Shippey, international journalist and former
features editor, *The Christian Science Journal*

"There is a much healthier kind of doubt I suggest you consider. . . . In his
just-published book, *Faith After Doubt,* McLaren made this affirmation."

—Rev. Paul Graves, *The Spokesman-Review*

"In a culture in which the self-appointed gatekeepers of Christianity insist
that faith equals certainty; belief is adherence to an exacting checklist of
principles and politics; and belonging is an insular, exclusive membership, Brian McLaren is a heroic gate-crasher. In *Faith After Doubt,* he
invites us into an honest, vital conversation about the pain and shame
created by inherited certainty, and the powerful usefulness of thought
and doubt."

—Glennon Doyle, #1 *New York Times* bestselling
author of *Love Warrior* and founder of Together Rising

"McLaren gently moves us away from the notion of God as vengeful and
petty, ready to punish those who question and challenge beliefs that no

longer harmonize with their evolving experience and honest understanding. Brian encourages the reader to embrace a deeper, wider, and more authentic faith that doesn't fear doubt but welcomes it as an ally in their spiritual growth."

—Bishop Yvette Flunder, author of *Where the Edge Gathers*

FAITH
AFTER
DOUBT

Also by Brian D. McLaren

Do I Stay Christian?

Cory and the Seventh Story

The Great Spiritual Migration

We Make the Road by Walking

*Why Did Jesus, Moses, the Buddha,
and Mohammed Cross the Road?*

Everything Must Change

The Secret Message of Jesus

A Generous Orthodoxy

The *A New Kind of Christian* trilogy

A New Kind of Christianity

FAITH
AFTER
DOUBT

WHY YOUR BELIEFS
STOPPED WORKING AND
WHAT TO DO ABOUT IT

BRIAN D. MCLAREN

ST. MARTIN'S
ESSENTIALS
NEW YORK

Published in the United States by St. Martin's Essentials, an imprint of St. Martin's Publishing Group

FAITH AFTER DOUBT. Copyright © 2021 by Brian D. McLaren. All rights reserved. Printed in the United States of America. For information, address St. Martin's Publishing Group, 120 Broadway, New York, NY 10271.

www.stmartins.com

Designed by Meryl Sussman Levavi

The Library of Congress has cataloged the hardcover edition as follows:

Names: McLaren, Brian D., 1956– author.
Title: Faith after doubt : why your beliefs stopped working and what to do about it / Brian D. McLaren.
Description: First edition. | New York : St. Martin's Essentials, [2021] | Includes bibliographical references.
Identifiers: LCCN 2020035306 | ISBN 9781250262776 (hardcover) | ISBN 9781250262783 (ebook)
Subjects: LCSH: Faith.
Classification: LCC BT774 .M35 2021 | DDC 234/.23—dc23
LC record available at https://lccn.loc.gov/2020035306

ISBN 978-1-250-82837-8 (trade paperback)

Our books may be purchased in bulk for promotional, educational, or business use. Please contact your local bookseller or the Macmillan Corporate and Premium Sales Department at 1-800-221-7945, extension 5442, or by email at MacmillanSpecialMarkets@macmillan.com.

First St. Martin's Essentials Trade Paperback Edition: 2022

10 9 8 7 6 5 4 3 2

Contents

✼

PART THREE
LIFE AFTER (AND WITH) DOUBT

PREFACE:
PERMISSION TO DOUBT

❧

It was as though he had been hurtling toward this point for weeks, months, maybe even years, but now he had come to an abrupt halt, run out of road.

—J.K. Rowling, *Harry Potter and the Deathly Hallows*

It's Sunday night, and a fourteen-year-old boy named Jordan is lying on his bed, his face buried in his pillow so his family won't hear him cry, his shoulders heaving in long, heavy sobs. He recently joined a youth group at a local megachurch where the handsome young pastor just gave a talk about sin, and especially sexual sin, and most especially "the lifestyle choice of homosexuality, which is never God's best for anyone." Of course, Jordan has never told anyone his secret, the secret he has known since he was twelve. Nor has he ever told anyone his more recent secret, that he has a head-over-heels crush on his youth pastor. At the end of the sermon just a few hours ago, Jordan walked down the aisle and asked to "receive deliverance from lust." The pastor laid hands on him, rebuked the devil, and shouted and shook as he prayed. On and on he prayed, his volume rising, rising, rising, then falling to a whisper. But nothing happened. Nothing. And at this moment, Jordan can't stop thinking about how good it felt to have the pastor's warm hands on his shoulders as he knelt before him. "What's wrong with me, God?" he sobs in his cracking, almost-baritone voice. "Do you even hear me? Why don't you answer my prayer? Why you don't change me? Are you even there? Are you even real?"

It's Monday morning, and across town, Meg, a young pastor of thirty-two in her first appointment, is pacing her office in a Methodist church, back and forth, like a wild animal in a cage. She picks up her phone and begins to make a call but then quickly punches *End*. She begins the call again and again ends it before it rings. The third time, she lets the call go through. "Jack," she says, "it's Meg McDaniel over here at First. I need to tell you something. It's not good news. I think I need to resign." There's a pause as her district superintendent responds, and then Meg replies, "No, no. It's not that. It's that . . . well, I might as well just say it. I think I'm losing my faith. I can't do this anymore. I can't preach things I . . . no longer am sure I believe." She lets out a long sigh and then adds, "There. I said it." There's another pause, as Jack asks a question. "No, no. I still feel my call to ministry. It's just . . . I'm having a problem with certain doctrines . . . you know, hell, atonement, even miracles and prayer, to be honest. And lately, I wonder sometimes if I even believe in God, at least, the Supreme Almighty Father in the creeds."

Fast-forward to Tuesday afternoon, and Sharon, a first-year college student, is taking notes in her Biology 101 lecture hall. The lights are dim as the professor talks through a slide presentation about evolution. Suddenly Sharon's face flushes red, her eyes brim, and her pulse pounds in her ears. Her hands start shaking, and she drops her pen as she holds her hands over her heart, as if to keep its thumping from disturbing her fellow students. "Another panic attack," she thinks. She has been having a lot of them lately, especially in biology and English classes. Her Pentecostal pastor taught her that evolution is a lie from the devil, intended to undermine her faith in a literal six-day creation as taught in the "inspired and inerrant Word o' God." She thinks back to her senior thesis at Victory Christian Academy, which she wrote to disprove evolution. Mr. Hunt, her science teacher, gave her an A, but she can still see the handwritten note at the bottom of the page: "This is well-written and your arguments are well-constructed. But I do hope you'll keep an open mind when you go to college." She showed that note to her parents, they called the principal, and Mr. Hunt was almost fired for advocating "open minds." "Do I dare to do it now?" she asks herself in the dark lecture hall. "Do I dare to open my mind as Mr. Hunt said, even though my faith might escape me forever if I let some new ideas in?" She looks around. Her fellow students seem bored, looking at their phones, a few quietly napping. "How strange that this is just another class for them," she thinks, "but for me, this dark classroom is a spiritual battleground, and I feel I have to choose between opening my mind and saving my soul."

It's Wednesday night, and Evelyn, a real estate agent by day and a lay leader at St. Francis parish by night, is sitting on a metal folding chair beside a plastic folding table in the drafty, poorly lit church basement. Rumors have been swirling for weeks now, but tonight the truth has come out: Father Ron has admitted to a long-term affair with a woman in the church. Evelyn has never told anyone of her own affair with Father Ron several years ago. She remembers Ron's tears as he pleaded with her not to destroy his ministry by revealing their secret. "He's at it again," she thinks. "I wonder who fell for him this time?" She feels ashamed, yes, but another feeling suddenly slides down her neck like a chill: disgust bordering on nausea. "None of this is real," she thinks. "The hymns, the offerings, the sermons, the prayers . . . it's all a front, a facade. This church is Ron's harem. It's Ron's personality cult. It's a chance for Ron to dress up, be the center of attention, and make us all love him and give him power over us. We're all an accessory to Ron's narcissism." She tries to pay attention to the conversation but can't. "I'm through," she whispers to herself. "Through with this whole damned thing." She gathers her things, gets up, and quietly leaves.

On Thursday afternoon, a seminary professor realizes in the middle of a lecture that he used to believe what he taught. Somewhere along the way, though, that changed without him even noticing. His faith evaporated quietly, hardly leaving a trace. In a split second between sentences, he realizes that even though his faith is gone, it doesn't really matter. He's a teacher and this is his subject and he'll still get paid, either way. He doesn't know whether to laugh, cry, curse, or sigh.

At a restaurant on Friday, a nun in her seventies confides to a niece over lunch that she stopped praying years ago. "I just didn't really see the point of it anymore," she says. "God never seems to answer, at least not in the way I was taught."

On Saturday evening at bedtime, an eight-year-old boy asks his mom why it was OK for God to kill all the animals on earth in Noah's flood when they hadn't done anything wrong. His mom thinks, "What's wrong with me that I never asked that question myself?" Suddenly, her whole religious life—the church, Christianity, God, the Bible—seems like an elaborate fairy tale that even a child should see through.

The next morning, another week begins, and in big cities and small villages around the world, a new batch of stories like these unfolds. I know, because for twenty-four years I was a pastor in whom thousands of people confided. And in the fourteen years since leaving the pastorate, thousands more people who have heard me speak or read my books have reached out to me. They write long and anguished letters or emails, full of apologies for taking so much of my time, or they approach me after speaking engagements, daring to trust me with their secret, often with tears. To protect their privacy, I've changed many names and details in this book, and on some occasions, I have combined elements from multiple stories into one. When I have created specific details and dialogue (such as the specific words of a prayer), I have tried to do so in ways that will help readers imaginatively enter the real experiences of others. Of course, that shouldn't be hard for them to do, because many readers will be brimming with stories of their own, full of resonance.

I understand, because I too am a doubter. And I am a believer. And a doubter. Sometimes I flip back and forth five times in one day, and sometimes, I'm both at exactly the same time. My friend Rachel Held Evans has often used a phrase that captures how many of us feel: "On the days when I believe this . . ."*

My first sustained spell of doubt came over me like a fever when I was in high school. I thought I could fight doubt and vanquish it, and it would never return.

Some years later, when wave after wave of doubt kept rolling in, I thought that doubt would vanquish me and my faith would never return.

I felt that I was peeling an onion, layer by layer by layer, and feared that when I was done, there would be nothing left but the burn and sting of tears.

Eventually, I came to realize that doubt was a companion, every bit as resilient and persistent as faith, and she wasn't going away. I realized that

---

* Rachel passed away from a sudden illness not long after I wrote these words. All of us who knew and loved her will always miss her, and we grieve for what this loss will mean to her husband and children, to the faith community at large, and to each of us who found her writings and friendship such a rich source of joy and insight.

she had some things to teach me, and I decided that since I couldn't shut her up or drive her away, I might as well learn from her.

She has turned out to be a tough but effective teacher and a difficult but faithful friend. In this book, I'd like to share some of what I've learned from doubt, starting with this: *you and I don't have to keep our doubts a secret any longer.*

Some people tell me they never have doubts. Faith comes easy for them, they say, at least it has so far. But many, many, many of us do have doubts, and sometimes our doubts seem far more powerful than our beliefs. It's hard enough having doubts; it's impossibly hard to have them and feel you must pretend that you don't.

Right now, let's grant one another permission to doubt. And let's see the doubt in ourselves and each other not as a fault or failure to be ashamed of, but as an inescapable dimension of having faith and being human, and more: as an opportunity for honesty, courage, virtue, and growth, including growth in faith itself.

I promise you: there is faith after doubt, and life after doubt, and life with doubt. If you thought life before doubt was good, wait until you see where doubt can lead you and what doubt can teach you.

You don't have to feel ashamed or be afraid.

INTRODUCTION:
MOMENTS OF TERROR

✤

> Doubt isn't the opposite of faith; it is an element of faith. . . . Sometimes
> I think it is my mission to bring faith to the faithless, and doubt to the
> faithful.
>
> —Paul Tillich

Sometimes, one big issue suddenly pounces on you from behind like a stalking leopard, a marauding bear, a mugger, a killer.

Sometimes, a hundred little questions descend on you gradually like a swarm of mosquitoes at dusk.

And sometimes, like a thousand small charges on a credit card, your doubts drain your faith account so far into the red that it can become frozen.

Sometimes doubt is terrifying. But sometimes, it's—can I say it?—a little bit funny.

I remember a drive home from church thirty years ago when my son Brett was in first or second grade. I asked him, "So how was Sunday school today?" "Oh, Dad," he said, "I don't want to go into it." I asked what the problem was, and he said, "Dad, the teacher tried to tell us that once there was this group of people trying to get away from a big army, and they were trapped between the army and this big sea, and then the water opened up and let them cross, but when the army came through, the water crashed in and drowned them all." His summary was accompanied by a massive eye-roll.

I recognized this as the Exodus story from the Bible, and I realized that Brett had never heard it before, and he apparently didn't think I had ever heard it before either. I could tell by the tone of his voice that he was a little embarrassed by the whole thing.

"So what did you think?" I asked.

"It sounded pretty far-fetched," he replied, shaking his head and rolling his eyes again.

I laughed, first, because I had never heard him use the term *far-fetched* before, second, because I loved his unvarnished honesty, and third, because I was happy he felt free to tell his dad exactly what he thought, even though his dad was also the lead pastor of his church.

Lots of us still don't feel as free as my son to acknowledge that some of our beliefs are kind of hard to believe. We have to wait until we're much older, maybe until a stern grandparent or anxious parent has passed away. Only then can we acknowledge out loud that some part of our inherited belief system feels far-fetched and our beliefs seem like make-believe.

Back in 2011, Richard Rohr wrote a book called *Falling Upward*. Richard, a warmhearted Franciscan brother, Catholic priest, insightful teacher, and bestselling author, is founder of the Center for Action and Contemplation, and I am honored to call him friend, mentor, and colleague. *Falling Upward* resonated with hundreds of thousands of readers because it told a secret that few dare to tell: somewhere in the journey of our lives, the faith we inherited often stops working. We go through a transition period, a period of letting go of many things and holding on to a precious few. To me, the title is perfect, because it simultaneously tells a painful truth and raises a hopeful possibility: the experience of doubt feels like falling, but could it actually be an *upward* fall?

Richard rightly identified how, for many, this faith crisis hits in the middle of life, and I've found that to be especially true among baby boomers and older generational cohorts. But for younger generational cohorts, the tide of doubt seems to flood in at younger and younger ages, suggesting that this epidemic of faith-struggle is more a *stage of faith* than a *stage of life*, reflecting a massive cultural shift that is making traditional beliefs less and less viable for more and more people. If they don't find genuine understanding and intelligent support to face and process their doubts while they're still in the first half of life chronologically, by the second half of life, they'll be long gone from religion and finished with faith for good.

Sixty-five million adults alive in the United States today have already dropped out of active religious attendance, and that number grows by about 2.7 million more every year.* Their reasons for dropping out are complex. Some leave because they begin to doubt God or the Bible or some of the doctrines and practices required by their churches. Many leave because they begin to doubt the church or synagogue or mosque itself as an institution worthy of their trust and support. Whatever the focus of their doubts, at this very moment, hundreds of thousands of people are watching their doubts grow and their religious identity weaken.

You may be one of those people.

If you muster the courage to raise your questions aloud, chances are you will be treated to a menu of facile clichés, unsatisfactory platitudes, or even threats of excommunication in this life and hell after death. If you keep your questions a secret, you may feel increasingly divided, even hypocritical, showing the mask of a happy believer on Sundays but living with a growing inner disillusionment the rest of the week. "Why does faith always feel like pumping water uphill?" you wonder. "Why does it take so much effort to maintain?" You understand why so many people decide to drop out of religion entirely.

The church I served for twenty-four years in the Washington, DC, area was full of people like you. Many were raised Catholic, Methodist, Baptist, Lutheran, Presbyterian, or Pentecostal but dropped out either because their questions were unwelcome or because the church's answers were unsatisfying. But over time, life outside of a faith community was also unsatisfying, so one way or another, they found themselves in our company. Many told me our church was their last hope: if we couldn't help them, they were done with religion forever.

Year after year, these spiritual seekers would come to our church and then get up their courage to make an appointment with the pastor. They would enter my office full of hope and caution, some with long and well-articulated lists of questions and nearly all with a vague but pervasive sense that, on the one hand, their beliefs weren't working for them, but on

---

* See, for example, Josh Packard and Ashleigh Hope, *Church Refugees* (Group, 2015); Josh Packard and Todd Ferguson, "Being Done: Why People Leave the Church, But Not Their Faith," SAGE Journals, September 21, 2018, https://journals.sagepub.com/eprint/jy3gSxWe2iKAtuwkyNwH /full; and Jeremy Myers, "65 Million American Adults Have Left the Church?" redeeminggod .com, https://redeeminggod.com/adults-have-left-the-church/.

the other hand, those beliefs connected them to something real that they couldn't walk away from.

They would leave my office with my best answers, and I would often be left with their toughest questions.

Between their doubts and my own, it's no surprise that I went through my own intense period of faith deconstruction. Doing so is hard for anyone at any time, but doing so while being paid to believe and spread belief can feel like a combination of temptation and torture. It's made all the more difficult when all of one's professional peers are similarly being paid to believe.

I was fortunate: a member of my church leadership team came to me one day and said, "We need to decide if the journey you're on—this journey of rethinking your faith—is just your journey, or if it's our journey too." I begged him not to bring this question up to the leadership team; I was afraid he would precipitate my being fired or half of my board quitting. Thankfully, he did not do what I asked but did what he felt was right, and the whole board responded with a message that brings tears to my eyes decades later as I write these words: *This is not just your journey, but a journey we're on together,* they said. *Please lead us through it. We trust you. And we need you.*

That pivotal moment made it possible for me to remain in the pastorate and explore, question, learn, and grow with this congregation for over two decades. We walked together into the valley of the shadow of doubt, and I wouldn't have survived as a pastor or as a Christian without their companionship.

Since I left the pastorate, I've continued to grapple with my own questions. And I've also kept exploring why this "blessed unrest" is so pervasive in every religious tradition I've encountered. As doubt heats up and as old certitudes seem to melt like glacial ice, I've worked with clergy and denominational leaders to help them respond to the changing religious climate. I've seen firsthand that nearly all church leaders have both newcomers and old-timers coming to them with tough theological questions, and truth be told, nearly all leaders struggle with some doubts of their own.

This book distills forty-plus years of personal struggle, heart-to-heart conversations, and cross-disciplinary research about doubt: why it's unavoidable; why, in fact, it's necessary and valuable; and how to live with it and learn from it.

The research component is significant, because insights from psychologists, neurologists, evolutionary biologists, sociologists, anthropologists, and even political scientists can help us understand the many interrelated dimensions of our doubt. When we bring their research into conversation with theologians and other scholars of religion, everyone has something to learn.

But of course, all this scholarly insight must be put into conversation with down-to-earth stories. Then, we need to translate our best insights into practical guidance that is accessible to normal people who are simply trying to make it through another week without losing faith, without falling into despair, paralysis, complacency, or dishonesty.

I've organized *Faith After Doubt* in three movements. In Part One, *Your Descent into Doubt*, I try to help you understand why your doubts can be so scary and painful. In Part Two, *All in Doubt*, I present doubt not simply as a deterioration process but as a growth process that provides you with an opportunity to mature intellectually, spiritually, morally, and relationally. I base this section on a four-stage theory of faith development that integrates the insights of many major theorists in the fields of human, moral, intellectual, and spiritual development.

In Part Three, *Life After (and with) Doubt*, I turn to the future, exploring how to live with doubt as a companion rather than an enemy on the journey of faith. In the book's final chapters, we'll telescope out to explore how old assumptions are being challenged in nearly every area of human life, not just theology, religion, and spirituality. In this way, we'll see how, by living constructively with doubt, we can contribute to a larger growth process in our faith communities and in the larger human community as a whole.

At the end of each chapter, you'll find a *Reflection and Action* section that offers specific questions, exercises, and practical guidelines to help you engage more deeply with the chapter as an individual or with a small group. At the end of the book, you'll find several appendices offering lists of resources for doubters, including books, podcasts, events, and classes. You'll also find additional suggestions for using the book in group settings.

A few years ago, during a stressful time of exhaustion and transition, I had two very powerful dreams within a few days of each other. Back in those days, I seldom remembered my dreams or took them seriously, but these were so powerful and vivid that they woke me up and I couldn't help but write them down. I felt that some deep part of me that I wasn't listening to in my waking life was trying to get my attention.

In the first dream, I was standing on a beach with the waves crashing in. All around me on the sand were water bottles that were filled not with clean water but with a milky substance that looked like dirty dishwater. People started coming to me from all directions. I handed each one a bottle and told them, "I know this looks like dirty water, but it's actually a special potion that can heal the world's oceans. Please bring a bottle back to your home and pour it into the ocean where you live."

In the second dream, I was again on a beach. Little airplanes kept flying in and landing on the sand. They would drop off canvas bags full of dried corn kernels. I took a long piece of heavy rope and tied it from one bag to another. I then waded into the water. I knew that my job was to swim out to the middle of the ocean, pulling these bags of dried corn behind me, to nourish the sea and feed its fish.

As I reflected on these vivid dreams with the help of a spiritual director and therapist, I was struck that in both dreams, the interconnected oceans of the world were poisoned or undernourished or in some way in trouble. In the first dream, I felt a responsibility to encourage others to play their part, and to offer them an unlikely resource for doing so. In the second dream, I felt my own personal responsibility, that I had to do my part, to swim out into the depths and deliver what I had been given to heal and nourish what was polluted and hungry.

Looking back, I feel that some hidden part of me was acknowledging that something is wrong, dangerously wrong, not just in my religion but in all the interconnected religions of the world. These dreams did not give me a sense of grim pressure or duty but a feeling of purpose, vocation, motivation, and even joy. I awoke with the feeling that people like you and me can play a part in detoxifying and healing our religious traditions, and that doubt can play a surprisingly constructive role.

I know doubt looks like dirty dishwater to many people, and I know that canvas bags of dried corn may not seem like much. But what if our doubts are actually like medicine, like nourishment, and we need them, and so does our world?

PART ONE

Your Descent
into Doubt

🍃

Doubt as Loss

There are recovery programs for people grieving the loss of a parent, sibling, or spouse. You can buy books on how to cope with the death of a beloved pet or work through the anguish of a miscarriage. We speak openly with one another about the bereavement that can accompany a layoff, a move, a diagnosis, or a dream deferred. But no one really teaches you how to grieve the loss of your faith. You're on your own for that. . . . It became increasingly clear that my fellow Christians didn't want to listen to me, or grieve with me, or walk down this frightening road with me. They wanted to fix me. They wanted to wind me up like an old-fashioned toy and send me back to the fold with a painted smile on my face and tiny cymbals in my hands.

—Rachel Held Evans, *Searching for Sunday*

From: Michael Walker
Subject: Greetings From South Florida
Date: January 22, 2019 at 9:53:35 PM EST
To: replies@brianmclaren.net

My name is Michael, and I am a minister for a fundamentalist congregation in Hendry County. Since Fall of last year, I've been reading a lot of Rob Bell, Richard Rohr, and Pete Enns. I've been listening to *The Bible for Normal People*, and I just got to your episode. I heard you mention Lee County, Florida, in your talk, and I just so happen to lead a study there on Tuesday nights each week for a house church. I understand that you are a county over, and I would love to get together with you sometime to talk about some of the things I've been studying recently. You put language to a lot of the things I've been thinking about. I hope to hear from you soon.

Michael Walker

P.S. I'm part of the 81 percent, but since last fall, I have slowly evolved where that is concerned as well.

Over the years, I've received hundreds of emails like Michael's: honest, direct, intelligent, polite, and, underneath the surface, in real pain, if not a little desperate. I respond to some of them on my blog (being careful to protect the authors' privacy), but I receive too many to respond to each one.

Something about Michael's message motivated me to set up an in-person meeting. I suggested a wildlife preserve halfway between us. I've found that sensitive conversations of a spiritual nature often go best outdoors. Sure, coffee shops, living rooms, kitchens, and offices work fine. But there's something about the logic and mystery of wind and water, trees and birdsong, together with the unhurried pace of walking and resting, speaking and listening, that creates just the right setting for conversations about matters of ultimate concern.

So Michael's story poured out under cypress trees and among painted buntings and snowy egrets. He was raised in a small, super-conservative Christian denomination in the Midwest, and at a young age he was identified as an emerging leader. By nineteen he was preaching. By twenty he was a pastor. And by twenty-three, he had been fired and disfellowshipped (or excommunicated) by his congregation.

There had been no sexual misconduct or financial mismanagement, no secret drinking or drug problem, no unsteady work ethic or weakness in his preaching or pastoral care. Nor had Michael denied some central tenet of Christian faith. His fireable offense? He questioned the little church's highly speculative doctrine of how the world will end.

If getting fired and disfellowshipped weren't traumatic enough for a sensitive young man, those who fired and disfellowshipped him included his grandfather and his parents.

He was a newlywed at the time, working hard to finish his bachelor's degree part-time while being employed as a pastor full-time, albeit with a pathetically small part-time salary. Suddenly, he had no salary at all.

What could he do? Was his short ministry career already over?

An older pastor in Florida who was nearing retirement heard through a friend of a friend that a precocious young pastor was available. Soon Michael had an interview and a job offer, and he and his bride were moving south to a town a couple hours northeast from where I live.

The small congregation began growing numerically. The people loved Michael and his wife. All was going well. Except for one thing. Week by week, when he studied the Bible in preparation for his sermons, new questions kept arising. Some things he read in the Bible seemed in tension with what he had always been taught. The more questions he asked, the more new questions arose.

Recent political developments brought additional intensity. Michael wondered if some of his members were more influenced by the Fox News of Rupert Murdoch than the good news of Jesus Christ. Michael only spoke to them during one hour on Sunday, but many of his members watched archconservative cable news pundits for three hours each weeknight, and during the day, they listened to radio talk shows with an identical slant. If Michael's sermon disagreed with the monologue of a media pundit, the pastor, not the pundit, would be assumed to be wrong.

Perhaps if Michael could have suppressed his doubts he would have, but he couldn't. Like a beach ball submerged in a swimming pool, his buoyant bubble of doubt kept popping up.

So he did what any number of budding critical thinkers before him have done: he secretly read books by authors that his tribe didn't approve of. First he read *Velvet Elvis* by my friend Rob Bell, a book that acknowledges the inability of religious language to ever fully capture the depths and richness to which it points. Then he read a book by Richard Rohr, who writes about a spacious "alternative orthodoxy" that seemed far more hospitable than Michael's inherited system of belief. Not long after that, he started listening to a podcast by yet another friend, Pete Enns, a biblical scholar who helps "normal people" have intelligent conversations about the Bible. Now, it wasn't just one esoteric doctrine of the end of the world that Michael was coming to question. It felt like the system of beliefs that he had spent his whole life perfecting was wobbling and perhaps beginning to crumble.

To make matters worse, he was letting some of his questions slip out in his sermons. He couldn't help it. Some people were relieved by his honesty; he was giving them permission to express their own questions and doubts. But predictably, others were suspicious. One fellow in particular seemed to be positioning himself as an antagonist.

What would happen if he lost another job? Could any young pastor survive two firings before the age of thirty? Far more serious, was he on a slippery slope that would land him in hot water (or some other deep or hot substance) with God as well as his congregation?

Only once did I see his eyes brim and only for the briefest moment. But I could tell that behind this young man's clean-cut, well-controlled exterior, deep emotions churned. My heart went out to him.

Truth be told, I saw myself in him.

I too was a child of fundamentalism. I too became a pastor at an impossibly young age and without traditional training. I too faced traumatic early setbacks. And I too wanted nothing more than to grow from a good and faithful boy into a good and faithful man, to follow in the way of my father and mother, my grandfathers and grandmothers. But I too was plagued with a curious mind. When as a young teenager I dared to ask questions and received thoroughly unsatisfactory answers, I remember a terrifying yet liberating thought arising, unbeckoned, from somewhere deep within me: "I'm only fourteen. Four more years and I'll be eighteen, and I can get out of here."

However, not long after that I was ambushed by an unexpected spiritual experience that I'll recount later in this book. In large part because of that experience, I found myself staying within the fold of the faithful. But I quickly moved to the margins of my traditional conservative Evangelical/fundamentalist heritage. When I discovered the Jesus movement and the charismatic movement, I jumped in, a little timidly at first, then more fully, and they provided new spaces to grow. But by my senior year in high school, I had questions for which I could find no answers.

It was an English teacher who helped me. He had formerly been a Jesuit priest, and I could tell that for him, questioning was a good thing. But I also knew that his form of open-minded, open-hearted Christianity would be considered liberal and dangerous by both my fundamentalist elders and my Jesus movement peers. "An open mind is like an open window," one of them warned me. "You need a good screen to keep the bugs out."

By my freshman year of college, my faith crisis was intensifying. Every time I'd run into a Christian friend on campus and he or she would ask, "How are you?" I felt I was plunged into a moral crisis. If I said, "I'm fine. How are you?" I felt like a liar. But if I said, "To tell you the truth, I'm having serious questions about the Bible, about hell, and, increasingly, about the existence of God, and I'm in deep inner turmoil," I knew that prayer groups around campus would soon be praying for me, and people would be "counseling" me if not rebuking me, which would only make my situation worse. Neither option—hiding my truth or speaking it— seemed practical.

Thankfully, I had some friends, all a few years older than me, with whom I could speak freely about my doubts. They introduced me to a whole new library of books by smart writers for whom the phrase *thinking Christian* wasn't an oxymoron. Francis Schaeffer and C. S. Lewis were chief among them. I devoured nearly everything they wrote. Buoyed by their good answers, like young Michael Walker, I was identified as a spiritually precocious young leader and helped lead a church while I was still a college student.

So as Michael's story unfolded, I listened with empathy because it resonated so deeply with my own.

Your path into doubt may be very different from Michael's and mine.

You may be Catholic, and it was the pedophilia scandals that rocked you, or the male hierarchy's obsession with controlling women's bodies, or the sense that the church was more interested in taking offerings than offering help to those in need.

You may be mainline Protestant, and you have been driven to doubt because your church's institutional bureaucracy seems to betray its talk about moral urgency, leaving you feeling impatient, suspicious, even jaded. You may feel that the church only continues because of a conspiracy of ambiguity; if the church became clear about what it was actually for and against, half of its members would leave in a huff and the remainder wouldn't be able to pay the bills.

You may be Jewish or Muslim or from some other religious tradition, and even though my references to Christian issues differ from your own tradition in details, you may be going through a similar process with a similar flood of emotions.

Whatever your background, you picked up this book because you want to deal with your doubts in a positive way. You're seeking guidance. You're seeking answers. You're hoping to discover you're not alone, and maybe even that your descent into doubt could ultimately lead you upward.

The origin of the word *doubt* helps name the pain. *Doubt* derives from the same roots as *duo* and *double*, suggesting that to doubt is to be in two minds, one that believes and one that doesn't. The two minds wrestle and writhe in tension, pulling you in two directions, leaving you in *di-stress*. You can see with eyes of faith and you can see with eyes of skepticism, leaving you with double vision or internal *di-vision*.

Before doubt, you simply believed. You were in one innocent and undivided mind, seeing with one vision, feeling a comfortable confidence rather than distress. But that innocence, that simplicity, that peaceful unity of mind and clarity of vision now slip away, the first casualties of doubt.

Doubt inflicts other losses too. In one period of doubt, I tried to capture my feelings of loss in a song lyric, comparing my faith to a map.

> *All my road is before me, but*
> *All familiar paths lie far behind me.*
> *My map's here in my hand, but*
> *I have ventured past its tattered edges.*

For many of us, faith is our map of reality, our map of the universe. It tells us where we are, where we've been, where we're going, where to turn. But as soon as our trusted map stops matching reality, we feel disoriented. We have no idea where to turn, what to do, how to survive.

Perhaps you've had the experience of using a paper map or a GPS guidance system and realizing that because of some glitch or a flaw, it's leading you astray, or taking you in circles, or telling you to keep going straight or turn right when you're actually at a dead end.

Academics often call these mental maps paradigms, and when a paradigm fails and we need to seek a new one, we go through a paradigm shift. That intellectual language might make it sound like we're dealing with a strictly theoretical problem, but people experience the failure of a mental map, paradigm, or worldview as personally traumatizing. Even scientists, when their conceptual maps fail them and they must challenge some of their fundamental scientific assumptions, use emotionally charged language to describe the experience.

Listen to Werner Heisenberg, known for his famous "uncertainty principle," describe what it felt like when he and Niels Bohr lost the certainty of their trusted scientific maps:

> I remember discussions with Bohr which went through many hours till very late at night and ended almost in despair; and when at the end of the discussion I went alone for a walk in the neighboring park I repeated to myself again and again the question: Can nature possibly be so absurd as it seemed to us in these atomic experiments? . . . Here the foundations of physics have started moving; and . . . this motion has caused the feeling that the ground would be cut from science.*

Albert Einstein used almost identical language when he described the experience of coping with data that took him off the edges of his scientific map:

> It was as if the ground had been pulled out from under one, with no firm foundation to be seen anywhere, upon which one could have built.†

If the loss of a scientific map or model creates anxiety, how much more does the loss of a religious worldview? This loss threatens us with another even greater loss: the very loss of God or of God's favor, love, and protection. What could be more terrifying for a sincere believer?

---

* Quoted in Margaret Wheatley, *Leadership and the New Science* (Berrett-Koehler, 1992), 3–4.
† "Autobiographical Note," in P. A. Schilpp, ed., *Albert Einstein: Philosopher-Scientist* (Northwestern University Press, 1949), 45.

This terror is especially real for people like Michael and me, who were taught that God is an almighty supreme being who demands absolute perfection and submission, a strict and demanding father, and a tough and exacting judge. Yes, we were also taught God is loving, gracious, and forgiving, but the one requirement God demands above all others is precisely the thing that doubters struggle with most: God demands *firm, unwavering faith*, which we understood to mean correct beliefs. To question those beliefs throws open the terrifying possibility that God might at any moment turn against us, punish us, reject us, maybe even send us to hell if we don't get our beliefs straight and hold them tight, without doubt.

Now it's scary to be a sinner falling into the hands of an angry God, but it can be equally scary to be a doubter falling into the hands of angry believers. Doubt can breach the psychological fortress in which we've felt safe, tear up the internal map by which we've navigated the world, and threaten to separate us from God's favor and love. Then, beyond all those losses, it can rob us of the relationships most near and dear to us. ·

I felt a less dramatic version of this loss one day as a young pastor. I was meeting for breakfast with a trusted colleague from a church across town. I got up my courage and told him I was having some doubts about the inerrancy of Scripture, a doctrine that was deeply important to Evangelical Christians like us. He looked up from his scrambled eggs and made unblinking eye contact with me. "If you lose the inerrancy of Scripture, you lose the inspiration and authority of Scripture too. And if you lose that, you lose everything. I'll never doubt that for a second."

And that was it. No empathy. No encouragement. No inquiry about the reasons for my doubts. Not even an offer to pray for me. Just a warning and a self-distancing, a line drawn in the sand between us.

Before that breakfast, I had been able to confide deep personal struggles to this friend, and he to me. But my doubt crossed a line, and I knew instantly that he was no longer a safe person with whom I could speak freely from my heart. Frankly, our relationship was never the same, and I was left not only with my doubt but with one less friend to help me face it. (At least, that's how I interpreted his response at the time. Now I wonder if I misinterpreted his intention. Perhaps he valued our friendship so much that the fear of losing me as a colleague in ministry motivated his firm response. Or perhaps my admission of doubt resonated with secret doubts of his own, and his response to my doubt was a way of suppressing his own.)

To lose or damage a friendship is a significant thing, but the toll of doubt can be even more costly.

One day, my friend Susan Cottrell received a phone call from her daughter, a college student. Her daughter confided that she was attracted to women, and in spite of trying to "pray the gay away," she was not changing. Susan brought this news to a small group of her closest friends at her church, and they immediately told her that her daughter was sinning, and it would be a sin for her to accept her daughter as gay. She recalls, "I was being asked to choose between the two most important parts of my life: my child and my church." Then, through tears, she adds, "I chose my child."* She no longer fit in with her church, and on top of that, half of her family turned away from her, many refusing even to speak to her.

Sadly, when faced with a choice like Susan's, many people choose their religious community. Reversing a famous parable of Jesus, they stick with the ninety-nine sheep and cut off the lost sheep forever.

Just as caregivers have identified five stages of grief† when we lose a loved one, doubters go through predictable stages as they grieve the loss of a simple, unquestioned faith:

Denial: I'm OK! Everything is fine! Praise the Lord!

Anger: It's *their* fault that I'm having doubts. It's that preacher, or friend, or church, or radio show, or denomination, or book that's to blame!

Depression: I guess I've lost my faith and I'm going straight to hell. I'm doomed.

Bargaining: Maybe if I go to church more often, or go on that retreat, or take that class, or pray more, or read that book, or send money to that religious organization, or try harder, the doubts will all go away.

Acceptance: OK. Doubts are here. What am I going to do about it?

---

* You can watch Susan share her story here: https://www.youtube.com/watch?v=rPo1bH9Ljf4.

† One of the world's leading grief experts, David Kessler, has proposed a sixth stage to the grieving process: *finding meaning*. This book could be seen as an attempt to find meaning in the experience of doubt. For more on Kessler's proposal, see *Finding Meaning: The Sixth Stage of Grief* (Scribner, 2019).

Now, someone might tell you that along with the devastating losses that accompany doubt, you will also lose some of your illusions, and that is a good thing. But disillusionment is only a good thing in retrospect. When you're going through it, it feels like hell.

Reflection and Action

1. If you were in a really safe place, how would you name the doubts that you are currently struggling with?
2. Do you know of anyone who could provide a safe place to talk about your doubts? Have you ever consulted a trained counselor, psychologist, or spiritual director with whom you felt safe? Who comes to mind as a safe person whose presence would help you open up about your questions and doubts?
3. In what ways has your faith felt like a road map? How is the map helping or hurting you these days?
4. Reflect on where you are in the stages of grief—denial, anger, depression, bargaining, or acceptance—as you face your current and threatened losses associated with doubt.
5. Heisenberg and Einstein compared their questions and doubts to having the ground fall away under their feet. Try to finish this sentence with as many comparisons as you can: To me, doubt feels like . . .
6. Consider starting a journal as you read this book and recording your answers to the "Reflection and Action" questions at the end of each chapter. And, if possible, write a poem, or lament, or letter to yourself, or even a prayer if you're able, in which you name and grieve the losses you are experiencing through doubt. Take time to listen deeply to your soul and see what arises. Pay attention to your dreams in coming days, because often when we begin to face our doubts and associated losses we dramatize our struggles in our dreams.

2

DOUBT AS LONELINESS

Doubts are the ants in the pants of faith. They keep it awake and moving.

—Frederick Buechner

I love to ride horses. Years ago, I was invited to participate in a four-day trail ride deep in the wilderness of northern Pennsylvania's Allegheny Mountains. I will spare you a detailed description of the first day, when we got lost and had to spend twenty-three hours on horseback to reach our campsite. (Actually it was eight or nine hours, but it really, really felt like twenty-three.) Nor will I share the details about how the next morning as I crawled out of my tent, I discovered agony in parts of my anatomy I didn't even know were capable of pain. Nor will I try to convey the corresponding ecstasy I felt halfway through our trip, when my body and mind seemed to drop into a deep rhythm with my horse and with the natural surroundings, maybe akin to the endorphin-induced euphoria of runners and the "inner smile" of yoga practitioners.

Instead, I want to share something the horses taught me during our days together that helps me understand the loneliness of human doubt.

From the first trot to the last gallop, what seemed to interest the horses most was neither their human riders nor the environment around them. Apart from the few moments when a bear entered our campground and the times we stopped to feed and water them, our mounts were obsessed with only one thing: one another. Tucker hated to be behind Zeus. Thunder loved to walk behind Daisy. Rain despised Plato so much that she would kick him if he came up behind her, and Plato was restless if he

wasn't somewhere near Thunder. At every moment, the horses were turning their heads to the left or right, lifting or lowering their ears, angling
their bodies on the trail, snorting, flicking their tails, and otherwise sending body-language messages to the other horses before and after them.
We humans were looking at the scenery, but the horses were tuned in
to one another. I mentioned this observation to our wrangler, and he
confirmed my hunch: "They're herd animals," he said. "They have power
struggles, friendships, rivalries, and alliances just as we do. It's like their
brains are wired together in a network, and each is constantly monitoring
the others."

The social life of horses helped me understand my own behavior when
I was struggling through a deep period of doubt as a pastor. On my
day off, whenever possible, I would get in my car and drive two hours
away, up into the mountains of western Maryland, to the C & O Canal
towpath along the Potomac River. I thought I was going to fish, because
fishing relaxes me. (So much so that my wife, when she notices I'm tense
or testy, says, "Maybe you should go fishing?") But looking back, I now
realize it was not the company of fish but the absence of people that I so
desperately needed. Why did I need some distance between me and other
human beings?

Because thinking, it turns out, is a social act, and to think freely, to
think differently, to think independently, you sometimes need to escape
from the herd. If you can't get physical distance from your clan, tribe,
herd, or hive, you'll at least need to create some emotional distance, perhaps by retreating into a book (as you're now doing). This need for withdrawal helps explain at least in part why contemplatives and other mystics
have always upheld the value—no, the necessity—of solitude as a spiritual
practice.

Biologically and culturally, we humans evolved to live interde-
pendently with other humans. We instinctively fear being left out or shut
out, as any brokenhearted child who didn't get invited to a party, picked
for a team, or "liked" on social media knows. By early childhood most of
us have not only learned to speak but we have also developed a powerful
sensitivity to the facial expressions and body language of those around
us. We register each hint of a smile, nod, frown, raised eyebrow, pursed
lip, or furrowed brow. We scan every gesture for praise, disagreement,

disapproval, affirmation, inclusion, or opposition. Some of us have even felt our faces flush or our shoulders rise in tension when we realized that our unexpressed thoughts are out of sync with the norms of a group we are part of. Our physical reactions show that we have internalized group norms, and those norms are policing even our secret thoughts.*

When my companions think as I do, it's effortless to speak freely and to think creatively. But the more out of sync I feel with a group, the more guarded I feel, and the harder it is for me to speak or even consider ideas that don't fit in. A friend once asked me what it's like to be part of a group where I am not respected or even wanted, and I replied, "When I'm with them, I feel like I'm thinking in molasses."

We often speak of "thinking outside the box," as if the box is a limiting structure we create ourselves. But I've come to believe that many of the boxes in our heads are not simply of our own making, nor are they easily escaped. Our brains, it seems, are equipped at birth with empty files waiting to be filled with the norms and expectations transmitted by our companions, whose acceptance and approval our brains have evolved to want and need. The box of internalized norms in my head corresponds roughly with the boxes in the heads of all my companions. We all come equipped with an evolutionary predisposition to first learn and then obey the norms, rules, and agreements that we transmit to each other and impose on one another in our primary belonging groups.

Two of my friends have helped me understand this process more clearly. Dr. Jerome Lubbe is a specialist in functional neurology, and Dr. Jeffrey Olrick is a clinical child psychologist.† While they use different terminology, they both understand the human brain as modular. To put it in highly simplified terms, your singular human brain functions like a three-member committee.‡ Each of your three primary modules includes

---

* For more on social norms, see Cristina Bicchieri, Ryan Muldoon, and Alessandro Sontuoso, "Social Norms," in *The Stanford Encyclopedia of Philosophy*, ed. Edward N. Zalta (Winter 2018), https://plato.stanford.edu/archives/win2018/entries/social-norms/.

† See Jerome Lubbe, *Whole Identity*, available here: https://www.wholeidentity.com/. And see Jeffrey and Amy Olrick, *The Six Needs of Every Child: Empowering Parents and Kids Through the Science of Connection* (Zondervan, 2020), with more information here: https://growingconnected.com/.

‡ See http://thriveneuro.com/. Drawing from the early work of Jerry Fodor and Noam Chomsky, neurologists today posit from 22 to 52 specific modules, and some posit thousands of discrete modules that have evolved over millions of years and contribute to brain plasticity. Because the

many distinct submodules that in turn contain even smaller submodules, and the interactions among these modules and submodules are so fast, so complex, and so overlapping and interconnected that your brain can hardly even begin to understand its own inner workings.

Your oldest primary module, sometimes called the primitive or reptilian brain, includes your brain stem and cerebellum. It controls your basic bodily functions, including a highly evolved set of unconscious reflexes and responses to novelty or danger: alertness, hunger, thirst, sexual desire, anxiety, fear, terror, panic. This *instinctive brain* comes online before you are even born, and its job is to keep you alive in a dangerous world.

Next, shortly after birth, a second member of your brain committee wakes up and becomes engaged. This mammalian or limbic brain module orients you toward attachment by generating emotions that strengthen relationships, relationships that are necessary for a helpless infant's survival. The need for connection, for example, draws you toward caregivers who offer comfort, companionship, and protection. Feelings of affection and loyalty keep you from easily discarding these essential relationships. Like the reptilian brain, this mammalian brain operates at super-high speeds, deeper and faster than you can consciously keep track of. For that reason, we can call this second member of the brain committee the *intuitive brain*.

Before you even learn your name, before you are even conscious of your own existence as an individual, your instinctive and intuitive brains are already hard at work, forming connections, learning to work together, keeping you safe, and keeping you connected with those upon whom your survival depends. Then, gradually, especially after the age of about two, your third brain committee member, consisting of the neocortex and its components, begins to assert itself. Often called the primate brain, it's the logical, rational, analytical member of your brain committee. This module is the seat of intellect, and it enables you to use language and to think critically and creatively. This *intellectual brain* is essential to help you become both an independent self and an interdependent agent in human society.

---

field of brain science is still in its infancy, most theorists hold current theories loosely. For a brief introduction to the idea of a modular brain, see https://inside-the-brain.com/2011/09/29/is-the-mind-modular/. Also see https://en.wikipedia.org/wiki/Modularity_of_mind. For a highly readable general overview of contemporary brain research, see Mike McHargue's *You're a Miracle (and a Pain in the Ass)* (Convergent, 2020).

People sometimes refer to these three committee members as the gut (the instinctive brain), the heart (the intuitive brain), and the head (the intellectual brain). We could also refer to them as the survival module, the belonging or relational module, and the meaning module. When we speak of healthy, mature, or well-rounded human beings, we are referring to people who integrate their survival, belonging, and meaning modules (and all their submodules) in ways that bring benefit and pleasure to themselves and others.

At this very moment, each member of your brain committee is negotiating with its colleagues, making deals, having arguments, and forming two-to-one alliances that constantly shift power. At one moment, you might defer to your instinctual survival module, which activates fear to protect you from danger. Right after that, you might follow your intuitive belonging module, which seeks secure connection with the herd. And then, you might lean on your intellectual meaning module, which uses language and other symbolic systems (like math or theology) to think consciously, critically, creatively, and independently. By the time a conscious thought emerges in your meaning module, your survival and belonging modules have already engaged in a lengthy set of complex negotiations with unimaginable speed and efficiency.

Now before we continue, it's worthwhile to pause and think about what we mean when we say the word *faith*, and how that word involves the whole brain. To think consciously about the meaning of faith, of course, we're primarily using our meaning/intellect module. The stories of faith, the doctrines or statements of faith, the content of songs and poetry of faith, the symbols of faith, the history of faith traditions . . . all of these require real engagement of the more rational, analytical, and independent member of our brain committee. But that's not the whole story. We learn and practice faith in groups, which engages the intuitive/belonging module as well. Without our existential need for belonging, religion and faith as we know them may never have developed. In addition, many of us see faith as a matter of survival, in this life and beyond, which energizes the survival module too. Faith is, we could say, a matter of head, heart, and gut; of meaning, belonging, and survival; of intellect, intuition, and instinct. It's a whole-brain or whole-self proposal.

Sometimes, though, faith engages different people in different ways.

For example, some people don't think much about their faith. For them, it's primarily a matter of belonging (*I enjoy being part of a church, synagogue, mosque, temple, or dharma group*) or of survival (*I don't want to go to hell; I want to maintain God's blessings of health and wealth for my continued well-being in this life*). They haven't had an intellectual question or doubt about their faith for years, or maybe ever, because for them, the conceptual side of faith simply isn't that important, especially in comparison to its social and survival dimensions.

Even though your brain works at lightning-fast speed, it's easy to imagine hours, months, or even years of argument among the three members of your brain committee about whether to stay or go, comply or protest, confess or deny, speak or remain silent. Your head might tell you to go or speak, your heart might tell you to stay or remain silent, while your gut may be torn between the two.

Now when it comes to intellectual doubt, you're dealing primarily with your meaning module, the part of your brain committee that thinks critically and analytically. But your meaning module's independent thought processes are constantly being monitored and even censored by your belonging and survival modules. They constantly whisper their respective warnings: "If you think or say that, you won't fit in the herd and you might even be banished from the herd. If you're banished from the herd, you'll be alone and in great danger. You need the herd to survive! Without your secure place in the herd, you might die! Danger! Danger!" In this example, it's easy to imagine how your belonging and survival modules can try to keep your meaning module in line. But sometimes, the opposite can also happen.

Just as your meaning module might raise intellectual objections ("I can't honestly accept that the earth was created in six literal days less than 10,000 years ago," or "I can't honestly believe the pope—or Bible—is infallible"), your belonging module might raise relational, social, and ethical objections: "I can't go along with stigmatizing gay people, because that would mean I am betraying my friends Bob, Jill, Grant, and Pat"; or "I know what the Bible says and what the church says, but I can't go along with treating women as second-class citizens. Doing so makes me feel like I'm harming my mother, my wife, my sisters, my daughters, and my female friends"; or "How could I treat people of other religions as if they are inferior and damned by God? Ahmad, Soraya, and Asha are among the finest people I know. I can't throw them under the bus."

That's your intuitive belonging module at work, and it leaves you feeling torn among competing loyalties, affections, and relationships. In response, you can imagine your meaning module scolding the belonging module, trying to get it back in line: "But this church is doctrinally orthodox and was established on divine authority! These positions have been part of the church tradition for centuries! I can logically defend our policies with chapter and verse! You can't put mere emotions above truth!" Then you can imagine your belonging module shouting back, "I don't care about doctrines! I care about how I treat people, and I feel dirty and unethical when I treat people the way our faith community requires!"

When the meaning and belonging modules are out of alignment like this, with one feeling safe and the other feeling insecure, you can be sure that your survival module, the third and senior member of your brain committee, is reflexively emitting stress hormones like adrenaline, cortisol, and norepinephrine. These hormones prepare you to fight, flee, freeze, or appease as instinctive responses to danger. Their whole purpose is to make you uncomfortable with the status quo, which is why, to state the obvious, stress is so stressful.

That's also why thinking outside the box of doctrinal norms or "feeling outside the box" of social and ethical norms feels so uncomfortable, even unbearable, for herd animals like us. Both thinking and feeling, even though they feel like private or personal experiences, have social consequences.

Once more, play out the possibilities: if your meaning module votes to differ from the list of socially acceptable ideas contained in your internalized box of doctrinal norms, your belonging module will pull the fire alarm. If your belonging module votes to differ from the written or unwritten list of relational policies in your internalized box of social norms, your meaning module will pull the fire alarm. Either way, your survival module will sense a threat to your safety as a member of a trusted herd. It will immediately activate your danger reflexes, and your body will punish you with feelings of stress until your committee feels safe and at peace once again.

Your survival module seems to have a special kind of veto power in matters of belief. If something threatens your survival, safety, or security—including your financial security—the senior member of your brain committee can make it nearly impossible to believe it. Just imagine a person employed by the oil, coal, tobacco, or gambling industries being asked for their beliefs about global warming, lung cancer, or gambling addiction. "It is difficult to get a man to understand something, when his salary depends on his not understanding it," Upton Sinclair said, and we could easily substitute the word *believe* for the word *understand*. As our brain committee navigates the constant barrage of rewards, punishments, threats, and opportunities that life presents us, our survival, belonging, and meaning modules must constantly negotiate conflicts of interest. That internal struggle often makes doubt even more difficult and costly.

Feel the tension: many of us are drawn to faith communities because they are places of warmth, safety, and belonging. But sometimes, they are among the most dangerous zones we enter. You are reasonably safe in your racial group as long as you don't change the color of your skin. You are reasonably safe in your national group as long as you observe the laws and don't defect to another nation. You are reasonably safe in your cultural and political groups as long as you speak the shared language, celebrate the shared heroes, and observe the shared taboos. You are reasonably safe in your professional group as long as you do a good job and follow professional protocols. And you are reasonably safe in your familial group as long as you show up for Thanksgiving and Christmas and appreciate Grandma's cooking (or at least don't insult it).

But in many religious contexts, the terms of belonging are different and more demanding. They depend on professed doctrinal or intellectual beliefs, a meaning module function, and on relational or ethical beliefs, a belonging module function. You can't be safe or secure in your belonging unless you conform, and if you don't conform, your survival module smells smoke. And that's where things get tricky, because in a real sense, you can't choose your beliefs.

Yes, you can choose *to say* you believe something. But whether you actually and authentically do believe it is less choosable than it seems. For example, consider these different statements of belief from everyday life:

Personal belief: I believe that my spouse is a loving person who never lies to me and is committed to my well-being.

Historical belief: I believe that Abraham Lincoln was the sixteenth
   president of the United States.

Aesthetic belief: I believe that every entrée should contain hot sauce.

Scientific belief: I believe that light travels at about 186,000 miles per
   second.

Moral belief: I believe that sexual relations that do not involve two
   consenting adults of the opposite gender are sinful.

Dispositional belief: I believe that people are basically good and only
   behave badly by necessity.

Now go back over the list and ask yourself if you could choose to believe
or disbelieve any of these statements. If you just caught your spouse lying to
you and cheating on you, could you choose to believe the first statement? If
you checked relevant history books and websites and found that all agree that
Abraham Lincoln was the sixteenth president, could you choose to believe
he was the first, or third, or twentieth? If you hate spicy foods, could you
choose to believe the third statement? Could you will yourself to believe that
light travels at 7 inches per second instead of 186,000 miles per second? If
you are deeply opposed to LGBTQ equality, or if you are deeply committed
to the idea of innate human goodness, could you simply choose to switch
sides on the final two statements? Yes, you could lie and pretend to believe
or disbelieve these things, and yes, you could at some point in the future
be confronted with evidence or have an experience that might cause you to
change your belief, but right now, being who you are, could you freely choose
to believe or disbelieve any of these statements simply by an act of will?

   What makes religious doubt so challenging is that in almost every
religious community, the box of normative beliefs contains beliefs of
each kind—personal, historical, aesthetic, scientific, moral, and dispositional (and more—this list is not complete). To make matters worse,
it is seldom clear *how* a faith community expects me to hold this or that
belief. For example, when I am invited to say, "I believe there is one God
who exists in three Persons," am I making a statement of historical and
scientific belief, on the same level as "Abraham Lincoln was the sixteenth
president" or "Light travels at 186,000 miles per second"? Or is my
statement more personal (*I trust those who told me this is true*), or more
aesthetic (*This is a beautiful thought to imagine*), or dispositional (*This is*

my working hypothesis, because my disposition is to defer to authority figures in my community)?*

Things get really complicated when we realize how powerful authority figures—we could call them gatekeepers—first articulate the box of norms that members must follow, then police conformity, and then impose punishments or dispense rewards accordingly.[†] They're like a dominant horse who can drive any other horse out of the herd.

I'm sitting at my desk, looking out the window, remembering that trail ride, and seeing myself as a herd animal. A series of questions arises, questions I can't simply put aside:

How do I actually know what I believe, since I may simply be succumbing to pressure from gatekeepers whose groups I need or want to be part of?

Whom have I sold out to maintain my secure place in a religious group?

Why would I ever want to be part of a group that pressures me to say I believe things I may not even understand, or be capable of forming an opinion about?

Why would I want to believe something under threat, promise of reward, or some other form of pressure or duress? Shouldn't sincere belief be unforced and free?

How might a community hold beliefs as something other than tests of belonging?

What is the alternative? Could a faith community use a standard of belonging other than beliefs as a membership requirement? How would that work?

These questions bring back some of the most difficult dimensions of my years as a pastor, when sometimes I was the gatekeeper, sometimes I was the one being threatened by other gatekeepers, and sometimes I was

---

* In addition to all the explicitly stated beliefs in my mental box of in-group norms, there may be large numbers of implicit, unspoken beliefs as well, like "Organ music (or rock and roll) is what brings us closest to God."

† Some groups claim to have no leaders or authority figures. Others doubt this claim and make their case by asking, "Why do you have no authority figures?" Whoever answers, they say, is revealed as a covert authority figure.

the one caring for the sheep being pushed out of—or kept out of—the fold. It was a difficult challenge, because on the one hand, I was responsible for helping the community stay unified, but on the other hand, I was teaching individuals to be honest and have integrity as a moral duty. If I tried to preserve unity, I had to pressure doubters away from integrity by asking them to minimize their doubts. If I encouraged doubters to honestly face and express their doubts, I undermined unity.

That's not an easy challenge for herd creatures like us to navigate, especially since our brain committees and social networks are far more complex than those of horses. It's not easy being a horse, I'm sure, with horse politics to deal with, plus people on your back. But when we doubt, we have people on our backs too, exerting pressures and burdens that are hard to bear.

Reflection and Action

1. Which of my questions at the end of this chapter most resonates with you, and why?
2. This chapter introduces the idea that thinking and believing are social acts, not just individual acts. Do you feel I am overemphasizing the social dimensions of faith? What experiences have you had that lead you to confirm or question this idea?
3. In a footnote in this chapter, I say, "In addition to all the explicitly stated beliefs in my mental box of in-group norms, there may be large numbers of implicit, unspoken beliefs as well, like 'Organ music (or rock and roll) is what brings us closest to God.'" Can you articulate two or three implicit and unspoken beliefs that are normative in a religious group you are or have been part of? How did those unspoken beliefs sit with you?
4. Many of us, when confronted with doubts, consulted books of apologetics, books aimed to defend traditional doctrines and bolster our intellectual module with evidence and arguments for our beliefs. If you consulted books like these, how helpful were they to you?
5. This chapter began with a story about horses as herd animals. Can you share an experience about a time when you consciously differentiated yourself from the herd or felt bad for not doing so?

⚘

3

DOUBT AS CRISIS

It was like I'd been reading the sheet music all my life but had never heard the song.

—Bryant Russ

I never planned on being a pastor. I wanted to be a literature teacher. But I had this knack for inviting people over for dinner, and then drawing dinner guests into deeper-than-average conversations. While I was in graduate school, one little dinner group gradually evolved into a little faith community. I still didn't plan on becoming a pastor, but that too evolved gradually. First, I prepared sermons and did other pastoral duties as a volunteer, and then I was paid part-time, and finally I left teaching entirely and became a full-time pastor. As much as I loved studying and teaching Emily Dickinson, Franz Kafka, Jane Austen, and Walker Percy, I realized that I was even more devoted to teaching Jesus, Mary, Paul, and John.

My new bride, Grace, was a high school chemistry teacher, and she thought she had married a fellow teacher. We had looked forward to having summers off and spending winter nights grading papers together in front of a warm fireplace. But she felt the calling too, even though it meant we didn't have summers off, or even weekends!

So this little experimental faith community started in our living room, and then we began meeting in rented space in a succession of elementary, middle, and high schools, along with one college thrown in, before eventually buying land and building our own facility.

A moment comes back to me from those years as part of a vagabond church in rented facilities. We were meeting in a high school, which meant early arrival to set up chairs, Sunday school rooms, a sound system, and the like. The service was about to begin, and I ran into the bathroom to check my hair. (I still had a little back then.)

"Wow," I thought, looking in the mirror, a row of urinals arrayed behind me, the pungent scent of urinal disinfectant blocks masking any more organic odors. "I'm going bald. And my beard is showing more salt mixed in with the pepper. And I'm not sure if there really is a God."

If you've never been close to a pastor, priest, or rabbi (or been one yourself), hearing me admit this might upset you, but I assure you, it happens more frequently than most folks (including most seminarians) think. But it was a shock to me, seemingly popping out of nowhere.

Before becoming a pastor, I thought more time in Bible study, more time in prayer, more time exposed to hymns and worship songs, more time in Christian fellowship meant my doubts would decrease, not increase.

But when I became an insider to the religious industrial complex, I saw things I hadn't seen before. I saw how petty and shabby religious people can be under their *Hallelujah*s and *Praise the Lord*s. I saw how often money reigns, even in the so-called kingdom of God. Speaking of money, I saw how much of it is expended (along with time and effort) for relatively little personal and social transformation. I encountered a significant minority of my fellow religious professionals who were arrogant, insecure, or emotionally enmeshed with their congregations, creating a narcissist/ co-dependent syndrome that often resulted in outward success (measured in money, facilities, and attendance) and inward misery (measured in anxiety, fatigue, hostility, self-hatred, and depression).

To make matters worse, because I was preparing two, three, or four sermons and Bible studies each week, I was reading the Bible more than I ever had, and as you'd expect, with all that exposure, I started noticing things. I noticed tensions—I couldn't yet let myself call them contradictions—between versions of stories told by different storytellers. I noticed passages where God seemed infinitely loving and kind just a few pages away from other passages where God seemed horribly cruel and vindictive. Of course, I read books that tried to resolve these tensions, but they often struck me as contrived excuses rather than convincing explanations. No matter how hard I tried, I couldn't employ those excuses when others came to me with their questions about things they were noticing in the Bible.

When members came to me for counseling, I observed how much relief and comfort traditional Christian theology brought to some people. But for others, it did the opposite. It confused them, terrified them, even traumatized them. And it emboldened some to be even more arrogant, judgmental, or insecure than they would have been otherwise. When I compared notes with my fellow pastors, I realized that many of them were struggling with similar observations.

All these observations piled up like a stack of firewood, and that morning, looking into the mirror in a dingy high school bathroom, I could smell smoke.

I combed my thinning hair, looked myself in the eyes, and said, "You have a sermon to preach," and in lieu of a self-administered pep talk, I silently prayed something like this: "God, you know my thoughts. You know that at this moment, I wonder if you even exist. But you also know that I'm asking you for help, which is an act of faith. Help me, a tangled mess of faith and doubt, to do my job this morning and preach well, for your sake and for the sake of the people who will be here today. And help me work through my doubts well, too, before they destroy me or do harm to my congregation."

That wasn't the last time a wave of doubt came over me right before a sermon, or in the middle of a counseling session, or (more understandably) at the end of a difficult board meeting. Years later, when I read that Mother Teresa confessed to literally years when God felt neither present nor real to her, I instantly thought, "I get it. I know how that feels."

Not long after my bathroom-mirror moment, I was taking a walk with a fellow pastor ten or fifteen years my senior. "You really seem to be at the top of your game," I said. "Your church is thriving, your family is thriving, everything is coming together for you."

Something in my voice evoked my friend's compassion. "You seem to be . . . at a different place," he said. Unexpectedly, my eyes went hot, and all I could do was swallow and nod.

"How old are you?" he asked.

"Thirty-eight," I replied.

"Ah, thirty-eight to forty-two. They were the hardest years of my life. I almost left ministry."

We walked on a bit further. He offered no sermon, no advice, no pep talk, except, "Better days will come, my friend. Better days will come."

They did. But a ton of agonizing days came first.

The "me" I saw in that bathroom mirror had been formed by my faith. God sat at the top of the pyramid of my conceptual universe, like that weird eye on the back of the U.S. dollar bill. If I lost faith in God, if I lost faith in Christianity, what would be left of me? Who would I be then? My marriage was a Christian marriage. My wife and I were committed to being Christian parents. My parents were Christians and knew their son as a Christian. My closest friendships had formed in the context of Christian community. I had never even thought about how to be a husband or dad or son or friend apart from my faith.

Yes, there were other complications, practical matters like the question of how I would make a living if I lost faith. But the deepest question that stared me in the face was not financial or professional. It was existential: who would I be without God, without Jesus, without the Holy Spirit, without Christian faith? Would there even be a recognizable me left if I lost my faith?

I felt another fear: if I lost my faith, how would I change morally? Without the "fear of God" in me, would I succumb to all the temptations I had been more or less successfully resisting? Would I decompose morally into a heavy-drinking, drug-indulging, womanizing, vows-breaking, kids-abandoning, seared-conscience libertine? Was I only staying moral because I was staying religious?

That question was intensified by a ritual-like conversation that recurred pretty frequently among my colleagues in those days. The ritual almost always began with the same four words: *Did you hear about . . . ?* Then the name of a fellow pastor would follow, along with the breaking news of his departure from ministry, most often due to a sexual affair but sometimes due to alcohol abuse, anger mismanagement, arrogance, divorce, or financial malfeasance. "Lose your moral and theological certitude, and you'll be next" was the implicit warning that came through the *did you hear about* ritual.

Of course, now that I'm a bit older and have had my own skirmishes with self-sabotage, I've come to wonder if my colleagues and I had it all wrong. It wasn't moral and theological *certitude* that helped some of us stay more or less moral; it was moral and theological *honesty*. The greatest threat to our moral and spiritual health wasn't questions or doubts but rather dishonesty or pretense *about* our questions or doubts. I've come to suspect that many of our former colleagues felt questions and doubts arising within them just as I did that day in the high school bathroom, but for reasons even they may not have understood, they dismissed their questions, denied their doubts, and refused to face and grapple with them. Publicly, they beamed a happy, confident, doubt-free smile to the church and the world, but privately, they hid a frightened, doubting, troubled heart and probably suppressed their questions even from themselves. Hypocrisy and self-deception proved to be far greater dangers than uncertainty. Once they practiced denial, deception, and cover-up in one area, they found it easier and easier to practice them in other areas.

When I look back on the *did you hear about* ritual, I now wonder if some of the unexpected departures were more deliberate than they seemed. Perhaps when someone is hiding doubts, a member of their inner brain committee tries to end the charade by hatching a plan to self-sabotage sexually, relationally, or financially. An act of ministry suicide is painful, but less painful, perhaps, than living the lie.

Even if you're not a religious professional who is, in a sense, paid to believe, you too have practical concerns that make it hard for you to lose some or all of your faith. What would your mother think, or your father? How would you survive Thanksgiving with Uncle Harold and Aunt Marie? And no less intense: like a person at the end of a long marriage, you wonder, "Who will I be now?"

Since leaving the pastorate almost fifteen years ago, I've continued to make a living in the faith world as an author and speaker, so in a sense, I am still under the pressure of practical demands and expectations. But interestingly, especially as I near the age of retirement, the practical concerns fade. If I wanted to leave faith now, if I wanted to "come out" as an agnostic or atheist or as spiritual-but-not-religious or whatever, as a sixty-something adult I could do it more easily than ever. But it's interesting:

the more free I feel to *not* identify myself as a person of faith, the more free I feel to do so . . . in ways that feel honest and authentic, of course.

Something in us wants to belong. But something in us also wants to be free, to be authentic, to be the truest, most genuine version of ourselves that we can. Those two desires can be in tension.

Something in us wants to be honest. But something in us also wants to be liked by those around us. And those two desires can be in tension.

Something in us wants to be good. But something in us also wants to be *thought of* as good by others. And those two desires are often in tension.

Something in us wants to be consistent. But something in us also wants to keep growing, and growing often means changing. So those two desires often conflict.

When enough conflicting desires wrestle within us, the faith crisis becomes an identity crisis. With so much to lose, we face the temptation to trade away our integrity and honesty for the security of belonging. If we do, our good faith decomposes into bad faith and we become stagnant and divided persons, wearing masks and hiding secrets.

In the middle of an identity crisis, whether we're standing in a bathroom and staring at a mirror or lying in bed at night and staring up at a dark ceiling, many of us engage in a profound cost-benefit analysis, weighing the benefits of external conformity (belonging, approval, familiarity, continuity, salary) against the benefits of honest questioning (integrity, curiosity, authenticity, new discovery). This internal debate puts the intellectual, social, and moral structures of our identity under acute psychological stress, and it pits our survival, belonging, and meaning modules against one another. To relieve that stress, we often make small decisions in the direction of conformity and dishonesty. As a result, the costs to personal integrity keep mounting gradually and often go unrecognized.

This gradual process often leads to a moment of choice, when our growing stack of doubts suddenly ignites and we realize that the whole house is in danger of burning down. Who will we be if we don't put out the fire? What will we become if our house burns to ash? Where will we belong if we take our questions seriously? And who will we be, what will we become, or where will we belong if we try to deny or suppress our questions?

In the world of addiction recovery, folks often speak of hitting bottom . . . that "come to Jesus" moment when you can no longer deny that you have a problem. Many of us have a similar moment regarding our faith: our questions and doubts are real and they're not going away. We have to face them head on.

To our utter surprise, it's only at the bottom that we find a trapdoor. It opens to a tunnel that leads us to better days.

Reflection and Action

1. At the end of this chapter, I make an analogy to hitting bottom in addiction recovery. What powerful desires, drives, or needs might tempt you, like an enticing drug, to sacrifice your honesty and integrity in matters of faith and doubt?

2. In some of my other books, I share other moments, like the bathroom-mirror moment, when I had to face a question, misgiving, or doubt. Could you share one or two of your moments of honesty and realization about a question or doubt?

3. Respond to this passage from this chapter: "It wasn't moral and theological *certitude* that helped some of us stay more or less moral; it was moral and theological *honesty*. The greatest threat to our moral and spiritual health wasn't questions or doubts but rather dishonesty or pretense."

4. Respond to this sentence from this chapter: "The more free I feel to *not* identify myself as a person of faith, the more free I feel to do so . . . in ways that feel honest and authentic, of course."

5. How would you describe your identity as a person of faith at this season of your life: solid and stable, solid but with a few small cracks, a little uneasy, deeply conflicted, in full-blown identity crisis, or something else?

6. In any area of your life, have you ever been at a "bottom" and found a trapdoor that became a doorway to better days?

✌

4

DOUBT AS DOORWAY

> I like the scientific spirit—the holding off, the being sure but not too sure, the willingness to surrender ideas when the evidence is against them: this is ultimately fine—it always keeps the way beyond open—always gives life, thought, affection, the whole man, a chance to try over again after a mistake—after a wrong guess.
>
> —Walt Whitman, *Walt Whitman's Camden Conversations*

For Sam, you might say, life was rocket science. As a young aerospace engineer and project manager, he approached not only his profession but also his whole life with mathematical precision, clearly defined desired outcomes, and rigorous quality control. He designed his faith with the same intensity he used in designing satellites and testing them before launch.

Not long ago, he found me at a conference where I was speaking. He had one of my books in his hand, and very politely asked if he could have a few minutes of my time. "Sure," I said. "What's up?"

"For most of my life," he said, "I've been addicted to certainty. I'm just beginning to understand that certainty and faith are vastly different things. That's what brought me to this conference."

He went on to explain that he had grown up in a conservative denomination, and in college he got involved with a campus ministry that his denomination recommended. "I went on a retreat in my first semester as a freshman," Sam told me, "and the speaker kept talking about something called *the biblical worldview* or *the Christian worldview*. I'd never heard that term before, and it intrigued me."

By the end of the retreat, he was sold: "The speaker was the most educated Christian I had ever met, and he promised us that if we developed a biblical worldview, we would have, literally, *God's view* on every important subject, from evolution to abortion to economics to politics to sexuality to interpersonal relationships. All we had to do was base everything on the solid foundation of the Bible, and then build on that foundation with solid principles of interpretation. We would have absolute certainty, from the bottom up. Who wouldn't want that?"

So through his late teens and twenties, Sam studied the Bible, and to learn to interpret it correctly, he read stacks of books, listened to scores of sermons, attended dozens of conferences, and took part in lots of courses, classes, and study groups: "I played with Legos as a kid, and that's what theology felt like to me: a massive Lego project. I would pick a question, say, the age of the universe. Then I would look up all the Bible verses that could possibly be related to that question. I would consult theologians who shared my view of biblical inerrancy and see what they had to say. Then I would come up with a belief that was as well defined as a little blue or white Lego. So on the age of the earth, something I had to confront in my physics and astronomy classes, I would conclude that, yes, the earth had *apparent* age in the billions of years, but its *actual* age couldn't have been more than about 10,000 years, because that was clearly the event horizon offered by the Bible."

He snapped that belief brick into place, added more as he developed them, and soon had a whole system of beliefs that formed a tight-fitting wall. "I felt that I was creating my spiritual home, my fortress of faith," he explained. He looked forward to spending the rest of his earthly life safe and secure in that fortress, after which a heavenly mansion would await him. From the high walls of his fortress, he could look out across the landscape of history and culture with the bomb-proof confidence he was promised, repelling all attacks of skeptics and maybe even convincing others to join him by building their own faith fortress as part of the ever-expanding Christian kingdom.

"It might have been different if I had been a biology major or an art major," he said. "But this approach to faith fit in perfectly with my chosen profession. Faith was about perfecting my biblical worldview fortress. It was a design project for me to manage with an efficient linear aggressiveness."

Sam worked diligently, even fervently. Sermon by sermon, book by book, retreat by retreat, conference by conference, he engineered his theological structure. After graduation, he even filled his daily commute and workout sessions with radio shows and podcasts that could add to his knowledge and fortify his faith. But eventually, something happened to Sam that happens to many, maybe most, and maybe even all of us.

One small brick became a problem.

For Sam, it started in the young adults Bible study group at his church. All the other group members believed that because a certain political candidate wanted to criminalize abortion, that position justified all his other behaviors, no matter how uncharitable, antisocial, or even antidemocratic. To make matters worse, Sam had become convinced of the reality of climate change: for him, the scientific evidence was undeniable. Every cause has an effect, so pumping millions of tons of carbon into the atmosphere could not be without effects. Yet this candidate called it a hoax, and that deeply offended Sam. The pill felt unswallowable.

So privately, Sam gave himself permission to hold an opinion different from that of his Bible study members. He decided to chisel out that one small "abortion trumps all else" brick and replace it with another brick. It would be his secret, and he would differ from his faith community just this once. Then everything would be perfect again. And it was, until one night, during a prayer time in the group.

Someone prayed for the political candidate in question, that he would be protected from the satanic attacks of his opponents and would prevail "in Jesus' name." Sam tensed up. Having Jesus' name associated with this candidate elicited an almost convulsive reaction in Sam's body. He made it through the prayer time and remained silent through the rest of the meeting, but his jaw was clenched tight and he felt hot, angry, and edgy. He noticed that his hands were even shaking a little.

During the refreshment time after the meeting, Sam spoke to the group leader, trying to project calm even though he was seething inside. "Do you really believe that opposition to abortion should trump every other concern in politics?" he asked. The leader responded with sincerity mixed with concern: "Yes, I do, with all my heart. Don't you?" Sam shook his head: "I find that really hard to accept. It seems like you're saying that character doesn't matter, honesty doesn't matter, morality doesn't matter, science doesn't matter . . . nothing else matters except that one issue?"

The group leader's answer sent a chill up Sam's spine: "I think you're on a slippery slope, Sam. Question one moral absolute and you'll soon be questioning everything."

Sam could see a dozen flaws and weaknesses in his group leader's argument. But he could also see that the leader's mind was closed and any further discussion would get nowhere. "Thanks," he mumbled, and excused himself.

Driving home that night, it was as if a dam broke. Questions flooded into his mind: *Was the earth really created in six literal days? Why would God create the universe with a deceptive appearance of age? Is an all-male church leadership really required by Jesus Christ? Does God actually send everyone who doesn't believe what we believe to hell, forever? Might our predictions about the end of the world, based on speculative readings of the books of Daniel and Revelation, be wrong, and even harmful? Is the church never allowed to change its mind on such things?*

Sam couldn't fall asleep that night. First, he felt anxious about the group leader's warning: would he soon start questioning everything? Then he felt worried that he soon might not fit in the young adults Bible study group anymore. That made him feel sad, even a little hurt, because these were some of his closest friends, and he wondered why the group couldn't tolerate more room for difference of opinion. Anxious, worried, sad, hurt . . . the churn of emotions was too much for him, and sometime after midnight, Sam made a desperate, last-ditch decision.

He chose to double down and force himself to stop questioning, because his church meant everything to him, and he couldn't risk being rejected by it. He processed his anxiety, worry, sadness, and hurt into blame and anger . . . not directed at his fellowship or his church, but at every outside force that kept him from being able to be a happy, compliant member. He vowed to stop listening to secular radio and TV. He promised himself he wouldn't go to websites that would challenge the political stance of his church. He vowed to intensify his Bible reading. He even decided to vote for the candidate whose character (or lack thereof) had precipitated his crisis. And he turned all of this resolve into a heartfelt prayer.

Many of us do something similar. Hoping to suppress inconvenient questions and doubts, we become more rigorous than ever before in defending what we say we believe and in attacking all those who see things differently. By battling as good soldiers and valiant warriors for our fortress, we hope to whip ourselves into a fighting frenzy of firm belief. We trade our innocent certainty for a commitment to suppress and hide all uncertainty. But the louder we fight and the more angrily we argue, the more dishonest we feel, desperately and even pathetically performing our certitude in public to compensate for the insecurity we feel in private.

Like Sam, in my younger years, I was often on the giving end of this kind of combative desperation, I'm embarrassed to say. I wonder how many arguments and sermons I directed at others in an attempt to convince myself.

In my older years, I've more often been on the receiving end. A few years ago, for example, I was speaking at a Christian college in the Midwest. In the Q & R, a man who looked at least twice as old as the students was the first to the mic and asked, very aggressively, "Who do you think you are to make up your own doctrines and create your own version of Christianity? Why don't you just admit you're a heretic and stop calling yourself Christian?" I tried to respond as gently as possible, but he didn't appear at all satisfied.

To my surprise, when the lecture was over, this same fellow came up to me and said, "I'd like your email address. I'd like to be in touch with you."

As a rule I never give out my email address, especially to pushy or aggressive people who are going to send me a barrage of emails with lots of Bible verses and CAPITAL LETTERS warning me of HELL and DAMNATION. I usually tell people they can reach me through my website, and very few go through the effort to do so. Frankly, because of his aggressiveness, I was worried he'd find my contact information and distribute it to others who would join him in a coordinated barrage, because that sort of thing had happened to me before.

But I felt a little nudge somewhere in my heart telling me to take a risk on this fellow. So I scribbled my email address on a piece of paper and gave it to him. The next morning, this email was waiting in my inbox:

Thanks for answering my question last night. Sorry if I was rude.

I have one more question. What do you say to a pastor who is losing his faith?

I am that pastor.

It's often the case that the people who attack and argue most loudly are doing so to convince themselves. For some, I suppose, it works, at least for a while.

But eventually, for many of us, even after doubling down against doubt for days, weeks, or even years, after fighting the good fight as good soldiers, we reach an impasse. We find ourselves in the position of Saul in the Book of Acts (Acts 9): we have tried to convince ourselves that we are fighting for God, but we begin to wonder if we're actually fighting against God.

First we chiseled out and replaced one brick in our fortress of beliefs, but then two or three more began to bother us. After we replaced them, plus seven or eight more, the whole fortress *did* feel a little less steady, just as we had been warned. We began to fear that the whole thing might come crashing down on our heads at any moment. Eventually, the fortress that once gave us a sense of security feels like a haunted house or a prison, and it produces a claustrophobic anxiety. The immovable clarity that once bolstered our confidence now stirs up stress. The simple, easy answers that we once took pride in now embarrass us.

So we start looking for an escape route from our maximum-security fortress turned prison. If the doors are locked, we'll use a window. If the windows are locked, we'll dig a tunnel through the floor or cut through the roof. We need a way out, an emergency exit, an escape tunnel.

Even after the idea of escape becomes more appealing, we often reach the threshold and hesitate, facing the outside world with a heart full of mixed feelings. We lean through the door and face the unknown. Then we pull back, often many times, before we gain the courage to push through. We may feel that we face an all-or-nothing choice: believe the whole package we're taught or throw the whole thing away. Or we may feel that we need to go through a sorting process, leaving extra baggage behind and carrying other treasures forward. But which beliefs are trash and which are treasure? It's hard to know, hard to choose, hard to live in tension between a desperate desire for certainty and an equal and opposite desire for honesty and charity.

Sam spent nearly two years on this threshold, in a state of liminality, wondering if he should stay or go, torn by tension. "I suppose I was in denial about my addiction to certainty," he said, "and I needed to hit bottom, as they say."

For him, that bottom came when he started to doubt some of his own religious experiences, wondering whether he faked them or was coerced into them. If his biblical worldview collapsed, that was bad enough. But if his spiritual experience went down too, he felt there was nothing of value left. That thought terrified him: were morality and meaning nothing more than illusions or delusions? Was he nothing more than a meaningless cog in a cosmic machine? A line from *Macbeth* that he had memorized way back in his high school English class returned to haunt him: would his doubt flatten out the universe and empty it of all meaning, reducing his existence to nothing more than a tale "told by an idiot, full of sound and fury, signifying nothing"?

"Looking back," Sam said, "I can see that I had bought into all these assumptions: that certainty is the same thing as truth, and that there can be no meaning without certainty, and so on. But at the time, I felt that years of hard work had been wasted, and I didn't know if I could admit that to myself. Honestly, a few times some scary thoughts entered my mind. I couldn't imagine life outside my fortress having any meaning at all. I had invested so much."

I remember watching a friend in graduate school make this kind of passage. When we began our studies together, he was a thriving United Methodist youth leader. But one afternoon a few years later, we were standing in line to order a pizza. "You're reading the same philosophy books that I am," he said. "You're engaged in the same critical thinking processes that I am. How are you holding on to your faith?"

"It's not easy," I said. "Sometimes I feel like I'm holding on by a fingernail."

"Don't give up," he replied, looking away. "It's not easy losing your faith, either. Believe me, it's not easy."

Like my friend in graduate school, Sam could feel how much was at stake. So he lingered on the threshold, leaning out the door, pulling back in . . . becoming an aggressive defender of the fortress, then secretly reading books that might provide him an escape route from it.

"You wrote a few of those books," he said, "including this one I brought with me today. That's why I came to this conference. I wanted to talk to you. To thank you. When I read your books, I felt a little less alone. You helped me stay in liminal space long enough to gather my courage to leave the Lego fortress behind and venture out into the world outside.

"Gradually, I realized I was trapped by a false dichotomy, an impossible choice between two unacceptable options," he explained. "Stay in the fortress of certainty and at least pretend to be satisfied with the answers I had been given, or leave the fortress and experience absolute, utter meaninglessness." There had to be a third option, he thought.

The title of the book he was holding gave him an answer: *We Make the Road by Walking*. "Maybe faith was never supposed to be a fortress," he said. "Maybe it was supposed to be a road. And maybe it was a road that led into the unknown." That shift in metaphor—from fortress to road—helped him see doubt not as a dead end but as a doorway out of the fortress and onto the road. "Finally," he said, "I reached a decision I could live with. I would keep faith, but rather than a faith that forbids all doubt, I would move forward with a faith that any God worth believing in would be able to love me as a doubter, and would rather me be honest than a pretender. I guess I finally realized that faith was never meant to be an engineering project."

Even though he suspected that his current church wouldn't be comfortable with his new approach to faith, he decided to make an appointment with his pastor anyway, just to be sure. First, Sam thanked the pastor for all he had learned and gained at the church, and then he explained his dilemma.

The pastor listened with empathy and finally offered his recommendation. "Sam, I really wish I could tell you this will be a safe place for you to go on the journey you have to go on, but I can't," the pastor said. Then, to Sam's surprise, he added this: "The truth is, I don't feel so safe here myself. If I didn't have kids in college, I'd probably be leaving with you. I wish I had your courage."

"It's not courage, really," Sam said. "It's actually a feeling of freedom that came to me a few weeks ago during one of your sermons."

The pastor was preaching on the beatitudes, a series of provocative statements at the beginning of Jesus' Sermon on the Mount in Matthew 5. Sam found himself reading ahead as the pastor spoke. "You have heard it said," Jesus said in Matthew 5:21, and then added, "but I say to you." He read ahead farther and found a total of five times when Jesus repeated this phrase. Each time, Jesus took an ancient and generally accepted belief and dared to say *but*, implying that the conventional belief was only partial, or temporary, or otherwise insufficient. Each belief needed to be challenged, subverted, expanded, reinterpreted, or in some other way further developed. These conventional beliefs didn't have the last word. They needed to be given a second thought. *They deserved to be doubted.*

Then Sam came to the passage where Jesus said he had not come to abolish the law and prophets but to fulfill them. He vaguely remembered me addressing this passage in *We Make the Road by Walking.** "It was like a spell was broken," he told his pastor. "Literally, like I was blind and then I could see. The ancient truths weren't the destination. They were like milestones or road signs, inviting people to reach them and then keep moving, looking for the next milestone or road sign, and the next, and so on. Jesus wasn't abolishing them; he was fulfilling their intention. Their intention was to invite people to growth, to keep exploring, to continue the journey on the road of faith. But so many churches are using them to hold people back and keep them from growing. We've turned milestones into roadblocks."

When their conversation came to a close, the pastor thanked Sam for coming, said a prayer for him, and walked him to the door of the church. After they embraced, the pastor assured Sam he was always available as a friend, whether or not Sam ever came back to the church. As Sam pulled out of the parking lot, he looked back in his rearview mirror. The pastor was still standing there, watching him go. Sam felt strangely blessed, strangely hopeful, and something else: "For the first time, I felt like a spiritual grown-up. I had given up my Legos."

Relatively few people I've known have experienced as gracious a departure as Sam did. Many pastors come down hard on people who no longer can live within a fortress faith. I've heard so many heartbreaking stories: of people being threatened with hell, or being "prophesied over" and told that if they leave their church, they will get cancer and die, and so on. Pastors who are all smiles and warmth on Sundays can become surprisingly harsh and authoritarian by Wednesday or Thursday.

---

* I address this passage in Chapter 28 of *We Make the Road by Walking* (Jericho, 2014).

Of course, pastors are just people, as I know better than most, having been one for over twenty years. Some of them who respond harshly are just doubling down, trying to keep their own questions and doubts at bay. In contrast, Sam's pastor literally walked him to the door and sent him off with a hug and a blessing, and I can't help but think that at that moment, he was as good a pastor as he had ever been.

For some of us, faith is a fortress of certainty we will defend to the death. For others, faith is a prison to leave behind forever.

Many of us linger at the threshold as Sam did, afraid to move ahead but unable to stay where we are.

If we dare take a first step, we discover that faith can be a road, a doorway out of the fortress prison of certainty and into the adventure of living. Before us lies the unknown, which is our life.

Reflection and Action

1. Sam described himself as "addicted to certainty." Can you relate to that description? What about certainty is addicting?

2. How would you describe the differences among certainty, uncertainty, and faith?

3. In this chapter, I describe how some people "double down" and become aggressive toward others as a way of tamping down their own doubts and questions. Do you think you've ever doubled down in this way?

4. Sam describes a moment when he felt like "a spell was broken" and he realized some beliefs, even beliefs held as certainties for centuries, "deserved to be doubted." Explain in your own words: what from Jesus' teaching in the Sermon on the Mount gave Sam permission to doubt in this way? (You may want to read the passage from Matthew 5 for yourself.)

5. Sam contrasted milestones to roadblocks. How would you put his insight into your own words?

6. How would you describe your own faith using the metaphors of fortresses, prisons, thresholds, doorways, roads, and adventures?

5

※

Doubt as Growth

May we face [the future] with the steady serenity of a tree—that supreme
lover of light, always reaching both higher and deeper, rooted in a network
of kinship and ringed by a more patient view of time.

—Maria Popova, *Brain Pickings*

During my first career as a college English teacher, I was invited to a free
half-day professional development class. Never one to pass up something
for free (my dad said this was part of my Scottish heritage), I attended
with no idea how those four hours would change my life.

The presenter began like this: "As college instructors, adjuncts, and
professors, most of you got graduate degrees in your specialty area, not
education, and many of you have never had a single course in education.
Now, here you are, working as educators, brilliant in your subject area but
often beginners in the craft of teaching.

"Even those few of you who studied traditional K–12 education likely
feel unprepared for the unique challenges of teaching young adults in
their late teens and twenties. That's why we've invited you here today.
We're going to explore how young adults learn and how they grow intellectually, so you can better teach them."

She then presented the work of an important educational theorist
named William Perry, who developed a nine-stage schema to describe
typical patterns of adolescent intellectual development.*

---

* See William G. Perry, Jr., *Forms of Intellectual and Ethical Development in the College Years: A
Scheme* (Jossey-Bass, 1998). For a good short summary of Perry's work, see https://ii.library

By the end of the afternoon, I felt that I was on the verge of an out-of-body experience. I was only in my mid-twenties, so what we were learning about young adult learners also applied to me. And it applied to me not just professionally but also personally, because nearly everything she introduced applied to my life as a Christian as well as my work as an educator. As I walked from the training back to my nearby apartment, I remember feeling ecstatic: "I might not be outgrowing faith after all," I mused, "but instead, I might be growing out of one stage of faith into another."

Over the next few decades, I searched out and studied multiple theories of human development in addition to William G. Perry, from William Blake to Paul Ricoeur, from Søren Kierkegaard to Ken Wilber, from Sigmund Freud, Karl Jung, and Jean Piaget to James Fowler, Lawrence Kohlberg, and Richard Rohr, from Ken Blanchard and Scott Peck to Claire Graves and Don Beck.* Some years later, when a friend pointed out that this field was (like many others) dominated by men, I investigated leading female theorists who challenged and augmented the research done by their male counterparts, including Mary Belenky, Blythe Clinchy, Nancy Goldberger, and Jill Tarule,† Nicola Slee,‡ and Carol Gilligan.§ I also studied the

---

.jhu.edu/2013/12/13/perrys-scheme-understanding-the-intellectual-development-of-college-age
-students/.

* You'll find a table summarizing their theories in Appendix III, and you'll find additional information about a fifth stage (Stage Zero) in Appendix II.

† In *Women's Ways of Knowing* (Basic Books, 1997), Belenky, Clinchy, Goldberger, and Tarule challenge and augment the work of William G. Perry. Thanks to Diana Butler Bass for introducing me to the important work of these feminist scholars.

‡ In *Women's Faith Development* (Routledge, 2004), Nicola Slee challenges and augments the work of William Fowler. In particular, she differs from Fowler by emphasizing the apophatic (beyond words) dimension of mature faith for women, and she focuses on the ways that women prioritize social connectedness as they grow spiritually. She offers six processes or strategies by which women develop in faith, which she calls "conversational, metaphoric, narrative, personalised, conceptual, and apophatic faithing." See https://www.academia.edu/3851527/APOPHATIC _FAITHING_IN_WOMENS_SPIRITUALITY. In this light, the work of contemporary feminist theologians, scholars, and spiritual writers becomes all the more significant. Doubt suppression can be seen as an aspect of religious male dominance, and the freedom to question and doubt can be seen as a needed feminist challenge to that dominating theological regime.

§ In *In a Different Voice: Psychological Theory and Women's Development*, Carol Gilligan (Harvard University Press, reprint edition, 2016), challenged the work of Lawrence Kohlberg. Kohlberg had concluded that fewer women broke through to what he described as more advanced levels of moral reasoning, but Gilligan noted that Kohlberg's research had focused only on upper-class white boys and men. She demonstrated that women approached moral reasoning in ways that were different, but not inferior, suggesting that Kohlberg's categories carried an inherent gender (and racial) bias. In fact, after considering the work of female scholars in the field (especially Carol Gilligan and Nicola Slee), I suspect that many women would be propelled more quickly to more advanced stages of moral reasoning than men because they experience the downside of

groundbreaking work of racial identity theorists including Bailey Jackson, Bernardo Ferdman, Placida Gallegos, Jean Kim, Perry Horse, Rita Hardiman, Charmaine Wijeyesinghe, William Cross, and J. E. Helms.* I saw clear patterns of resonance across many of the theoretical frameworks, and I integrated them into a simple four-stage schema that has proven helpful to me and many others in the years since. I call this schema *the four stages of faith development*.

Doubt, it turns out, is the passageway from each stage to the next. Without doubt, there can be growth within a stage, but growth from one stage to another usually requires us to doubt the assumptions that give shape to our current stage.

Now any schema clarifies by simplifying, and many people are rightly suspicious of stage theories for that reason. Stage theories can easily be abused, especially by people who, let's say, create a four-stage theory and put themselves at the top in stage four and judge everyone "beneath" them as inferior. I'll deal with that concern later (in Chapter 9), but for now, I hope you'll dispense with the idea of climbing a ladder or stairway, and instead, I invite you to imagine a tree.

As you know, trees in temperate climates have periods of growth (spring and summer) and dormancy (fall and winter), and those periods show up as rings in a cross section of the tree. The dark, thin lines represent the dormant season, when the tree consolidates the last season's growth, and the lighter, wider spaces between lines represent the growing season, when the tree adds new substance.

We'll call the growth period of the innermost ring Stage One, and we'll call the next growth period Stage Two, and so on. Each new stage, like a

---

male-dominated systems. A similar case could be made that marginalized people would often be similarly propelled to more advanced stages of moral development (or different patterns of development entirely) because their experiences of oppression and exclusion force them to see through and beyond the conventional moral reasoning patterns of those who marginalize them. These considerations are reminders of the limitations of any single theory or model of human development.

* See William Cross, *Shades of Black* (Temple University Press, 1991). For a short summary of racial identity theories, see https://www.racialequitytools.org/resourcefiles/Compilation_of_Racial _Identity_Models_7_15_11.pdf. I especially recommend Charmaine L. Wijeyesinghe and Bailey W. Jackson, III (ed.), *New Perspectives on Racial Identity Development* (NYU Press, 2012), which offers helpful summaries of black, Latino, Asian American, American Indian, white, and multiracial identity theories. Obviously, faith identity development and racial identity development are very different processes, but they have fascinating similarities and intriguing overlaps.

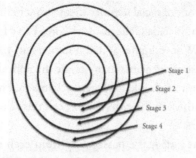

ring on a tree, embraces and builds upon the previous stage, while growing
beyond its limits. Or to borrow and invert a phrase from integral philosopher Ken Wilber, each stage includes and transcends its predecessors.

Before we look at the four stages in more detail, we should review what
we discussed in Chapter 2 about your internal brain committee. When
you were born, your survival module was already at work, serving as the
control center for all your unconscious, instinctive bodily functions: your
beating heart, your breathing lungs, your active digestive system, your
basic reflexes, your vigilance for danger. Your intuitive belonging function was quickly activated, that part of your brain that focuses on relationships that, for a completely helpless baby, are absolutely necessary for
survival. Around the age of two, your meaning module or intellect also
became more active, the part of your internal committee that could learn
language, ask a million questions to help you make sense of the world
for yourself, and make independent judgments, like, "No! I won't!" and
"That's not fair!" and "I want that toy *now*!"

Your ability to use language, to think independently, to walk and even
run out of your parents' reach, and to make your desires, needs, and dis-
agreements known marked your graduation into Stage One, and for most
of us, it happened around the age of two. As you became increasingly
independent, your parents had a new set of responsibilities: not simply
to provide for your needs and desires, as they had been doing since your
birth, but also to teach you how to provide for your own needs and desires
in appropriate ways.

To help you in this way, your parents and other significant adults began teaching you that some ways of meeting your needs and desires were
acceptable and others weren't, that some would be rewarded and others
would be discouraged. Smile, say *thank you*, share . . . and the Big People

responded one way. Scream, steal, bite, and hit . . . and the Big People responded another way. Adults around you had one primary teaching goal: to help you survive independently in human society and in the natural world by learning the difference between right and wrong, good and bad, safe and dangerous, appropriate and inappropriate, permitted and prohibited.

For us to become fully independent adults someday, we need to start life fully dependent on the guidance of older, wiser Big People. They make the rules and we follow them. We ask questions and they answer them. They give commands and we obey them. We have problems and they solve them.

I call this first stage *Simplicity* because it revolves around a simple mental function of sorting nearly everything into one of two categories.

Is this berry edible or inedible?

Is that person or tribe a friend or an enemy?

Is taking your friend's toy permitted or prohibited?

Is telling a lie or using violence a clever and effective way to get what you want or is it a punishable offense?

Did this make me happy or sad, glad or mad?

For that reason, in Stage One, you set out to master the mental skills of dualism, of seeing the world in twos: this or that, in or out, right or wrong. Dualism may be simple, but it's not so easy when you're first getting started. That first, "No! You can't!" or "Yes, you must!" comes as a bit of a shock for an infant who is used to being coddled and given whatever she cries for. Her original innocence is disrupted by a new responsibility: to figure out what the Big People want, what they will reward, and what they will punish.

The Big People—your parents, grandparents, teachers, chiefs, and religious leaders—are central to your world in Stage One, because they're the ones who know the rules and show them to you. They're also the ones who enforce the rules. So Stage One is the stage of authority as well as the stage of dualism.

As far as you're concerned, the authorities know everything, and you don't, so you feel highly dependent on them. You trust them and want to please them, and you aspire someday to be as certain and all-knowing as they are. Sure, sometimes they make you sad or mad when they don't let you get your way, but in the end, they're the Big People, and until you become a Big Person yourself, you need to fall in line.

Before long, you find out that your Big People dislike or distrust some other Big People, and your dualism adds a new category: us versus them. Our Big People are good; their Big People are bad. We are right; they are wrong. Familiar and similar is safe; unfamiliar and different is dangerous. This social dualism creates a strong sense of loyalty and identity among *us*. It also creates a strong sense of anxiety and even hostility about *them*, the *other*, the *outsiders*, and the *outcasts*.

Stage One is built on trust, because for the child, trust is an absolute necessity, a matter of survival. If you distrust the authorities, you'll ignore their warnings and venture too far into the woods, where the wild things will eat you. You'll run out in the street, where the cars will hit you. You'll get too friendly with the other tribe, and they'll kidnap or corrupt you. If you don't trust, you won't obey, and if you don't obey, you won't survive. So you'd better not blur any edges or allow any shades of gray: life is a war, and your survival depends on you becoming a good, obedient, trusting soldier who follows orders as an absolute necessity.

Simple trust; simple obedience; simple, unquestioning loyalty . . . that's what matters in Stage One.

Nearly everyone you've ever known was born and raised into Stage One, and in fact, that's the baseline of what being *raised* means in our culture: being taught the basic dualisms of Stage One.* Many people spend their whole lives in Stage One. They submit to the authorities and follow the rules. Then, when it's time for them to become authorities themselves, they demand the same submission from the next generation that they themselves gave to the previous generation. It's that simple. For

---

* I should add here that those words *in our culture* are significant. I can imagine a culture in the future in which this four-stage model is no longer relevant, and I am sure that this model is already much less relevant or helpful in understanding some subcultures in today's world. When I say "in our culture," I mean the global/industrial/technological culture framed largely by four characteristics: patriarchy (rule by powerful and often violent alpha males), white (Christian) supremacy (rule or privilege for white-bodied people, especially if they're Christian), dualistic thinking (either/or, us/them thinking), and what I call "theo-capitalism" (a form of capitalism that inspires religious devotion, and in which the "invisible hand of the market" is seen as the divine hand).

that reason, it shouldn't be a surprise that faith and religion are a strictly Stage One phenomenon for millions, even billions, of people.

For Stage One Jews, Christians, and Muslims, God is the Big Person in the sky who sets the rules, demands trust, requires obedience, and mandates punishment when rules are broken. God authorizes Big People to exercise delegated divine authority, whether in the home, faith community, city, state, or nation, and if we trust our authorities enough to believe and do what they tell us, we can have the same absolute certainty that they have . . . the certainty that we are the good people, and all who are not part of our in-group are the bad people, the certainty that we will have a happy ending and those other people will not. So for the rest of our lives, it will be our job to avoid the bad people, to exclude them, eliminate them, control them, or convert them, because in the end, it's either us or them.

From the age of two to twelve or so, Stage One works pretty well for most of us. But as we mature into adolescence, we naturally desire more independence and we begin to chafe against Stage One rigidity. We may begin to question some of the rules that Big People have imposed on us since childhood. Our social circles widen, and we discover that some of *them* are every bit as nice as *us*, maybe nicer, so we see some of the dualistic judgments of our Big People as prejudices. With more age and independence, we read new books, make new friends, travel to new places, and we start to see that there are other groups with their own Big People and their own differing rules and beliefs, and they are just as human as we are. Still more questions arise.

Up until this point, Stage One may have felt like a school to help us learn the basic morals necessary for independence, but now it starts to feel like detention, a cage, even a prison.

The only way out is doubt. We may doubt that the authorities are always right. We may doubt that all the rules are always absolute and appropriate. We may doubt that *they* are as bad or dangerous as our authority figures warned us or that *we* are as good and exceptional as we were told. Add hormones, puberty, sexual curiosity, and changing bodies and brains to the mix, and Simplicity stops feeling so simple anymore.

Whether it happens at twelve or twenty-two or fifty-five, eventually, many of us doubt our way out of Simplicity and enter Stage Two: Complexity.

If Stage One is about dualism and dependence, Stage Two is about pragmatism and independence. We're not children any longer. We want to self-differentiate. We have our own lives to live, and we have to find a way to become who we are on our own, as self-reliant individuals who know what we want. Our new Stage Two challenge is to figure out how to get what we want when we want it.

In Stage One we were drawn to authority figures who told us what to think and do, but in Stage Two we seek out coaches who teach us how to think for ourselves and help us develop our own goals, along with our own skills to attain those goals. In Stage One, we saw life as a war, a matter of survival, but in Stage Two, we see life as a game, a matter of skill, a contest of competing and winning. Or better yet, we see life as a complex set of different games, and we have to master the rules and craft of each game. Remember when you were in high school, for example, and reflect on how complex your life became:

> **in your academic subjects:** *Will I get As, Cs, or Fs? Will I succeed or fail in math, language, history, science, and art, each a different game with different rules, requiring different skills? Which games should I specialize in because I have the best chance of winning, and which should I avoid because I'm certain to lose? How can I win in at least one or two of the many academic games I am forced to play?*
>
> **among your peers:** *Will I be popular or unpopular, liked or ignored, respected or made fun of, befriended or bullied? How will I win the game of social status and popularity? How will I handle peer pressure? Will I position myself as a nerd or a jock, a bully or a wallflower, a do-gooder or a delinquent?*
>
> **with your parents:** *Will they allow me to grow up and help me grow up, or will they fear the changes they see in me and clamp down? How long a leash will they give me? How will I win the game of freedom to be my own independent me?*
>
> **in your own body:** *How will I negotiate the rapid changes I see and feel, some of which are simultaneously powerful, exciting, and scary? How will I grapple with my adult body . . . its height, weight, shape,*

strength, hair, skin . . . especially in light of the ideas I've internalized
about how my body should be? How will I manage my sexual desires?
sexually: *How will I fare in romantic relationships? Will I be seen as desirable?*
Will I win the attention and affections of others whom I find desirable?
Will I win or lose in the dating game? What does winning even mean?
spiritually: *How do I integrate the complex information I'm learning—in*
science, history, philosophy, and psychology, for example—with the sim-
ple dualisms of right versus wrong, us versus them, good guys versus bad
guys, and truth versus error I was taught throughout childhood? How
do I relate to a God of rewards and punishment when what I really
need now is a God of coaching and encouragement?

Stage One preoccupied us with dualistic questions of right versus
wrong, good versus bad, us versus them. But in Stage Two we ask new
questions: "What good is being right if I'm not successful? What good is
being good if I don't get the rewards of being good? What good is being
part of *us* if *we* aren't winning against *them*?" For that reason, in Stage Two
we face a steady flow of pragmatic questions of success in multiple games,
each with its own skills and complexities. Back in Stage One, everything
was either known or knowable, but here in Stage Two, everything is
learnable and doable, if only we can find the right models, mentors, and
coaches and master the right techniques, skills, and know-how.

If you can remember this stage, you'll probably recall that your childhood authority figures had already taught you all the familiar dualisms
they had to offer. You began to tire of their constant lecturing and you
came to resent their constant policing. You may have actively run away or
rebelled, or you may have simply found ways to distance yourself, getting
space through a busy social life, extracurricular activities, or withdrawal
into your own imaginative world. Having gained some distance from
your Stage One authority figures, you found some models, mentors, and
coaches who gave you permission to explore and helped you learn the
skills of success so that you could become a winner (or at least not too big
a loser) in this complex adolescent world full of complex adolescent games.

The best parents, teachers, pastors, and other authority figures understand this distancing process, and they offer two generous gifts for the
emerging adults in their care. First, they begin to act less like police and

more like coaches themselves, and second, they welcome new mentors and models to share the spotlight they have previously had to themselves. Sadly, many parents and other authority figures don't understand how much a young adult needs a new and different kind of leadership from them, so they clamp down with even more force than before, trying to reassert control. This authoritarian move is especially common among parents and other authority figures who have never outgrown Stage One themselves. The results are predictable: either a stunted and damaged adolescent or a rebel who cleverly or defiantly finds space to become an adult. For parents who are themselves in Stage Two or beyond, the process is generally less contentious. In fact, instead of feeling that they're losing a child, they feel they're gaining a peer.

When I look back on my own adolescence, because I grew up in a very conservative Christian setting, Simplicity was the absolute norm for spirituality. But by the age of twelve or thirteen, I realized it wasn't working for me. I jokingly say that sex, facts, and rock and roll were my undoing.

Sex was never talked about, except when linked with terms like *sin* and *immorality*. I remember being sexually scandalized for the first time at about the age of eight. I kept hearing the word *circumcision* in sermons and in the Bible, but I had no idea what it meant. When I asked my parents at dinner one night, they used the word *penis* in the explanation. I was mortified that the Bible and God would have anything to do with such matters! It's no surprise that when I experienced ejaculation a few years later, I didn't even know the word to describe it, and my predisposition was to be ashamed, afraid that God would punish me for my arousal.

The insistent intensity of my hormone-infused body created a kind of feedback loop with my Stage One spirituality: the stronger my sexual desires, the stronger my shame. The stronger my shame, the stronger my need for grace and forgiveness. The stronger my need for grace and forgiveness, the more I read the Bible, prayed, and went to Bible studies, church services, and youth group. The more I did those things, the better a Christian I was. Looking back, I wonder how many thousands (or millions?) of young men and women have become passionate spiritually because they've been trapped in a Stage One shame cycle with a strong sexual component.* When I ponder this sex-shame-spirituality cycle, I

---

* For more on this process, see Tina Schermer Sellers, *Sex, God, and the Conservative Church* (Routledge, 2017); Linda Kay Klein, *Pure: Inside the Evangelical Movement That Shamed a*

can't help but think of Stage One religion as a kind of forgiveness racket, a mafia that increases our shame and then sells us forgiveness, only to expose us to more shame and then more forgiveness, world without end.

As a teenager caught in the vortex of this vicious cycle, I remember thinking, "This can't be healthy." And then I remember feeling ashamed for thinking that.

Sex was a problem but so were facts. My religious authority figures told me the earth was six to ten thousand years old, having been created by divine fiat in six literal days. There were a literal Adam, Eve, snake, and fruit. We knew this because an inerrant book told us so. But by middle school, I had an insatiable curiosity about science, especially biology. I read all the biology books for my age group at the local library and soon was checking out high school and then college textbooks. There, an old and evolving earth was the norm, and when the Big People of my Stage One faith community told me I had to choose between the facts of science or the facts of the Bible, I remember thinking that I probably would not be able to stay a Christian as an adult, since my authority figures also taught me that Stage One Christianity was the only legitimate form.

Rock and roll rounded out the trifecta. The energy, joy, and aliveness of music and other forms of art seemed so out of sync with the buttoned-down seriousness of Stage One religion. Where my religion demanded clear, simple, and certain answers to every question, the arts beckoned me to exploration, to mystery, to delight instead. Sitting in straight rows and singing four-part harmony from a hymn book brought a certain feeling of belonging and order, but dancing to a pop song or improvising on the sax or guitar brought a feeling of freedom, elation, and empowerment. The latter, our religious authority figures said, was fleshly and worldly, and the former godly and heavenly. I wondered why I had to choose.* Many years later, I read Chaim Potok's masterful novel *My Name Is Asher Lev*,

---

Generation of Young Women and How I Broke Free (Atria, 2018); and Nadia Bolz-Weber, *Shameless: A Sexual Reformation* (Convergent, 2019).

* Just as I was coming of age, fundamentalists were discovering that rock and roll could become a powerful tool of indoctrination, so many stopped fighting it and started using it, creating a powerful wing of the Evangelical Industrial Complex called CCM (Contemporary Christian Music). It blossomed with recording artists, concert venues (often megachurches), and radio and TV outlets that later became powerful tools of the Religious Right. I was a small player in that world for a short time, giving coffee house concerts and producing independent albums of original songs.

in which a young Orthodox Jew with a gift for visual arts faces a similar choice. I wonder, looking back, how I might have processed that book if I had read it at fourteen or fifteen.

I felt stuck: unable to leave and unable to stay, caught in the liminal space between Stages One and Two. That's when an unexpected invitation came. A fellow a few years older than me invited me to a Bible study. I wasn't interested, but he was persistent, and he drove forty minutes out of his way to bring me, so it was hard to say no. In that group, I experienced my first taste of Stage Two Christianity, and it tasted like freedom.

Instead of listening to a sermon by an authority figure, we learned methods of studying the Bible for ourselves. If I asked a question, instead of giving me the one right answer, the leaders would tell me three or four ways different Christian groups answered the question, leaving me space to choose which made the most sense to me. Sure, they might have had their preferred answer, but they acknowledged that other good Christians came up with different answers. Not only that, but they actually wanted me to learn all I could so I could make decisions of my own about controversial matters. They encouraged me to study Christian history and theology, and maybe even secular philosophy. Learning and studying, thinking for myself and reaching my own conclusions, it turned out, were part of what it meant to be a good Stage Two Christian. From that time forward, there would always be a few books beside my bed or in my backpack, because my appetite for Stage Two learning quickly became voracious.

I felt I was entering a wide new world of varied challenges: keep a prayer and Bible study journal, master the message of the Bible, read lots of other books to develop my own personal theology, learn to witness or share my faith with others, go on retreats to deepen my spiritual life, discover and use my special spiritual gifts, attend concerts and conferences to experience new depths of worship (and maybe even speak in tongues), go on special mission trips to translate my faith into action. All this, I now realize, was the meat and potatoes (or burger and fries) of classic Stage Two faith, and although there were difficulties, Stage Two brought me great joy, great growth, great relationships, and great opportunities that I never would have had in my Stage One version of Christian faith.

Back in those days, nearly every household in America was trading in their old black-and-white TVs for color sets, just as they were trading in their old mono radios and record players for hifi stereo systems. I felt that I was doing something similar in my faith. What wonderful, exciting days!

I was a thoroughly engaged Stage Two Christian by the age of twenty, and for nearly twenty years, Stage Two worked pretty well for me. Of course, I had misgivings, and sometimes the complexity felt so overwhelming that I wondered if the whole complex system of beliefs and practices I was constructing was about to collapse under its own weight. Most annoying, Stage One Christians kept popping up in Stage Two settings. They acted like they owned the space, and their narrow-mindedness, dogmatism, naive ignorance, and unselfconscious arrogance drove me nuts.

But there was always more to learn: sixty-six dense and challenging books in the Bible, twenty centuries of Christian history, dozens if not hundreds of different schools of thought in different denominations. I was a dry sponge, eager to absorb as much as I could as fast as I could. I was always looking for the next must-read book or must-hear album of Christian music, the next retreat or conference, the next teacher or dynamic leader, the next experience or insight. I had this sense that life was good and would only get better if I just kept consuming more and more and more Christian goods and services. Meanwhile, many of my Jewish, Muslim, Buddhist, and other peers were having similar Stage Two experiences in their traditions.

Phrases like *engage the culture* and *change the world* set my Stage Two imagination on fire. God was on the move in the world, and I wanted to be part of the movement. My initial induction into a Stage Two movement mindset was the Jesus movement, which overflowed and intermingled with the charismatic movement, which in turn was absorbed by the larger Evangelical movement, which eventually was captured and co-opted by the Religious Right.

And that's where Stage Two stopped working for me. Stage One introduced me to the joy of being right. Stage Two introduced me to the joy of being effective. But what happens when you start to think that you are becoming highly effective at achieving the wrong ends?

I soon found myself in my deepest and most significant period of doubt yet. I started looking for an exit ramp.

I had a few friends who shared my concerns, but we were a tiny minority among our baby boomer cohort. In the seventies and eighties, the vast majority of our peers either dug in their heels with Stage One faith or jumped with both feet into Stage Two faith, and there they have made their stand ever since. They've invested so much in their early-stage faith that it would cause deep psychological trauma to acknowledge that it's no longer working. So the only faith they will ever know is either the authoritarian, dualistic faith of Stage One Simplicity, or the pragmatic, independent faith of Stage Two Complexity.

People in Simplicity and Complexity have become a significant religious market. Every year, they need more sermons, books, radio and TV shows, podcasts, conferences, courses, retreats, camps, churches, and mission trips to help them maintain and strengthen their stage of faith. Many preachers become celebrities—some of them, super-rich celebrities—by proclaiming the six steps to this, the five principles of that, the nine secrets to something else. People are willing to pay a lot for the promise of answered prayers, sweet marriages, and smiling children who will never come out as gay and never need counseling, not to mention the promise of eternal heaven after blessed success in this life. They're willing to pay a lot for the promise of prosperity at or above middle class and for the privilege of being part of a growing megachurch with great facilities, lots of dynamic programs, and connections with the rich, famous, and powerful, not to mention the prestige of being one of God's chosen people, called out and set apart from the leftovers of sinful humanity. Aided by an ample supply of religious products and professionals, the faithful lay a solid foundation of Stage One Simplicity upon which they build an elegant mansion of Stage Two Complexity. From the top floor, the view is amazing and life is abundant.

Except when it isn't.

That's when some feel so stuck, so trapped, and so stagnant they decide to burn down the whole structure. On their way out of the burning building, many grab for some mementos of faith to save. Others barely make it out alive, saving nothing but their lives.

When the smoke clears, all is in doubt.

Reflection and Action

1. How do you feel about the way I introduce developmental stage theory in this chapter? Do you see both the value and potential abuses of a multi-stage approach?

2. How would you tell your own faith story using the categories of Simplicity and Complexity?

3. How would you describe your congregation and denomination using these categories?

4. I describe doubt as "the passageway from each stage to the next." Does that match your experience? Can you describe your current experiences of doubt as helping you leave your current stage?

5. I also say, "Without doubt, there can be growth within a stage, but growth from one stage to another usually requires us to doubt the assumptions that give shape to our current stage." Try to describe, from your own experience, ways that you've grown "within a stage."

6. Describe what is most fulfilling and rewarding about Stage One faith. Do the same for Stage Two faith. Then describe how Stage One and Stage Two may begin to feel less fulfilling and rewarding.

7. The phrase *all is in doubt* in the last sentence might seem overly ominous or dramatic. How do you respond to it?

PART TWO

ALL IN DOUBT

6

DOUBT AS DESCENT

If Christ spent an anguished night in prayer, if He burst out from the Cross, "My God, my God, why have you forsaken me?" then surely we are also permitted doubt. But we must move on. To choose doubt as a philosophy of life is akin to choosing immobility as a means of transportation.

—Yann Martel, *Life of Pi*

I met Walt at a gathering for people concerned about environmental issues in my state. We chatted over refreshments after the meeting, and he invited me to his farm, where he was doing all he could to preserve and protect some pristine wildlife habitat. I gladly accepted his invitation. A few weeks later, as we walked the hilly trails through the meadows and forests on his property, we shared our stories. When Walt learned that I was a pastor, he did what many people did: explained why he didn't go to church, as if I expected an excuse.

"My wife and I used to be Catholic," he said. "Then we got 'born again' and 'Spirit-filled' and joined the Assembly of God. But we found out they had a whole lot of rules, like no drinking alcohol, so we switched to Presbyterian. We enjoyed being Presbyterian for a while, but then my wife got into an argument with the pastor because she didn't like how he interpreted the Bible. So she became Methodist for a while, but then she had problems with that pastor too because the minister performed secret weddings for gay people. Now she's something called Independent Charismatic."

"You're still Presbyterian?" I asked, trying to keep track of when *we* switched to *she*.

"No. I felt like our religion bus was making too many sharp turns, so I pulled the cord and got off after Presbyterian," Walt replied. "I guess I stopped seeing the point. I studied some Buddhism with a teacher at the community college, and now, mindfully walking these trails has become my church. It's a little lonely, but it's better than singing songs and reciting creeds I don't believe anymore. I guess out here, on these trails, I walk out my unanswered questions."

When people run into problems with Stage One or Two Christianity, many make what I call a lateral transfer. They move, like Walt's wife, from a Stage One Catholic to a Stage One Pentecostal, or from a Stage Two Presbyterian to a Stage Two Methodist. (I think similar transfers happen between religions: a Stage One Christian might become a Stage One Muslim, for example, or vice versa.) They don't have doubts about the basic product, whether it's more dualistic or pragmatic, authority focused or success focused; they're just dissatisfied customers who want the same religious goods and services with improved features (anti–gay marriage or pro–biblical literalism) or a better price point (it's OK to drink alcohol). Luckily for them, there are plenty of religious retailers eager to cater to the demands and tastes of dissatisfied Stage One and Stage Two religious consumers, as Walt's wife discovered.

Sometimes, people make forward rather than lateral transfers. When they move from Stage One into Stage Two, the transition often requires a change in churches, denominations, or religions. So a Stage One Roman Catholic becomes a Stage Two Methodist or Buddhist. The new faith community offers room to grow in a new stage of faith. It feels like a step up, because developmentally, at least, it is.

A few disillusioned Stage Two Christians may temporarily or permanently revert to Stage One Christianity, making what I call a regressive transfer. Sadly, a regressive transfer often leads the spiritually troubled into cults or cultlike groups, which are fiercely devoted to rigid Simplicity. For those who regress, the fear of what lies beyond Complexity feels so terrifying, or the sense of belonging that is often found in strict Stage One communities feels so alluring, that they willingly resubmit to Stage One authority, or even authoritarianism.

For most Stage Two believers, though, there's no going back, at least not in the long term. After trying lateral transfers among two or three (or seven or eight) Stage Two faith communities, many start doubting the whole Stage Two project.* They get sick of sermons about the three easy steps to marital bliss, the five certain cures of depression, and the seven proven keys to biblical prosperity. Real life, they realize, is more mysterious, less formulaic, and more messy than that. Stage Two feels a little shallow, a little fake, and they're craving depth and honesty. "Faith shouldn't feel like an infomercial," one disillusioned Stage Two fellow said to me, "and especially not a slick one." It's better, many find, to "walk out their questions," even if doing so means walking alone.

It often takes a faith crisis to force someone into a forward transfer out of Stage Two. Perhaps a trusted religious leader experiences a public setback, failure, or scandal: *If all those easy steps, cures, and keys to success didn't work for the Stage Two leader who taught them, why should I trust them?* they wonder. Sometimes, the pain is more personal: *I followed the three easy steps, and I still got divorced; I tried the five certain cures, and I still feel depressed; I've been working the seven keys to biblical prosperity, and I'm deeper in debt than ever (while the prosperity preacher keeps getting richer).* When a Stage Two religious teaching or program doesn't produce the results that were promised, many sincere Stage Two believers simply amp up their effort, assuming the fault is their own. But eventually, their confidence cracks like a breached hull, the doubts pour in, and their Stage Two project starts to sink.

Often, they feel they must go down with the ship as a final act of loyalty. It may have been easy to transfer from one community to another within Stage Two, but leaving Stage Two entirely for something beyond it? That's not so easy.

Stage Two leaders often "poison the well" by telling their followers that such communities are liberal and therefore evil. Better to be a non-Christian entirely than to be a liberal or progressive Christian! From this perspective, when Stage Two Christianity fails for you, you can't go back to Stage One, so Christianity fails for you, period.

A young Ugandan journalist once captured this feeling for me. I was a

---

* The pragmatic orientation of Stage Two folks often makes them comfortable with church shopping and church hopping. Loyal Stage One members tend to leave a church only when the church is exposed as bad, incorrect, or wrong, but Stage Two folks have no problem asking, "What works best for me?" So when something that looks better comes along, it only makes sense to check it out.

guest at a gathering of East African Christian leaders near Kampala, and she was covering the event for the local paper. African Christianity, like American Christianity, is largely a mix of Stage One Simplicity and Stage Two Complexity. Because the continent has so many practical problems, like poverty, sickness, and violence, pragmatic Stage Two faith often predominates in the form of the Prosperity Gospel, which promises miraculous provisions of money, healing, and protection. As the conference was ending, the journalist approached me, asking for an interview. After a few minutes, she turned off her recorder and said, "I have one more question. This isn't for publication. This is for me. Would that be OK?" I assured her that would be fine, and she asked, "Do you *really* have hope for African Christianity?"

I told her I did, but I was intrigued by her question. "I have lost hope," she said. "Every week, my job as a religion reporter requires me to cover the latest scandals committed in the name of religion. I've come to see much of Christianity as a criminal enterprise. Just last month, for example, I covered a pastor who prophesied that there was a woman in his congregation with HIV, and she was praying to be healed, but her prayers could not be answered because there was a curse on her land."

At the altar call, the journalist explained, a woman came forward, crying and trembling, because she felt his description fit her: she had HIV and she owned the land she inherited from her late husband, who had died of AIDS the previous year. "The Lord says that your healing will only come if you give your land to the *man of God*," the preacher said, referring to himself. She gave him the deed to the land. Then, a few months later, she died of AIDS.

"That is tragic," I said. "It does sound like a crime. Extortion, fraud, theft."

"It only got worse," she continued. "When her brother discovered what the pastor had done, he hired a hit man to kill the pastor, which forced the pastor to hire a group of armed bodyguards to accompany him everywhere, even into the pulpit. Of course, the pastor tried to play the victim, that the devil was attacking him for preaching the Word. Week after week, that's the kind of story that I cover. That's why I have lost hope for Christianity in Africa."

Of course, I could think of equally depressing stories from my side of the Atlantic. (In fact, I read recently of an American megachurch pastor who is under investigation for trying to hire a hit man to take out a rival!)

Millions of people around the world have reached a breaking point just like this young journalist did. She has reason to doubt whether the claims of religion are true, but in addition, she now doubts whether religion can even be considered good or safe. Where do people like her go? They've never seen anything beyond Stage One dualistic religion and Stage Two pragmatic religion. Many conclude they've reached the end of the road in what religion has to offer. They may decisively drop out or they may gradually peter out, staying on the rolls but participating with less and less frequency, showing up three or four times a year instead of three or four times a month.

Eventually, some pull the cord, get off the religious bus, and make a lateral transfer, becoming Stage Two nones. They're still pragmatic, focusing on "what works for me." It's just that now, they're honestly finding more help in their quest for success, fulfillment, and personal development outside the world of faith.

But others aren't so easily satisfied. Like Walt, they walk out their questions. Having felt increasingly alienated both from Stage One dualism and Stage Two pragmatism, they lose faith in both the authoritarian leaders of Simplicity and the success coaches of Complexity, whether inside or outside the church. Both types of leaders make promises they can't deliver on, and neither type is honestly facing life's deeper questions and challenges.

This quest for honesty and depth burns like a fire in the belly and baptizes people into Stage Three: Perplexity. Life, folks in Stage Three feel, is more than simple *and* more than complex: it is downright mysterious, downright *perplexing*. What physicists say about quantum mechanics is true for all of life: reality is not only stranger than we imagine, but stranger than we *can* imagine.* Looks deceive. Appearances lie. Full truths are far less convenient than half-truths and lies. Confident people are often con artists, and their simple rules and promises are often little more than tricks for controlling the gullible and making a profit at their expense.

---

* Variations on this quotation are attributed to both J. B. S. Haldane and Arthur Stanley Eddington.

My friend Chuck, the son of a famous Stage One preacher, once captured the spirit of Stage Three Perplexity in a single sentence. "I wish that everyone at their baptism could be presented with a state-of-the-art BS detector," he said, "because they're really going to need it in the church."

His statement, of course, is actually an understatement, as Stage Three people will readily admit. It's not just the world of religion where people need a BS detector. The domains of politics and economics, romance and sex, friendship and family, the arts and the academy are also full of fog, smoke, false claims, deceptive orthodoxies, overblown ideologies, dishonest games, and convenient lies. What you're taught in high school doesn't always hold up in college, what you're taught in college doesn't always hold up in graduate school, and what's said in a graduate school seminar often sounds silly or naive in the "real world." Ignorance, misinformation, and full-fledged BS abound in all sectors of life, not just religion.

That fact frustrates those of us who have found real value in religion: we think, or at least wish, that the domains of faith and spirituality would be different. Shouldn't faith communities be places where we find justice, truth, beauty, and love, not malarkey, baloney, hokum, and balderdash?

With questions like these glowing like hot embers in their hearts, many unsettled believers in Stage Two faith communities feel increasingly desperate for something, anything, beyond dualistic Simplicity and pragmatic Complexity. For many, the first signs of hope come in the form of books, podcasts, online chatrooms, classes, conferences, or graduate programs rather than as actual flesh-and-blood spiritual communities. That was Walt's experience. His Buddhist teacher at the local community college didn't require him to agree to a set of Stage One dogmas, nor did he make extravagant Stage Two promises of success and happiness. His teacher's tone was more humble: *here is a set of symbols, stories, principles, and practices that have been life-giving to me, and I'm glad to offer them to you so you can work with them yourself.* Walt took what he needed and put it to use as he mindfully walked the trails of his farm alone.

Stage Three doesn't seem to be an easy space in which to form anything as long-lasting and stable as a congregation. Stage Three communities tend to self-destruct in five different ways.

Structure: Because Stage Three people see the damage done by unchallenged structures and institutions, they distrust and challenge even their own institutions constantly, perhaps obsessively. Whatever Stage Three people construct, they feel an obligation to immediately deconstruct.

Authority: In contrast to Stage One people, who are dependent (or even co-dependent) on authority figures, and in contrast to Stage Two people, who seek success coaches who will help them in their quest to be independent, Stage Three people tend to be counter-dependent. For them, authority figures must be approached with de facto suspicion. It's hard for any leader to earn the trust of people in Perplexity and even harder for them to keep it. Stage Three groups, as a result, tend to use, exhaust, and discard their leaders quickly. The rare leader or teacher who survives Stage Three scrutiny is often deeply loved.

Purpose: Stage Three people often feel allergic to the level of confidence implicit in any call to action. Because Stage Three individuals specialize in critique and deconstruction, not goal-setting and action, they gravitate toward groups that focus on conversation and analysis rather than mobilization and mission. Mission statements and strategic plans evoke memories of conquest and colonization, so they opt out.*

Belonging: Stage Three embraces relativism, the idea that every viewpoint is relative to the point from which its adherents view the world. For example, rich white people generally see only what is visible from their downward gaze of privilege and power, and poor people of color see things uniquely from their vantage point of marginalization or oppression. To belong to a group wholeheartedly can too easily mean buying into its limited perspectives and blindnesses. For that reason, Stage Three folks feel more comfortable lurking on the fringes of a group rather than belonging squarely in its center. Even better, they might be fringe members of a number of groups, to gain a variety of viewpoints.

---

* Some readers may have noticed that many Stage Three people are drawn to social action, but interestingly, much of that action has a deconstructive and oppositional feel to it, characterized by resistance and involving only short-term intense involvement (marches, boycotts, Twitter rants, etc.). Short-term intensity is an essential dimension of social change, but the long-term work of building and reforming institutions is much harder for Stage Three people and often requires them to graduate to Stage Four, or to recruit idealistic Stage One and Stage Two foot soldiers who still have a stomach for institutional involvement.

It's hard for Stage Three individuals to build a sense of belonging in any single community when one of the primary qualities they share is an aversion to commitment.

Suspicion: Given their disillusionment with structure, authority, organizational purpose, and belonging, Stage Three individuals generally operate on what is often called a "hermeneutic of suspicion." They are keenly aware of organizational and institutional injustice, oppression, and hypocrisy, and so they enter any new organizational setting expecting the worst. Their suspicions are almost always confirmed, since wherever people gather, there are problems. (Of course, if Stage Three people turn this scrutiny on themselves, they may become disillusioned with their disillusionment, skeptical of their skepticism, and suspicious of their suspicion, which sometimes leads them to regress to Stage One or Two, or to progress to Stage Four.)

Unable to find a community that fits their stage, many Stage Three people have only one option: like Walt, they must walk out their questions alone. If they find community at all, it tends to be among alienated individuals like themselves. When these folk gather, they do so loosely and often temporarily in public or secular spaces, providing mutual benefits without long-term demands, perhaps forming a reading group, signing up for a college course, making online connections through a social network like Facebook, Patreon, or Twitter, or attending a retreat, conference, or festival.

For people who have outgrown Stages One and Two and who find themselves in the dynamic space of Stage Three, doubt and its cousins of deconstruction, suspicion, and relativism are not enemies to be kept at bay: they are doorways to insight and liberation. It is only by doubting institutions, authority figures, mission statements, limited perspectives, group-think, and the like that they can discover the inconvenient truths that are being carefully hidden on behalf of some individual or group's self-interest.

Not long ago, after one of my lectures on the four stages, a young minister named Joelle approached and told me she could remember the exact day she stepped into Perplexity. It was during her third week in seminary. Like many seminarians, she experienced her call to ministry through her high school youth group, which was a problem, because her denomination didn't believe in women ministers.

In high school, she actually found "grown-up church" pretty boring. It was, in the terms we're using here, firmly cemented in Simplicity, offering one right answer to every question. But youth group was different. It was all about Complexity, and to the teenaged Joelle, that was delicious. Her curiosity was welcomed. Her questions were encouraged. Her gifts were celebrated. To her delight, her youth group leader could offer her three easy steps to solve this problem, four different possible good answers to that question, and five spiritual practices to develop that virtue or skill. He gave her dozens of books, invited her to conferences and mission trips, and constantly shared podcasts and online resources, which she devoured. She was ravenously hungry for information that went beyond easy answers.

Her delight in Stage Two faith made her want to do for others what her youth group leader did for her, so during college, she joined a campus ministry, and each summer, she volunteered at her denomination's youth camp. Then, during her senior year, she found a new denomination that ordained women. In fact, her new pastor was a woman who celebrated Joelle's desire to enter ministry, and she helped Joelle apply and be accepted to her own alma mater.

Joelle's first class on her first day of seminary was a church history course. She was shocked to discover that the doctrines she assumed had always been held by all Christians everywhere actually took shape through controversy, dispute, and even violence over several centuries. The next day, she started a Bible survey class. Again, she was shocked to learn that the process of assembling the biblical texts was long, messy, and far less confidence-inspiring than she had always been taught. For a seminar class on worship in the second week, the professor had the students read several articles defending and critiquing various understandings of the meaning of the Eucharist, all centering on the phrase *for your sins* found in both the Gospels and I Corinthians. She had never once even wondered what the phrase meant, because it always seemed obvious. After that class, though, she was genuinely perplexed.*

---

* The subject that Joelle was being introduced to, "theories of atonement," has been addressed by a number of authors. See, for example, Chapter 23 in my *Why Did Jesus, Moses, the Buddha,*

In her Christian ethics course later that second week, the class read and discussed sermons from the pre–Civil War period that defended slavery using the Bible. She never knew such sermons existed, and to make matters worse, she was disturbed by how similar they sounded both in style of communication and in method of interpretation to contemporary sermons she heard in churches and on the radio.

She began seminary excited about studying theology, the Bible, and church ministry in more detail, but by her third week, she felt she had made a terrible mistake. "Forget becoming a minister," she said. "I wasn't sure I wanted to be a Christian anymore, or even a theist!" One question kept echoing in her mind: "Why didn't anyone ever tell me this before? Why did all the sermons, books, conferences, podcasts, and other teachings I devoured never even mention these things? Were they just ignorant, or were they intentionally trying to distract me with various spiritual shiny objects so I wouldn't discover this disturbing information?"

Joelle was in spiritual shock for the rest of that semester, but as time went on, she gradually felt invigorated by what she was learning, especially by the rare and liberating space her professors helped create. They encouraged her to think freely and pursue every question fiercely, without a predetermined answer in mind. That's why she now remembers seminary as some of the best years of her life. "I loved being part of a community of people whose job is to ponder the deepest theological, historical, philosophical, and ethical questions of life," she said. "When you described Stage Three as Perplexity, I disagreed. To me, after the initial shock, Stage Three was *Inquiry*: scholarship, education, critical thinking, and free, unlimited curiosity. What's not to love about that?" Joelle laughed.

Her laughter, touched with a bit of irony, perfectly captured the joy of Stage Three. Pleasing authority figures and fighting the bad guys, as in Stage One, often feels good, righteous, even heroic. Mastering complex information and skills to compete and win in the game of life, as in Stage Two, feels even better: exciting, expansive, competitive. But what could be better than deeply and honestly seeking truth and justice, insight and understanding, wherever they lead . . . especially for a person in Stage Three?

---

and *Mohammed Cross the Road* (Jericho, 2013), or Christopher Grundy's *Recovering Communion in a Violent World* (Cascade, 2019).

I've been on the board of directors of two seminaries and have taught or lectured at many more, and Joelle's experience is very, very common. I seldom meet a student these days who doesn't cherish their seminary experience. Yes, they quickly lose the naive certainty of Simplicity and the can-do confidence of Complexity, but they gain new treasures, gifts of Stage Three: honesty, humility, openness, curiosity, scholarship, and a commitment to understanding the truth, no matter the cost.

That cost, Joelle was discovering, can be high. For starters, when she graduated with her Master of Divinity degree, along with her new set of Stage Three skills, she had accumulated over $40,000 in debt and only one realistic career path to pay it off. And that career didn't pay very well.

To make matters worse, like thousands of young pastors with seminary loans to repay, she found herself preaching in a church composed almost exclusively of Stage One and Stage Two people, mostly older folks who were unlikely to grow beyond the stage in which they had rested comfortably for decades. They welcomed a young pastor in hopes that she would attract a younger crowd, but they certainly didn't expect to learn anything from her. They could only see her as their chaplain and employee, not their leader or teacher. They paid her to make them feel good about what they already knew, not to lead them into the unknown.

"That's my predicament," Joelle said. "If I preach what I learned in seminary, I'll probably lose my job, because most of the people in my congregation have no interest in a Stage Three message, especially the loyal members who pay the bills. Most of them come to church for comfort, for confirmation of what they already think, to hear old familiar hymns and old familiar themes presented with just enough freshness to keep them interesting. They want their sermons to be comfort food, and if I serve up a spiritual meal with kale, broccoli, and tofu rather than butter, salt, and sugar, there will be grumbling for sure. If I don't give them what they want, they'll just transfer to the spiritual restaurant down the street. And don't even get me started on the challenges of preaching about politics. That's a recipe for disaster!"

Churches in the United States (along with churches around the world influenced by U.S. churches) have long had a bipolar theological identity. On the right wing, people sing "give me that old-time religion" because it was "good enough for my father, so it's good enough for me." They've been trained to oppose the "liberals" who welcome critical thinking and scholarly study of the Bible and church history. Since about 1980, these theological conservatives have been organized into a political force (the Religious Right), embracing social and economic conservatism as well. There's a joke among these folks: calling seminary *cemetery*, because they see uncensored scholarship and critical thinking as the death of their brand of conservative orthodoxy. Meanwhile, all but the most conservative seminaries over the same period have engaged with liberation theology, black theology, feminist and womanist theology, eco-theology, and related movements. This engagement has fired up their graduates with a more robust theo-political vision, and it's almost always less conservative than what the folks back home are hearing.

To add to the difficulty, if young ministers like Joelle do try to introduce their congregations to new perspectives and insights, and if some members do begin to move in a more open and progressive direction, division is likely. That's because many of their older parishioners (who support the church with both loyalty and money) experience what I call multiple belonging. Yes, they are devoted members of First Methodist or Shiloh Baptist on Sunday, but from Monday through Friday they're devoted members of the 24/7 Fox News–watching community (or parallel radio and social media communities). Every day, the leading voices of these communities warn their Baptist and Methodist audience against the very messages that enthusiastic young ministers like Joelle feel called to preach.

For all these reasons and more, Joelle won't hear many "amens" if she passes on what she has learned. In fact, if she wants to keep her job, she has to play dumb and continue the same cover-up and conspiracy of silence that so disillusioned her back in those first few weeks of seminary.

Joelle's experience helps explain why so few seminary professors deeply involve themselves in local churches. True, some faculty members find intellectually curious churches where their critical scholarship is welcome, but many if not most seminary faculty simply can't find a church that doesn't require them to leave their scholarship at the door. Not surprisingly, they switch their primary allegiance to the academic community, which encourages rather than resists their life's work. We're left with an irony: many of the professors who train future clergy can't find a home in the churches those clergy will serve, which leaves Joelle and her friends without much in the way of hope and practical guidance in facing this challenge.

A few years ago, I was part of a group tasked with "reimagining theological education," and when I was asked for my assessment of seminaries, I said that I thought seminaries were doing a good job in their theological mandate. The problem wasn't the seminaries, I explained; it was resistance in local churches to the new ideas, information, and understandings the seminaries were presenting. In other words, the better the job that seminaries do in actually training their students to be responsible theologians, the more out of sync those future pastors will be with churches that hire them to maintain the status quo.

I can see only three possible solutions to this dilemma. First, seminaries can intensify training for seminarians in transformational leadership, equipping them to be change agents rather than chaplain-custodians in their future congregations (which is far more difficult than it sounds). Second, they can prepare more seminarians to start new local congregations from scratch where fresh perspectives are baked in from the beginning (which is also more difficult than it sounds). Or third, they can accept that it's OK for there to be a massive sorting out, with conservative and progressive members parting company and clustering in conservative and progressive churches (which seems to be happening anyway, and which brings with it a whole host of unforeseen and unintended consequences). In other words, in light of these three options, seminaries (and the denominations that fund them) will have to stop treating conservative-progressive division as a failure and start seeing it as an unavoidable reality or even as a strategic necessity. (Conservatives have, by and large, already made the choice to do so. By precipitating splits in several denominations, they have been free to rally their base, protect them from unwanted information, and perpetuate the old-time religion without disturbance or doubt.)

So there's Joelle's dilemma in a nutshell: if she dares to teach what she learned in seminary, she will either be fired or she will split her congregation. If the congregation splits and the conservatives leave, the remaining congregants will probably not be able to afford her salary. Either way, she'll be left without a job and with a huge student debt. But if she hides what she's learned or pretends not to know it, if she suppresses what inspires her because her congregation won't appreciate it, she will lose something even more valuable than a job.

"This tension is waiting for me like a backpack full of lead every single morning when I wake up. Sometimes I feel like I'm being paid to carry on a charade, and that's depressing," she said. "If there really is such a thing as Stage Four, I need to tell you, I can't see it yet. I've been in this tunnel for a long time, and the only light I see looks like the headlight of an oncoming train. I'm going down, down, down, and I don't know how much longer I can last."

At the Center for Action and Contemplation, one of our core teachings is "the path of descent," the idea that the spiritual life will eventually require us to descend into a dark tunnel, to descend into unknowing and doubt, to descend into a loss of certainty, to descend through a process that feels like dying. As with Jesus in the Gospels, we find ourselves crying, "Let this cup of suffering be taken from me," and "My God, my God, why have you forsaken me?"

It doesn't help to be told that from this descent and death, resurrection will come, true as that may be.

Deep in that tunnel, you just can't see it.

Yet.

If you're like Walt, you walk the trails in solitude, up one hill and down the next, quite certain that no faith community or tradition has anything to offer you.

If you're like Joelle, you keep showing up but wonder how long you'll last. It's hard. Really hard.

Reflection and Action

1. Walt described his post-church experience as "a little lonely, but it's better than singing songs and reciting creeds I don't believe anymore." He "walked out" his questions in solitude. How have you handled times of questioning and doubt? Has it been lonely for you?

2. Have you made any lateral transfers in your spiritual growth, from one Stage One or Stage Two faith community to another? What

made that lateral transfer desirable, and how did it work out in the long term?

3. Have you had any temporary regressions, moving from Stage Two back to Stage One, for example, or from Stage Three to Two? How did they work out?

4. If you find yourself in Stage Three (or beyond), what about Stage Two stopped working for you?

5. Many people are taught that Stage One and Two Christianity are the only valid forms, which means that if Stage One or Two Christianity fails you, "Christianity fails for you, period." Does this match your experience?

6. My friend Chuck said, "I wish that everyone at their baptism could be presented with a state-of-the-art BS detector." Share an experience when your religious BS detector sounded an alarm.

7. Summarize in your own words why, according to this chapter, it's hard to find a stable, long-term Stage Three faith community. Does that match your experience?

8. Were you surprised to hear, through Joelle's story, that many seminarians have a faith crisis early in their studies? Did anything else from her story surprise you?

9. Share an insight about your own spiritual journey that arises as you reflect on this chapter.

❧

7

Doubt as Dissent

Expressing or even entertaining doubt sometimes takes so much courage that we may say it takes real faith to doubt.

—Lloyd Geering

Stage Three has its exhilarations, but often, it feels conflicted and heavy, like a "backpack full of lead," as Joelle said. Others describe it as a downward slide, plunge, or fall, like Dante's protagonist dropping through various levels of hellish loss toward an inferno of abject despair. The language used by people in doubt across the centuries reflects this feeling of descent and loss: falling away, falling from grace, slipping, backsliding, losing faith, losing footing, losing ground, losing God.

What a contrast to Stage One, which was about being raised, ascending, gaining, growing, accumulating knowledge of right and wrong, gaining confidence about why *we* are the good guys and *they* are the bad guys, always climbing toward acceptability and correctness, and rising higher in the eyes of our authority figures. With some combination of intention, effort, and grace, in Stage One we ascended to the heights, became masters of Simplicity, stars of certainty, heroes of dualistic thinking, legends in our own minds.

Similarly, in Stage Two we trekked up rugged trails of independence, up steep slopes of performance, higher toward the summit of spiritual success. We mastered the skills our faith community taught us, from interpreting the Bible (our way) to sharing our faith with others, from grasping the complex concepts of our systematic theology to replacing some of our bad habits, from praying in public to keeping a journal in private, from serving with distinction on a church committee to baking a first-class casserole for the church potluck. People watched us develop as Stage Two believers, maybe even as leaders, and although we experienced occasional failures and setbacks, we learned to recover and rebound *successfully*.

But Stage Three, even though it brings new gains, feels like the loss of all that we worked so hard to attain, descent from the heights we worked so hard to surmount. Stage Two built so naturally on Stage One, and even the portal of doubt between the two was a relatively easy passage compared to Stage Three. Stage Three feels different, disruptive. Everything we constructed, we now deconstruct. The summits we climbed, we now leave behind. We cut our losses but secretly fear: will anything be left, or will we end up in a state of spiritual bankruptcy?

So much time, so much energy invested in building a faith portfolio, and now its value plummets toward nothing.

We find ourselves in a free fall from doubt into deeper doubt into doubt that feels utterly bottomless.

Over time, we will come to see that our grim "all is lost" assessment isn't the whole story. For example, in Stage Three, we still retain powerful and valuable treasures that we gained in Stage One. We learned, through dualism, to care about whether we're doing right or wrong. We learned to tell the truth. We learned to stand for something. Now in Stage Three, our courageous commitment to honesty in the face of great cost and loss shows how well we learned the moral lessons of Simplicity. (People who don't learn those essential lessons of Stage One may reach great heights, but sooner or later, they'll tell one too many lies, make one too many financial missteps, blur professional standards one too many times, or cross one too many lines of intimacy or decency, and they'll discover how quickly all their success can go up in smoke.)

Similarly, in Stage Three we retain powerful treasures that we gained in Stage Two. We learned to be curious and flexible. We learned that different spheres of life are like games that operate by different sets of rules, and we became fluent in the complex rules of multiple games. We learned independence, too, and became self-motivated learners and self-managers, adults who began to take responsibility for their own successes and their own failures. (Again, people who don't do their Stage Two work and learn its vital lessons often flounder. They might have good ideas and lots of talent but they lack the Stage Two qualities of self-discipline, flexibility, cleverness, resilience, and persistence to maximize their potential.)

So in spite of the feelings of loss, Simplicity and Complexity actually produced lasting gains that now help sustain us in Perplexity. And Stage Three will do the same for Stage Four. The fact is, Perplexity brings some of the greatest spiritual gifts life has to offer. It's just that they don't always look or feel like gifts when they arrive on our doorsteps.

For example, Stage Three offers the gift of *humility*. We thought we knew so much in Stages One and Two, but now, we get comfortable admitting, "I don't know. I'm not sure." With each gain in Stage Three knowledge and understanding, the horizon of what remains unknown grows more vast, and with wider unknowing comes deeper humility.

When I was around twenty, I got the chance to have lunch with an author and spiritual leader twenty years my senior whom I greatly respected. There was an awkward moment during that meal that I now recognize as this fellow trying to help me, ever so gently, to see my own naive arrogance and excessive confidence. When I gushed about how much I had learned from his amazing teachings, his response was simple, his tone sincere, his message just what I needed even though it disturbed me: "Brian, I know a lot less now than I did when I was your age." The Stage Two me was instantly flustered. The more mature you are, the more certain you are, right? The longer you live, the more you learn and the more you know, right? His statement seemed like either nonsense or an admission of a terrible failure.

But as I took another bite of my sandwich, I remember feeling that a tender, humble, gentle truth from this man's wise heart was reaching out to an undeveloped part of me. That part of me, like a shy student raising a hand in class, ventured to speak: "Wow. Maybe his ability to say he doesn't know actually means he does know something that I don't." My companion knew how much he didn't know, and he had a sense of how much he would never know. And I didn't know either, at least not yet!

Acknowledging how little we know is, I think, at the core of mature faith. What we boast of as great faith may merely be a boatload of indoctrination and overconfidence.

Not long after that uncomfortable lunch, my long, slow descent into

Stage Three was well underway. I fought it with every step. I would descend four steps, and then scramble back three, desperately trying to get back to Stage Two, where I felt successful and knowledgeable and in control. But like a child trying to run up a down escalator, I discovered reality wouldn't cooperate with my desperate fear of descent. There was no climbing back.

I had been a singer-songwriter since my college years, and suddenly all kinds of angsty, alienated songs began to pour out of me, gnarly mile markers on my slide into Perplexity. I was giving a concert one night and was mortified to look across the crowd and see the face of a theologian whom I greatly respected. Like my lunch companion who admitted how much he didn't know, this gentleman was about twenty years my senior. I suddenly felt embarrassed by my songs, embarrassed to expose my doubts in front of him. Afterward, though, he found me and complimented me on my songs. I started to apologize for how dark and grim they were, but he put up a hand as if to indicate, "Stop! Please!" and said, "No apology. That is your *honesty* speaking, and your *sensitivity*." He named two great gifts of Stage Three.

I was so impressed by his kindness to me that night that I decided to sign up for a course on Christian mystics that he taught several months later. Of course, the Stage One me had been taught that mysticism was bad for a whole raft of reasons. For starters, most mystics were Catholic, which made them somewhat suspect for Protestants like me. Second, the Stage Two me saw mysticism as irrelevant, maybe even selfish. After all, there's so much work to be done in the world. Why sit around contemplating and meditating (whatever that is) when the world is going to hell (literally or figuratively, take your pick)? Third, I hungered and thirsted for clarity, certainty, information, and confidence; any talk of a "cloud of unknowing" or "experiencing mystery" described exactly what my knowledge-starved self was *not* looking for!

One morning, this fellow gave a lecture on three Catholic mystics. He spoke so tenderly of "Dear Julian" of Norwich, so warmly of "Beloved Teresa" of Avila, and so reverently of "Blessed St. John" of the Cross; I knew that he saw something deeply beautiful and precious in them. I had to admit I didn't yet see it and couldn't yet see it, but I wanted to see what he saw, if not at that moment, then someday.

By that time, I had already stumbled into some experiences that, looking back, were genuinely "mystical." But I interpreted those experiences as valuable only insofar as they motivated me to be right (Simplicity) and zealous (Complexity). It was as if I had lived my whole life in two rooms of a house without knowing that there were other rooms, wings, and even floors waiting to be discovered. (Like many people, I had recurring dreams about discovering these vast, previously unknown rooms.) Through this teacher's love for the mystics and contemplatives, I started hearing faint music from those unexplored spaces of my own soul, beckoning me to explore.

Later, when I studied the mystics on my own (studying on my own being a skill I can thank Stage Two for), I learned that they spoke often of purgation (or *katharsis*) as the portal to illumination (or *fotosis*) and union (or *theosis*). They saw purgation as the painful and necessary process by which we are stripped of know-it-all arrogance, ego, and self-will. Perplexity, I realized, was working like an X-ray of my soul, exposing much of my so-called spirituality as a vanity project of my ego, an expression of my arrogant desire to always be right, my desperate and fearful need to always be in control, my unexamined drive to tame the wildness of life by naming it and dominating it with words. The doubt of Perplexity, the mystics helped me see, was just the fire I needed to purge me of previously unacknowledged arrogance. In this way, *self-knowledge* was another gift that came, unwanted, during my Stage Three descent.

In the Christian mystics class, I was exposed to "the dark night of the soul," a period of desolation in which God feels absent, a period in which one can't see or understand what is going on, a deep valley during which one feels abandoned and lost. To my surprise, the mystics believed this was not something to be avoided, but rather it was a passageway into something deeper and greater. In fact, only the path of descent into spiritual dryness and soul-darkness could lead the soul to a deeper experience of union with God (or *theosis*). My friend Barbara Brown Taylor explored this reality in her warm and insightful book *Learning to Walk in the Dark* (HarperOne, 2014), but when I was descending into Stage Three back in the 1990s, I felt paralyzed by darkness, and the only walking I wanted to do was to flee out of darkness and back into bright light, as fast as possible!

I wanted union with God, but I fought the path of descent as if I were being dragged to my own crucifixion. My songs from that period reflect this ambivalence; I did not like what was happening to me, but I was holding out hope that what the mystics said might be true. Take the song "Vultures," for example:

> *Doubts fly like vultures, hovering hungrily,*
> *Catching wind currents,*
> *Their shadows are cast on my pathway,*
> *And nothing seems healthy. . . .*
> *I search for firm footing until my hands and knees bleed*
> *From falls that I've taken*
> *But my wounds give awareness of need,*
> *And my needs make me seek Him.**
> *Though the path of the pilgrim leads through the dark valley,*
> *It's then, in my need, when I see, though my faith*
> *May prove feeble,*
> *My Guide remains faithful.*

Looking back, I realize that at that stage I still felt obligated to end on some hopeful and faith-affirming note, even if I didn't feel very optimistic. In another song, "Sunken Corner," I was looking for consolation in the experience of what the mystics called desolation, and rather than ending with an affirmation, I ended with a question:

> *It's a rainy night. The streets are shining*
> *Like a carnival with colored lights:*
> *Flashing red and blinking yellow,*
> *Neon blue and mellow sodium white.*
> *I cannot see the lines they've painted.*
> *I'm trying to find the lane where I belong.*
> *So if you see me drifting, mister, it's just the weather.*
> *I ain't done nothing wrong.*
> *I have some friends snug in the inner circle.*

---

* In those days, I used male pronouns for God, something I now avoid.

You couldn't pay them to exchange their place with you or me.
But at least we have this consolation:
There's not much here in the way of false security.
I feel the blaze of revelation,
I feel the stir of inspiration . . . rumbling.
It's a process of elimination,
An interruption to our conversation . . . it's coming.
So meet me at the sunken corner.
There's a diner there that's light and cool and clean.
And while we taste our toast and coffee,
We can relate illusions that we've seen.
You find God in the strangest places,
Places you would never choose to be.
I feel like Moses on the mountain.
It's burning there . . . what can I do but see?
What can I do but see?

As the songs said, I didn't feel healthy. I was in a place I would never choose. But I was beginning to see some things that I would never be able to unsee, and that *insight* itself was another gift of Stage Three.

Again, these gifts didn't feel like gifts. My sense of belonging and, even more, my leadership status in my religious community meant so much to me. Would I have the courage to tell the truth about what I was seeing, feeling, questioning, doubting, and, yes, denying in the space of Perplexity . . . even if it meant losing that status and sense of belonging? Or would I hide, minimize, and pretend?

For some people, that courage comes easily. But I had been taught so deeply and thoroughly to submit to authority and adhere to what we called orthodoxy, with such grave threats of eternal consequences if I faltered, that I vacillated between courage and cowardice. In addition, I had invested so much in trying to reform my religious community that it seemed rash to risk that investment by making admissions that I knew my critics would use to discredit and dismiss me. On top of that, I had so few models or mentors who would understand and validate what I was going through. So just as I spent a long time in Stage Two Complexity because

I liked it so much, I spent a long time in Stage Three Perplexity because I hated it so much, and my struggle prolonged my experience there.

When I finally did "come out" about my questions and doubts, at first I was subtle, partly from fear but partly from the realization that if I wanted to bring people along, I had to do so with great gentleness and patience. I hid every teaspoon of honest medicine in a gallon of sugary, fizzy Coke, full of humor and affirmations of orthodoxy. I demonstrated obsessive care to appear "balanced," "orthodox," and "biblical." I'm embarrassed to say that I often justified my tiny moves "to the left" by finding someone farther to the left and then throwing them under the bus. In other words, I might be changing a little, but I wasn't a *liberal!*

Of course, the gatekeepers and watchdogs in my Evangelical community weren't satisfied with even these tightly controlled and highly edited expressions of honest doubt. They wrote articles and editorials in magazines, posted critical reviews on blogs and websites, and sent threatening letters to colleges and organizations that invited me to speak. I suppose their public criticisms and private opposition were intended to make me recant and drive me back into the fold. But they had the opposite effect. The shallowness and predictability of their counter-arguments, frankly, seemed intellectually embarrassing. ("Is that really the best they can do?" I remember asking myself on more than one occasion.) Beyond that, the meanness and vitriol of their tone struck me as a sign of weakness, not to mention a revelation of character. "I'm a friend," I thought, "a brother in Christ who is trying my best to play by their rules. If this is how they treat me, how must it be for women, for gay people, for Muslims, or for people who don't have white skin and other marks of insider privilege?"

So gradually, I lost my fear of the gatekeepers (yet another gift of Perplexity) and gained *courage*: the courage to differ, the courage to speak my truth, the courage of dissent.

As I watched the Religious Right gain power through the 1980s and 1990s, I reached a breaking point. I couldn't pretend to support their agenda or tactics, much less remain silent. So by the early 2000s, I began taking bigger risks and making bolder stands. I spoke and wrote with growing boldness about poverty and economic inequality, about the harm being inflicted on women and the LGBTQ community by religious patriarchy, about American militarism, about Islamophobia and anti-Semitism, about racism and white supremacy, and about the ways our economic system was literally destroying the earth for short-term profit. Predictably, the pushback from the leaders of my religious community intensified. Just a few years after being welcomed into many centers of power, I felt myself being shouldered to the margins. Still, I continued to speak from the "edge of the inside" while I still had the chance.

When I crossed the line by openly challenging the concept of biblical inerrancy, by affirming the full equality of LGBTQ persons, and by celebrating the beauty and wisdom of other (non-Christian) religions, it was *one, two, three strikes*, and I was pronounced *out*. Suddenly, a financial spigot was turned off, and a whole hallway of doors slammed shut. Evangelical bookstores wouldn't carry my books. Evangelical organizations stopped inviting me to speak. It was an effective, though informal, excommunication, a decisive silencing of dissent.

The unspoken message from the gatekeepers was clear: "If you're going to dissent, you're going to do so from the outside, not the inside."

Perplexity is a path of *descent*. It is also a path of *dissent*. It requires us to have the courage to speak our truth, even when we're threatened with punishments for doing so. That courage is not simply an intellectual matter; it is also an ethical matter . . . a matter of character, integrity, and morality, as Dr. Martin Luther King, Jr., noted: "It may well be that we will have to repent in this generation. Not merely for the vitriolic words and the violent actions of the bad people, but for the appalling silence and indifference of the good people who sit around and say, 'Wait on time.'"*

At first, I doubted ideas, propositions, beliefs: that the earth was created in six literal days less than 10,000 years ago, that evolution was a satanic hoax, that the Bible was God's inerrant textbook full of history and science facts, that God created the universe as a factory to produce human souls, some destined for heaven and some for hell. Then, I doubted the authority figures who defended these beliefs, people I got to see "behind the curtain," people whose motives, I came to understand, were often

---

* From *Remaining Awake Through a Great Revolution*, a sermon given at the National Cathedral in Washington, DC, on March 31, 1968, available here: https://kinginstitute.stanford.edu/king-papers/publications/knock-midnight-inspiration-great-sermons-reverend-martin-luther-king-jr-10/.

more about money, power, pride, and privilege than faith, hope, love, and service.

Finally, I began to doubt whole systems: the system of Christian empire unleashed by the bishops of the fourth century who sold their souls to Emperor Constantine; the system of racist colonialism unleashed by Pope Nicholas V with the Doctrine of Discovery in the 1450s; the system of white supremacist Christianity in America (and elsewhere) that justified land theft, genocide, slavery, and apartheid; the system of twentieth-century Protestantism as a chaplain of extractive capitalism; the system of an all-male, supposedly celibate Catholic hierarchy that covered up heinous sexual abuse; the system of the Religious Right that strained out gnats but eventually swallowed Donald Trump in one big gulp.

On more than one occasion, a chill ran up my spine as I remembered all the theological arguments that kept people of my conservative Christian religious tradition so intensely occupied, literally, for lifetimes. "Could it be," I wondered, "that these arguments are weapons of mass distraction, keeping us fixated on abortion and gay marriage, evolution and inerrancy, popes versus presbyteries, and guitars versus organs so that we don't talk about other things: racism, environmental destruction, militarism, economic inequality, and how the love of money is at the root of all kinds of evil?"

It's one of those things that's hard to see in Stages One and Two: that doubt is an ethical as well as intellectual matter. In Stage One, we "good guys" have to stay united to stay right, so we dare not differ. In Stage Two, we "winners" have to stay "on message" and "on mission" to keep winning, so we dare not differ. But Stage Three can lead us far enough down a path of descent that we see things from the underside, so to speak.* In that new place and posture, we feel an ethical summons to dissent, as our consciences become sensitized to the personal harm, social injustices, and environmental destruction perpetuated by the very authority structures and systems that demand our faith, devotion, and compliance. Stage One

---

* I should add that it takes quite a while for people of inherited privilege to reach this point. Oppressed and marginalized people are positioned to see from this perspective much more naturally. However, even they can be co-opted by dominant systems, and taught to see (and diminish) themselves with the eyes of their oppressors. The deconstruction and critical thinking of Stage Three can help both the oppressors and the oppressed to be liberated from the structures of oppression that write scripts for both.

and Stage Two gatekeepers often try to warn adherents about Stage Three, mischaracterizing it as moral relativism, but in reality, Stage Three is an attempt to see through false or incomplete morality to a deeper and more holistic understanding of good and evil, right and wrong.*

According to Jonathan Haidt and other teachers of moral foundations theory, whatever our religion or politics, we all use the same six basic lines of moral reasoning to defend our beliefs and opinions: justice, compassion, purity, loyalty, authority, and liberty.† People of a conservative temperament, theorists explain, often feel morally superior because they emphasize all six. Liberals or progressives, however, focus on two: justice and compassion.

Here's my hunch: more liberals and progressives have reached Stage Three, and as they have come to doubt authority figures and institutions, they have come to see how arguments based on purity, loyalty, authority, and liberty are often marshaled against justice and compassion. For example, perpetrators of genocide use the moral logic of *purity* to render their targets impure, dirty, savage, subhuman, and disgusting, disguising murder as an act of sanitation or fumigation. Similarly, every racist or bigot has used *loyalty* to the racial, religious, political, or nationalistic in-group to justify harming, oppressing, or persecuting their targeted out-group.

Every authoritarian political, corporate, familial, or religious abuser capitalizes on the logic of *authority* to consolidate their abusive power. And every one of us has at some point used the logic of *liberty* to absolve ourselves of responsibility for the common good, maximizing liberty for *me* and *us* at the expense of liberty for *you* or *them*. Really scary things can happen when purity, loyalty, authority, and liberty combine into an all-consuming identity in which individuals are invited to lose themselves, leaving behind what Jesus called "the weightier matters of the law," namely, justice, compassion, and faith (Matthew 23:23).‡

---

* In the biblical tradition, this was the work of the prophets, a role that Jesus also embraced, as the Sermon on the Mount makes clear (Matthew 5–7).
† For a good introduction to Jonathan Haidt's work, see his TED-Ed talk, "The Moral Roots of Liberals and Conservatives," December 31, 2012, https://www.youtube.com/watch?v =8SOQduoLgRw. For an overview of moral foundations theory, see Jonathan Haidt, *The Righteous Mind* (Vintage, 2013).
‡ See James Hamblin, "The Most Dangerous Way to Lose Yourself," *The Atlantic*, September 25, 2019, https://www.theatlantic.com/health/archive/2019/09/identity-fusion-trump-allegiance /598699/.

Ironically, moral foundations theorists point out, when progressives (often in Stage Three) downplay four of the six lines of moral reasoning for moral reasons, they seem less moral to the very people they might hope to influence. We might wish that people in Stage Three could integrate arguments from purity, loyalty, authority, and liberty in service of justice and compassion. But being sensitive to that level of nuance is not typically the forte of folks in Perplexity, whose levels of frustration and reactivity are high. It will probably take a passage into Stage Four for them to develop this capacity for moral integration.*

When I first became aware of moral foundations theory, I couldn't help but think of Jesus' moral reasoning in the Gospels. Obviously, the "weightier matters" of justice (which he said we should "seek first" in Matthew 6:33) and compassion (which he said was more important than sacrifice in Matthew 9:13) were central for him. But he didn't ignore the other four lines of reasoning. For example, he flipped the conventional understanding of *purity* (in Matthew 15:11–20), saying that it's not what goes into a person (such as taboo food and drink) that makes that person impure but rather what comes out of a person's heart (such as greed, hate, or vengeance). In this way, he disarmed purity as a weapon of dehumanization and rendered it a moral summons to self-examination. Similarly, by constantly including outsiders and outcasts in his circle of concern, by consistently welcoming the "other" to the table of fellowship, by repeatedly humanizing the other in parables like the Good Samaritan, and, most directly, by advocating loyalty and love for enemies, Jesus flipped the conventional understanding of *loyalty.* God's love is non-discriminatory and unconditional in its loyalty, he taught, and we should imitate God's example (Matthew 5:44).

Along with purity and loyalty, Jesus deconstructed typical understandings of *authority* and replaced them with aspirations to service (Matthew 20:25, 24:20 ff.), as he did with upholding service over individual *liberty* to pursue self-interest alone (Luke 22:27 and John 13:1–17; see also Philippians 2:1–11 and Galatians 5, where Paul celebrates service rather than self-interest as the very heart of Jesus' identity and teaching). In all these ways, Jesus dissented from the typical understandings of purity, loyalty,

---

* My short e-book, *Why Don't They Get It? Overcoming Bias in Others (and Yourself)* (2019), may be helpful in this regard. Available here: https://brianmclaren.net/store/.

authority, and liberty. Instead of neglecting them, however, he redefined them and in a sense recycled them in service of justice and compassion. For Jesus, justice and compassion were ultimately two facets of one thing: love. As Cornel West has said, justice is what love looks like in public, and we could add that compassion is the humanizing sense of empathy that opens the door of our hearts toward the other in love. To put love first and make love our highest goal integrates all six lines of moral reasoning and represents the most profound act of dissent possible in a world that puts so many other things first: money, one's nation or religion, power, prestige, pleasure, revenge.

So Perplexity, even though it is deconstructive, is not destructive. Even though it questions and challenges conventional moral thinking, it is not immoral. It is a constructive stage of dissent on its way toward love. Even though people in Simplicity and Complexity see dissent as a danger to avoid, the world would be ethically impoverished if conventional notions of purity, loyalty, authority, and liberty went unchallenged. In this way, Stage Three dissenters, by questioning and challenging beliefs, norms, authority figures, and systems that are harming people, help everyone, including those in Stages One and Two who don't approve of their dissent.

If Stage Three dissenters keep descending through Perplexity, they will face a moment of crisis, a moment of reckoning, a moment of decision. Will their Stage Three superpower of critical thinking become their Midas touch, a gift that undoes them? Will they use their X-ray vision to see through everything and determine that there is nothing of value left to see? Will they be sucked into a vortex of meaninglessness and despair? Or will the *seeing through* of skeptical doubt lead them to the *seeing into* of mystical or contemplative insight, so that they see through and beyond Simplicity, Complexity, and Perplexity to a deeper narrative, a more mysterious coherence, a revolutionary harmony that embraces and integrates all it includes?

Will they deconstruct each object of their scrutiny to its smallest fragments, until those nearly weightless fragments blow away like a dust devil contorting in the wind? Or will they be able, after their honest and even ruthless deconstruction, to step back again, discern new patterns of meaning among the fragments, and find some reason for hope, some way to see things whole again?

Will their *withheld consent*, their refusal to go along with unjust systems or conventions, keep them constantly on the sidelines, always saying "no" or "yes, but" but never being able to utter a wholehearted "yes" of commitment to anything? Or will a moment come when their pent-up withheld consent bursts forth as wholehearted assent to something better and deeper than never-ending quests for certainty, success, and scrutiny, namely, "the still more excellent way of love"? *

That phrase "still more excellent way of love" comes from Paul's letter to the Corinthians, where it introduces a passage commonly read at weddings (12:31–14:1), even though the scope of that passage is as broad as life itself. Paul makes clear that nearly everything religious people strive for will eventually be swallowed up in something deeper, and in and of itself, is of no real worth. Even faith and hope don't have the last word. Only love, he says, is the more excellent way. Elsewhere, he makes clear that love fulfills the law (Romans 13:8–14) and summarizes the whole law in one word (Galatians 5:14). In fact, he dares to say, *nothing else matters except faith expressing itself in love.*

Looking back on my own spiritual pilgrimage, I have come to see "the still more excellent way of love" as the telos whose gravitational pull has been drawing me first through *Simplicity*, then through *Complexity*, then downward through *Perplexity*, and then deeper still, toward an experience that is too profound for words, the experience of *Harmony*. When I loved correctness in Stage One, yes, correctness mattered, but the love with which I pursued correctness mattered still more. When I loved effectiveness in Stage Two, yes, effectiveness mattered, but the love that moved me to pursue it mattered still more. When I loved honesty and justice in Stage Three, yes, honesty and justice mattered, but the love that burned in my heart for them mattered still more.

I think back to the many people I have introduced you to so far in this book—Michael, the young pastor; Susan, the mom of a lesbian daughter; Sam, the engineer; Walt, the environmentalist; Chuck, the son of a famous preacher; Joelle, the minister in her first parish—and I see them

---

* See 1 Corinthians 12:31. Wendell Berry offers a pungent critique of undoubted certainty and success in his poem "The Objective," from *A Timbered Choir: The Sabbath Poems* (Counterpoint Press, 1998), available here: https://www.teachthought.com/learning/read-wendell-berrys-the-objective-voice/.

all being pulled through all of the simplicities and complexities and perplexities of faith toward this one treasure, this one pearl of great price, this one thing that truly matters: *love*.

Faith was about love all along. We just didn't realize it, and it took doubt to help us see it.

Reflection and Action

1. The chapter begins with words of *descent* and *loss*: falling away, falling from grace, slipping, backsliding, losing faith, losing footing, losing ground, losing God. How do these words resonate with your spiritual experience?

2. I tell the story of an older man saying, "I know a lot less now than I did when I was your age." Can you share an example of something you feel that you used to know but no longer do? What question did you use to have an answer for, but now you can only respond to by saying, "I don't know"?

3. Describe the role of purgation, illumination, and union (or *katharsis*, *fotosis*, and *theosis*) in relation to Stage Three.

4. Have you ever read any of the Christian mystics? Consider doing some research on one of the mystics mentioned (Julian of Norwich, Teresa of Avila, John of the Cross), or on one of the following more modern mystics: Thomas Merton, Howard Thurman, Evelyn Underhill, John Muir.

5. Share your understanding of the term "dark night of the soul" and any experiences you have had with it.

6. Describe the relationship between the six foundational moral values described in this chapter: purity, loyalty, authority, liberty, justice, and compassion.

7. Reflect on the two final sentences of this chapter, "Faith was about love all along. We just didn't realize it, and it took doubt to help us see it."

❧

8

Doubt as Love

To be a human being among people and to remain one forever, no matter in what circumstances, not to grow despondent and not to lose heart—that's what life is about, that's its task.

—Fyodor Dostoyevsky, *Letters*

Doubt was the portal from Stage One to Stage Two and from Stage Two to Stage Three. But once you're deep into Perplexity, doubt often feels like a Mobius strip: it only leads you back into deeper doubt.

I captured that feeling in this lyric from "X-Ray Eyes," a blues song (fittingly) that I wrote while in Stage Three:

> *It's so sweet to complain, such fun to criticize,*
> *To see the world through penetrating X-ray eyes,*
> *To find the bad in everything,*
> *To taste the honey and think of the bee sting.*
> *Winter's too cold. Summer's too hot.*
> *The things I wish were happening*
> *Are not.*
> *Summer's too hot. Winter's too cold.*
> *First I'm too young, and then*
> *I'm too old.*
> *Don't it bring a tear to your eyes?*
> *So sweet to complain and criticize. . . .*
> *There's just one problem*
> *With this way of living.*

The road gets narrower and narrower as you go along.
You look more and more.
You see less and less.
It gets harder and harder to find the things
That bring happiness
When you only see what is wrong.
It's fun for a while, but when you're through,
The judgment you give will roll back on you,
Back on you.

Interestingly, while I was in some ways looking "more and more" but seeing "less and less," in other ways, I was seeing things I hadn't seen before, even in the Bible. The Book of Job, for example, rang true in a new way. Job suffers one tragedy after another, and his sufferings defy the formulaic promises of Leviticus and Proverbs about things going well for good people. Job refuses to keep his questions and doubts to himself, and predictably, his friends pile on with typical Stage One and Stage Two judgment and advice. In the end, God gets a word in edgewise, and to everyone's surprise, God rejects the pious platitudes of Job's friends and celebrates Job's honest, defiant perplexity.

Similarly, before I entered Perplexity, the book of Ecclesiastes troubled me: "Why is this even in the Bible?" I wondered. But in Perplexity, the book became a source of great comfort. I remember reading "With much wisdom comes much sorrow" (1:18) and feeling that truer words had never been spoken. The fact that there was room in the Bible for a book of questions and doubts meant that there should be room in the community of faith for people like me, full of our own questions and doubts.

And, of course, Jesus looked more brilliant than ever in Stage Three. He seemed radiantly and radically different from the Jesus of the Stage One and Stage Two preachers, who loved to use his name (and, frankly, his blood) but didn't seem to "get" him because their boxes just couldn't contain him.

In Luke's Gospel, for example, at the original Eucharistic meal, Jesus offered a classic Stage Three political deconstruction of the concepts and deceits of power, leadership, and social status (or "greatness," Luke 22:25 ff.): "The kings of the Gentiles lord it over them; and those in authority over them are called benefactors. But not so with you; rather the greatest among you must become like the youngest, and the leader like one who serves. For who is greater, the one who is at the table or the one who serves? Is it not the one at the table? But I am among you as one who serves."*

I had a lot more to deconstruct than most folks, of course, having been so thoroughly indoctrinated and invested in Stage One and Stage Two. I was like a cancer patient who needed a lot of chemo and radiation to be saved. But I didn't feel like my doubt was healing me. I felt it was killing me. In stages. One "treatment" at a time.

I wish I could go back to that younger, agonized me and bring this message:

> I know that your perplexity feels like a dead end. But wait, wait, endure, persist, do your work, see it through, hang in there, trust the process, and it will become a passageway, a birth canal. You actually need this purgation and unknowing to prepare you for a new depth of living, knowing, and loving. There is much that deserves to be doubted, and if you really care about the truth, you must pursue it, using doubt as a necessary tool. (It's not your only tool, but it is one of your tools.)
>
> I know you feel that everything you value is slipping through your fingers. But don't clench your fists. Open your hands. Your open hands, open eyes, and open heart will prepare the way for new gains, not just new thoughts, but new ways of thinking. You have already added dualistic thinking, pragmatic thinking, and critical/deconstructive thinking to your skill set. You will soon learn a new skill: unitive or nondual seeing, in which knowing and unknowing, faith and doubt, clarity and mystery are not opposites, but complements.

Many sages, of course, were already offering this kind of reassurance, pointing me beyond perplexity, few more winsomely than the Romantic poet William Wordsworth. Every few years I would come back to his famous poem *Tintern Abbey* and see myself in his Hermit who "by his fire . . . sits alone." I felt Wordsworth was promising me something

---

* For a masterful analysis of how Jesus deconstructs "benefactors," see Diana Butler Bass, *Grateful* (HarperOne, 2018).

precious in lines like these: "with an eye made quiet by the power / Of harmony, and the deep power of joy, / We see into the life of things." Was such a deeper seeing possible? I wondered. What was this "power of harmony"? Even Wordsworth himself acknowledged his doubts, writing, "If this be but a vain belief." But later, he testifies to "a sense sublime / Of something far more deeply interfused, / Whose dwelling is the light of setting suns, / And the round ocean and the living air, / And the blue sky, and in the mind of man: / A motion and a spirit, that impels / All thinking things, all objects of all thought, / And rolls through all things."

Unfortunately, among my circle of close friends in those days, there were few if any Wordsworths. Almost none of my peers were even dipping their toes in Perplexity (publicly, at least), and of those who were, none that I knew of had made it through to anything beyond. So, without peers to help me see what I couldn't yet see, I kept struggling, studying, praying, and agonizing, hoping against hope that I would find the new "silver bullet" idea, the magic quick fix that would restore me to Stage One certainty and Stage Two confidence. But that was not to be.

Looking back, there was not a singular eureka moment for me. But I do recall several turning points in the process of moving from Stage Three Perplexity into Stage Four Harmony, several points when something fell apart and something else fell into place, and I felt that I was passing through the turbulence into a new calm on the other side.

I used to take long walks along the Potomac River on my days off. On one of those walks, after several days of summer storms, my doubts were churning in my mind and heart like the swollen river rolling silty and brown in its channel beside me. A verse I had memorized in my childhood came to mind: "Trust in the Lord with all your heart, and do not lean on your own understanding." For the first time, it dawned on me: there's a difference between doubting God and doubting my understanding of God, just as there's a difference between trusting God and trusting my understanding of God. Would I be able to doubt my understanding of God while simultaneously trusting God beyond my understanding? In a strange way, that question for the first time in my life allowed me to see God as a mystery distinct from my concepts of God.*

---

* Years later, I came across a quote from Greg Boyd, courtesy of Rachel Held Evans, that captured this insight: "The quest to feel certain becomes an idol when a person's sense of significance to

A few months later, sitting on a porch and overlooking a beautiful valley at a retreat center, I wrote in my journal that in one year, I would be out of the ministry and maybe out of Christian faith altogether. Writing those words felt both terrifying and liberating.*

Not long after that, I was on another retreat with some other pastors and my unquiet thoughts disturbed my sleep. I took an early morning walk in a desert garden and realized that my systematic theology, the system of beliefs that I had worked so hard to construct, was collapsing. It was no longer salvageable. There was no going back. And maybe that was OK.†

About a year later, another surprise came at a nonprofit board meeting. A gifted musician led our group in an extended time of worship, praise, and prayer. There was no hype, no pressure, just relaxed sincerity. I had not "felt God's presence" for a long, long time and, in fact, had largely given up hope that such a feeling would ever return. I found it hard to sing words that I was no longer sure I believed, so I just sat in silence, my eyes closed. Suddenly, without expecting it, there it was: a surprise, a sudden sense that God had been with me through all my doubts, that I had endured and passed a difficult test. Even after I had let go of so many of my certainties, even after so much of my naive confidence had slipped between my fingers, even after I had acknowledged that whatever God was, God was beyond both my present and possible understanding, there God was, still with me. It felt like I was leaving an old chapter behind and entering something new.‡

When I first began developing this four-stage schema, I called this final stage *Humility*. The name seemed fitting because for me, Stage Four involved a sense of embarrassment about my earlier arrogance and naivete. But it seemed even more arrogant and naive to say one had reached a stage of Humility. I toyed with calling it *Maturity*, not because I liked giving it such a presumptuous name, but because I thought the aspiration

---

God and security before God is anchored not in their simple trust of God's character, as revealed on the cross, but in how certain they feel about the rightness of their beliefs." "Faith, Doubt and the Idol of Certainty: An Interview with Greg Boyd," Rachel Held Evans blog, September 17, 2013, https://rachelheldevans.com/blog/greg-boyd-interview-doubt/.

* I tell this story in more detail in the introduction to *A New Kind of Christian* (Fortress, 2019).
† I tell this story in more detail in *The Great Spiritual Migration* (Convergent, 2016), Chapter 1.
‡ I tell this story in more detail in *Naked Spirituality* (HarperOne, 2011).

toward maturity would attract people in Simplicity and Complexity and invite them to risk the passage through Perplexity. I also considered calling it *Commitment*, following William Perry, because the ethical summons to commit to some purpose bigger than myself and my tradition was critical to my own entry into that stage. I also entertained calling it *Solidarity, Integrity,* and (following Paul Ricoeur) *Second Simplicity*. In the end, though, *Harmony* felt like the right name, primarily because it resonated with the new dimension of non-discriminatory love that became possible at this stage.

Richard Rohr has provided helpful language to describe this passage. What I call Simplicity and Complexity, he calls the "first half of life." In this stage of life, we "build the container," meaning we create the structures of personality necessary to live. Perplexity becomes a transition period, characterized by "great pain and great love," and Harmony is what he calls the "second half of life," when we focus on filling the container with meaning. The most significant difference between the two stages, he says, is that in the second half of life, we become capable of non-dual seeing and thinking, which is the way that contemplatives and mystics encounter the world. We learn to hold binaries in larger unities, to gather paradox and tension in a larger embrace, to welcome diversity without division, to hear difference without dissonance.

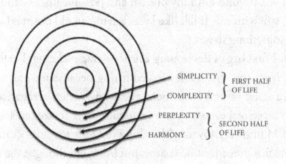

As I've said before, I prefer to describe these as stages of faith rather than stages of life because I see more and more people reaching Perplexity and Harmony at younger and younger ages. Rohr makes the same point: "When I say that you will enter the second half of life, I don't mean it in a strictly chronological way. Some young people, especially those who have learned from early suffering, are already there, and some older folks are still quite childish."* I expect the passage to Stage Four to become common at even younger ages in the future. For example, if more young adults reach Perplexity at age thirty rather than age forty, and Harmony at age forty rather than age fifty, they can provide a model for their children to develop the skills and habits of Perplexity and Harmony by the time those children are fifteen or twenty. For that reason, a book like this may not be necessary in twenty or thirty years, because our families and congregations, or at least some of them, will support the natural growth process rather than block, stunt, and frustrate it. One of the key functions of families and congregations will be to help people develop the sequential capacity for dualistic thinking (in Simplicity), pragmatic thinking (in Complexity), critical thinking (in Perplexity), and non-dual seeing (in Harmony).

You might think of it like this: dualistic thinking is the necessary work of Stage One. We learn to put everything we encounter into two simple bins: good/bad, like/dislike, familiar/unfamiliar, us/them, male/female, in/out. In Stage Two, we keep our dualistic thinking, but we complexify it. There's absolute good and bad, but there are also mixtures of the two in infinitely graded proportions: 50/50, 60/40, 30/70, and so on. Similarly, in Stage Two there is absolute in and out, but that's not the whole story, because some things are outside moving in, and other things are inside moving out, and some are straddling the line at any given moment. Stage Two invites us to move from bounded-set thinking to centered-set thinking and helps us see if not in full color at least in many shades of gray.†

In Stage Three, we come to see so much complexity that we wonder if there was ever any validity to our simplistic Stage One dualisms. We realize that the authority figures who taught us that *this* was good and *that* was evil (and *the other* was unimportant) had their own agendas, their own self-interest in getting us to buy into their set of judgments. In case after case, we discover that those binaries—male/female, communist/capitalist, human/non-human, us/them—obscure much even as they reveal much. And worse, those Stage One dualisms, when put into the

---

* Richard Rohr, *Falling Upward: A Spirituality for the Two Halves of Life* (Jossey-Bass, 2013), xvi.
† My friend Dave Schmelzer offers a good summary of centered-set thinking here: "Bounded vs. Centered Set Thinking," Vimeo.com, January 6, 2009, https://vimeo.com/2742653/.

ambitious hands of Stage One and Stage Two demagogues and pragmatists, are often used to bring harm: dehumanization, violence, genocide, even geocide, destruction of the earth.

Finding ourselves deep in Perplexity, and feeling disillusioned with our naive dualisms and pragmatisms, we face a stark and terrifying choice. Will we become cynical nihilists, seeing through everything with our X-ray eyes so that meaning, purpose, value, reverence, and wonder become increasingly, then utterly, invisible? For many people, this cynicism is the only intellectually honest option they're aware of, so they surrender the search for meaning and they surrender to perpetual Perplexity, all dressed up in critical thinking with nowhere to go.

But some people can't be satisfied with that choice. They begin to wonder, to hope, to imagine, and they dare to believe that there is another option beyond Stage Three. Their "graduation" may be aided and abetted through mystics and saints; through musicians and artists and filmmakers; through poets like Rumi, Hafiz, William Wordsworth, Mary Oliver, or Wendell Berry; through a beloved grandparent, wise mentor, or spiritual director; through a gentle priest, pastoral theologian, or sage friend; through a pilgrimage or mystical experience of some sort; or perhaps through all of the above. In one way or another, they catch a scent, a faint music, a hint of an undiscovered country beyond Perplexity.

Now that phrase, *undiscovered country*, is originally from Shakespeare's *Hamlet*, and in its original context, it refers to death. The allusion is somewhat fitting here, too, because there is indeed a kind of dying involved with passing through Perplexity into Harmony. You might call it a death to ego or pride, as we relinquish our right to judge, to know, and to control. You might call it a death to privilege, superiority, or supremacy, as we realize that all of us ultimately share in the human condition, and anyone who claims otherwise is either naive or hypocritical.

So it is often with some surprise when we find ourselves waking up to another day, still alive, still breathing, still with a future ahead of us, like a castaway washed up on the shore, like a survivor after an earthquake. We may feel a little embarrassed because after all our thinking, all our mental anguish, all our adventures in missing the point, this discovery of unifying harmony beyond disintegrating perplexity seems very simple, almost childish. It has come to us as a gift, a surprise, a dawning, and we can't honestly take any credit for figuring it out at all.

For this reason, Harmony has been described as a second naiveté, a second simplicity or innocence, where instead of seeing through everything, we see into everything, and at the core, we find not meaninglessness and banality but profound, inexpressible belovedness and beauty. Songwriter Bruce Cockburn captures it perfectly in a song lyric: "All these years of thinking ended up like this: in front of all this beauty, understanding nothing."*

Stage One and Stage Two people hear "understanding nothing" merely as a negation, but Stage Four people realize that it's a confession: a confession that the mystery we behold beyond Perplexity is deep beyond all knowledge, a peace that passes understanding, a beauty that surpasses all words, a new simplicity and an all-encompassing love that far surpass all comprehension, a "still more excellent way" that opened for us when we felt we had reached a dead end.

Father Zossima, a sage character in Dostoyevsky's masterpiece *The Brothers Karamazov*, captures this shift to Harmony. He sees beyond judgment and critique to a space where we lose the dualistic discrimination of early stages. So, he says, "Love a man even in his sin, for that is the semblance of Divine Love and is the highest love on earth." But then he goes even farther:

> Love all God's creation, the whole and every grain of sand in it. Love every leaf, every ray of God's light. Love the animals, love the plants, love everything. If you love everything, you will perceive the divine mystery in things. Once you perceive it, you will begin to comprehend it better every day. And you will come at last to love the whole world with an all-embracing love. Love the animals: God has given them the rudiments of thought and joy untroubled. Do not trouble [them], don't harass them, don't deprive them of their happiness, don't work against God's intent. Man, do not pride yourself on superiority to the animals. . . .
> Love children especially, for they too are sinless like the angels; they live to soften and purify our hearts and, as it were, to guide us. Woe to him

---

* From his 1988 album *Big Circumstance*, with lyrics available here: http://cockburnproject.net /songs&music/un.html/.

who offends a child! Father Anfim taught me to love children. The kind, silent man used often on our wanderings to spend the farthings given us on sweets and cakes for the children. He could not pass by a child without emotion. That's the nature of the man.

At some thoughts one stands perplexed, especially at the sight of men's sin, and wonders whether one should use force or humble love. Always decide to use humble love. If you resolve on that once for all, you may subdue the whole world. Loving humility is marvelously strong, the strongest of all things, and there is nothing else like it.*

And so, in the loving humility of Harmony, we begin to see things without the obsessive dualistic judgments of Simplicity, without the compulsive pragmatic analyses and schemes of Complexity, and without the deconstructing suspicions of Perplexity chattering away in our heads. Or perhaps that word *without* is an overstatement. Perhaps the chattering remains, but it no longer has the last word, because a new music begins, faintly at first but rising to a steady crescendo, a music of appreciation, empathy, wonder, and, yes, all-embracing love. That music is what Howard Thurman, one of America's most brilliant spiritual leaders, called the "sound of the genuine," a phrase to which we shall return in a later chapter.

Our quest for certainty was confident in Simplicity, determined in Complexity, and despairing in Perplexity. Through the whole process, it represented our desire to gain mastery or control over what we came to know: we needed to name whatever we encountered; then to judge it; then to determine its value in relation to our conquests, self-interest, and schemes; then to scan it for oppression, domination, and exploitation. But in the hot crucible of doubt we experienced in late Perplexity, we began to become cynical about our own cynicism, skeptical of our own skepticism, critical of our own critical thinking, doubting of our own doubtfulness. Our naive certainty, excessive confidence, and obsessive deconstruction began to burn away in a self-consuming blast furnace. We finally descended to a point so low that instead of looking down on everything, we had to look up at it from a humbled position of under-standing,

---

* Fyodor Dostoyevsky, *The Brothers Karamazov*, Book VI, Chapter 3, available here: https://homepages.bluffton.edu/~bergerd/classes/las400/handouts/karamazov/book6chapter03c.html.

you might say, and in so doing, we became capable of encountering something without needing to control it. Rather, we were able simply to see it, perhaps even to see it with love.

I remember the early stages of Harmony, when I as a Christian could for the first time encounter my Buddhist, Muslim, Jewish, or atheist neighbor in a new way, a way that previously I was utterly incapable of. For the first time, I began to show up as merely a human being, stripped of my labels, encountering a fellow human being without judgment, without agenda, without suspicion, and with curiosity, respect, and love. When I looked in the mirror, I was able to see myself with less shame and self-incrimination on the one hand, yet without a veil of defensiveness and self-deception on the other. I could accept my neighbor as neighbor and myself as self. We were who we were. If you had asked me to have encounters like these before developing the competencies of Stage Four, I would have tried. And perhaps for a few minutes or even hours, I would have gotten close. But eventually, inevitably, I would have found myself judging, competing, and critiquing. Encounter without control was not yet natural or habitual to me. I could attain it but not sustain it.

Philosopher Ken Wilber makes a helpful distinction between states and stages that can help us at this juncture, and I can explain it best through a story. My first powerful spiritual or mystical experience came when I was around fifteen. I was on a retreat with a youth group from a friend's church. A group of us arranged to sneak out of our dorms after we were supposed to be asleep and rendezvous on a hill nearby. We sat together under the stars just chatting for a while. Then I felt drawn to separate myself from my friends, so I walked a stone's throw away and lay back in the grass to look up at the night sky, which was blessedly free of light pollution. As I gazed at the glittering Milky Way, I began to feel myself strangely, unexpectedly gazed upon. I felt that from all directions, I was being seen by a loving presence. The joyful feeling of being inexplicably, irresistibly seen, known, and loved grew so strong, so utterly big within and upon me, that I began to laugh with joy and then to cry with tenderness. My stomach actually began to hurt because I was crying so intensely. Then I remember feeling that the Love that loved me also loved the stars, the cattle nearby, the grass, the dew, the earth, the air, every single thing. I was not only a beloved individual; I was part of a beloved universe. And then I thought of my friends, and the love I felt for them seemed so huge and uncontainable that I felt I might burst. As wonderful as the feeling was, I begged God to stop it because I felt I couldn't take it anymore. I dried my eyes on my shirtsleeve and went back to join my companions.

When I arrived, their conversation had turned to the fact that in a few years, we would all go our separate ways. One by one, my friends started saying how much they loved one another and sharing what they appreciated about one another. The beauty of that moment, of feeling surrounded by love, permeated by love, absorbed into love . . . I seldom speak of it because doing so too easily cheapens the memory.

That whole experience lasted maybe twenty minutes. You might say that for those twenty minutes, I entered Stage Four as a temporary *state*. I was transfigured or enveloped or abducted into Harmony. But it would be more than twenty years before I was able to enter into Harmony as a *stage*, a way of life, a habitual practice and normal experience. I'm thankful for the temporary state, even though it was so fleeting, because it marked me. It opened up a space in me, a capacity in me, that I didn't even know I had. It let me know that such a way of seeing and being was possible. I only wish that someone had told me that this mystical experience of belovedness and connection was like a short vacation to a place that I could actually migrate toward and live in someday, if I were willing to go through the processes, struggles, experiences, practices, and intervening stages that would make Harmony go from impossible to fleeting to hard to habitual to normative.

Of course, I'm not saying that I now live blissfully in Stage Four, perfectly and constantly possessed by revolutionary love, effortlessly seeing without judgment, relating without control, and seeing through critically without rendering invisible cynically. Of course not. Just as one carries the strengths of previous stages into the next stage, one also brings the weaknesses and temptations. But what was once impossible has become possible, through struggle, suffering, practice, growth, and . . . doubt. Especially doubt.

If I had not come to doubt the reactive dualism of Simplicity, Complexity would have been impossible. If I had not come to doubt the analytical pragmatism of Complexity, Perplexity would have been impossible.

If I had not come to doubt the suspicion and critical deconstruction of Perplexity, Harmony would have been impossible. Each stage contributed to Harmony, and so did doubting each stage. No stage was bad because it wasn't Stage Four. (That would be a Stage One thing to say.) Neither was any stage a distraction, delay, or obstacle to success because it wasn't Stage Four. (That would be a Stage Two thing to say.) Nor was any stage futile and in vain because it wasn't as mature and complete as Stage Four. (That would be a Stage Three thing to say.) Rather, each stage made a vital contribution, appropriate for a time, that made possible what followed, and each stage remained a central element of what followed. No stage was the destination, but each played a vital role in the journey toward and into Harmony, toward non-discriminatory, revolutionary love. (That is a Stage Four thing to say.)

If I began this book by saying, "Doubt is the doorway to love," it would have sounded like nonsense. But perhaps now I can say it and you will see it.

It's what I have wanted to say since the beginning: doubt prepares the way for a new kind of faith after (and with) doubt, a humbled and harmonious faith, a faith that expresses itself in love.

Reflection and Action

1. If you could write a letter to your "younger, agonized" self as I do in this chapter, what would you say?
2. Is there a movie, poem, or other piece of art that gives you a sense of this beauty beyond Simplicity, Complexity, and Perplexity, as Wordsworth's *Tintern Abbey* did for me?
3. I mention that I had very few peers (that I was aware of) who were grappling with Perplexity when I was. Do you have some peers with whom you are on this journey of faith and doubt? If so, be sure to thank them. They are a gift.
4. I share a few moments that marked turning points in my passage through Stage Three. Can you share any similar turning points, if this stage is where you are in your spiritual journey?
5. How does the image of tree rings help you think about the four stages?
6. Try to explain non-dual thinking in your own words. Can you

imagine a congregation that could teach dualistic, pragmatic, critical, and non-dual or integrative thinking and seeing?

7. I quote a song lyric from Bruce Cockburn: "All these years of thinking ended up like this: in front of all this beauty, understanding nothing." You can watch Cockburn perform the song here: https://www.youtube.com/watch?v=6Jay2_EFGCg. How do you respond to the song? What lines strike you, or what feelings does it evoke?

8. Put the difference between a state and a stage in your own words and see if you can share some experiences of a "state of harmony" from earlier stages in your life.

9. How would you have responded to the statement "Doubt is the doorway to love" if you had read it on the first page of this book? How do you respond to it now?

❧

9

A HUMAN PROBLEM

> Ladders and stages suggest leaving behind the previous rung or stage.
> Actually one adds new dimensions to what one is, like a tree adds rings.
>
> —Thomas Keating

In spending the last several chapters talking about the role of doubt as a portal from one stage of faith to the next, I imagine that I've made almost every reader at least a little uncomfortable for one reason or another.

For example, I can imagine some Stage One readers asking, "Shouldn't there only be two stages, wrong and right?" I can hear Stage Two readers repeating their most urgent question: "How can I get to Stage Four as efficiently and quickly as possible?" Stage Three readers, the ones for whom this book is especially relevant, probably feel more suspicious than anyone else: "Aren't you just imposing this human construct on other people to take advantage of them in some way, to assert your power and superiority over them? Isn't every stage-oriented schema ultimately a meta-narrative that is inherently colonizing?" And I imagine that even Stage Four readers are feeling a little impatient: "Can't we drop all this talk of stages and simply see people as people and love them?"

Here's where I can try to relieve some of your concerns, at least a little bit, with four provisos. First, let's acknowledge that *life is messy and difficult*, and any schema rightly used has to acknowledge that messiness and difficulty. That's why I encourage you to think of your current stage of faith as a base camp. On any given day, you might venture back a stage or forward a stage to cope with what life throws at you. In my own experience, I spent many years camped out in Stage Two, but I'd make brief forays ahead into Stage Three and even Four, or at times back to Stage One, based on people I was with or situations I faced.

I think of a young man I met a while back who told me several of my books really helped him when he was in college. "You were my favorite writer back then," he said. But more recently, he told me, he decided to return to his traditional beliefs, so he had stopped reading my work. When I asked what made him change his mind, he replied, "Eighteen months ago, my precious daughter was diagnosed with cancer. Right now, all I'm concerned about is her being healed. I feel like my daughter's life depends on my prayers, and my prayers depend on my faith, and my faith depends on everything being super clear and super literal. So I stopped reading people like you who make me think and question, and I just focus on books that help me claim a miraculous healing for my daughter." In the language we're using here, I think my books originally helped him when he was in Stage Two, leaning into Stage Three. But because of his daughter's illness, he decided to lean back into Stage One. Because it was a pragmatic decision, still rooted in Stage Two, he projected no malice in my direction, as he would have if he were firmly rooted in Stage One.

Of course, I could have warned him about people I had known who "claimed their miracle" with unshakable Stage One faith but whose miracles never came and who then faced a double crisis of personal grief and spiritual disillusionment. But I knew this loving dad would deal with that tragic possibility if it occurred, so I told him I would join him in praying for his daughter and I understood why he wanted nothing to do with my books for now.

Second, let's acknowledge that *the lines between stages are somewhat arbitrary, so there's nothing magic about the number four.* Different theorists have posited from two to nine stages. I've chosen four because it captures more nuance than two while remaining easier to remember than nine.* If you would like even more nuance, you might say there are twelve stages, since each of the four stages has an early period (like the shallow end of a pool) and a late period (like the deep end of a pool), with a section in between. Not only that, but we often find ourselves straddling stages, partly

---

* You can see my integration of a number of stage theories in Appendix III, and you'll find additional information about a fifth stage (Stage Zero) in Appendix II.

in late Simplicity and partly in early Complexity, for example. And to add to the nuance, we might function at Stage Three at school or work and at Stage One in church. Or we might feel like we're in Stage Three when we visit a Stage One church, but then feel ourselves reacting as if we were in Stage One when we read a book by a Stage Three author. The fact is, there is no more of a clear line between stages than there is a clear line between seasons. You can have warm days in winter and snowfall in spring, and just as calendars don't tell the whole story, neither can any schema.

Third, let's reiterate that *there really is no top or bottom or best or worst,* because these four stages are cumulative. Like a ring on a tree, each new stage *includes* the previous stage as it *transcends* it. My friend Phyllis Tickle wisely said that we have a rummage sale each time we move into a new stage. We sort through our belongings and put aside things we no longer find helpful (that's the *transcend* part) while carrying forward what we feel we'll want or need in the future (that's the *include* part).* As we've seen before, there can be no later stages without the earlier stages, and we accumulate and carry forward new skills with each new stage. What novelist and poet Madeleine L'Engle said about age is true about stage: "The great thing about getting older is that you don't lose all the other ages you've been."† The great thing about a new stage is that you get to keep what you learned and became in previous stages.

Finally, in addition to being cumulative, *the stages are iterative.* After you're in Harmony for a while, Harmony becomes your new Simplicity. And if you live long enough, you will surely face new levels of Complexity, which will lead to a new season of Perplexity, and so on. I know hearing this feels terribly depressing to folks who are just breaking through into Harmony and feel relieved to be leaving Perplexity behind. Now they have to imagine that an even deeper Perplexity may lie ahead! (Perhaps it's even more depressing for folks currently in Perplexity, wondering how anything could be harder than *this*!)

But after you cycle through the four stages a few times, you begin to feel that dualism, pragmatism, relativism, and non-dual holism have simply become four ways of seeing or four skill sets at your disposal.‡ After a

---

* Phyllis Tickle, *The Great Emergence* (Baker, 2012).
† Attributed to a *New York Times* interview, 1985.
‡ Recalling our brief discussion of brain modularity in Chapter 2, stages may be a way of

few runs around the spiral, you become less conscious of being "in" only one stage, and instead, you feel you constantly experience all of them. You can access all their strengths and fall for any of their temptations. Just imagine yourself a tree with sixty or seventy rings inside your bark, and you can see that for such a tree, autumn and winter would have stopped being a surprise long ago.

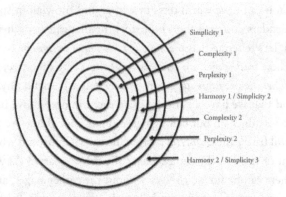

There is no shame, pride, or regret in being at the stage of development in which you find yourself. If there's anything to regret, I suppose it's refusing to grow when life invites you to do so, or rushing through your current stage without learning all it has to teach you.

With those provisos in mind, I hope you'll find the four stages a general pattern that can be helpful in understanding your own life story, the spiritual biographies of your friends, and the dynamics of human development that seem to work across many faith traditions. I trust you won't abuse the four-stage framework in a rigid, judgmental, or reductionistic way or overuse it in an obnoxious way. To that end, I'm going to refer to the first three stages less often from this point forward so that we can focus on the fourth stage, Harmony, the stage of faith after (and with) doubt.

Whether you're Jewish, Muslim, Hindu, Christian, Sikh, Buddhist, or whatever, chances are, you've probably noticed that the most vocal and assertive members of your tradition are not speaking from a place of Harmony. Granted, the most outspoken are intensely committed,

---

describing the gradual, predictable, but variable process by which we learn to integrate basic modules of thinking into higher-order, more comprehensive modes of perception.

passionately loyal, highly confident, and fully identified with their tradition, which makes them enthusiastic and passionate spokespeople. Often, their confidence is downright inspiring.

But as C. S. Lewis said, those most willing to suffer and die for their faith may also be those most willing to harm and kill for it.

Sometimes these passionate spokespeople attack people of other religions, using stereotypes and dehumanizing language that pave the way for violence. At least as often, though, these spokespeople function as gatekeepers who target even more viciously any members of their own religion who express doubt about group norms. Gatekeepers typically label these doubters as liberal, apostate, heretical, infidel, unwelcome, and dangerous.

Because of my role as a writer and speaker who raises questions and acknowledges doubt, I've had a front-row seat to witness the way a traditional gatekeeper often draws a doubter into a dance that makes them increasingly dangerous to one another. I know what it's like to have the figurative barrel of a gatekeeper's rhetorical gun pointed in one's direction.

And I'm sad to admit that I've also found myself more than once looking down the barrel in the other direction.

My first few books received generous and positive reviews, but around my third book, things began to change. As I brought some of my private questions, doubts, and dissent into public view by publishing them in books, articles, and blogs, the network of gatekeepers in my larger faith community took notice. On one occasion, a respected periodical published three reviews of my most recent book, one sympathetic, one critical, and one "hostile" (the editor's term). I was then invited to respond. I stayed up late for a few nights, fine-tuning my response. When I read my final draft, I was proud at first. I met each criticism point by point, demonstrating my rightness and superiority, exposing the false premises and logical flaws of my critics. But after a few re-readings, my heart sank.

What looked at first like a masterpiece of self-defense and clear argument seemed more and more like a disaster of defensiveness, passive aggressiveness, and tit-for-tat spitefulness. "Lord, is this how I want to spend the rest of my life, defending myself in this way?" I prayed. "Will this make me a better person? Will this make the world a better place?" I decided to hit *delete* and start over. I realized that if I argued with Stage

One people on Stage One terms, I would be strengthening their Stage One system. So I tried to respond from a Stage Four stance instead, even though I was still less than fluent in that space myself.

Of course, that didn't win over my critics. In fact, they responded with even more fire and fury. In a sense, they burned the bridge and made it clear that I was simply not wanted in the space they felt they owned. With less and less left to lose, I continued to speak out about my doubts and dreams, which only emboldened other doubters and dreamers to step out of the shadows, speak out, and stand together. Individual doubt evolved into group dissent, and group dissent threatened to become division, so gatekeepers became more desperate to regain control by any means necessary. Excommunication (informal but nonetheless real) was their only option.*

Contraction by contraction, my fellow doubters and I were squeezed out of our once womb-like denominations and traditions. Then, as "born-again doubters" (to turn a familiar phrase), we were left to fend for ourselves, spiritually homeless until we found or formed new communities. The community that "delivered" us quickly contracted to its former parameters, and loyal insiders continued toeing the line, being submissive to their gatekeepers, staying on brand and on message, and keeping "the faith."†

Our experience was, of course, completely predictable. The same diversify/purge (or expand/constrict) cycle repeats itself across denominations

---

* While Stage One gatekeepers often tell vocal Stage Three doubters that they are rebellious and heretical, Stage Two gatekeepers typically use different language to cut off doubters whose presence has become problematic. Two friends of mine, for example, both associate pastors in different megachurches, were let go within a few weeks of each other, one for being "off brand" and the other for being "off message," perfect Stage Two reasons for termination and excommunication.

† Live long enough and you'll see this same pattern repeat itself again and again: for a while, a community makes space for diversity as some of its members mature into Stage Two, Three, and Four. But eventually, Stage One warriors become alarmed. They institute a purge, full of righteous fear and fury, often aided by their Stage Two allies, who know that assisting in a purge is a better way to get ahead than being purged. It's stressful for a while, but the community soon returns to equilibrium, its members feeling pure and safe once again, although to outsiders (and the purged) they appear more harsh and rigid than ever. Before long, though, some of the Stage Two allies move into Stage Three, and eventually into Stage Four, and then the diversify/purge process repeats again. I have seen the reverse happen rarely, if ever: Stage Two enthusiasts or Stage Three purists instituting a purge of Stage One traditionalists. Stage Four people, in contrast, find purges as abhorrent as Stage One people find tolerance of diversity, so they tend to be buffers in this process, in my experience.

and traditions and centuries. With each cycle, a disproportionate number of young doubters are purged, so that only the most compliant (or most calculating) of the younger generation remain alongside their conservative elders. As a result, the average age among compliant loyalists often increases.* This phenomenon of shrinking and wrinkling faith communities is so widespread that just recently, nones, or the unaffiliated, became the third-largest religious identity (16 percent) in the world, behind Christians (31 percent) and Muslims (23 percent), and just ahead of Hindus (15 percent).†

For that reason, lots of smart people have reached the conclusion that religion is on its way out, going the way of the dodo and woolly mammoth. As a critical mass of humanity matures, religion will become unnecessary, they say, a once-useful but now-harmful adaptation of human cultural evolution. Just as frogs, toads, and salamanders needed gills when they were tadpoles or larvae wriggling in the water but outgrew them and learned to breathe air on solid ground, so the human race is now outgrowing its need to breathe religion. It can now breathe pure reason and stand tall on solid empirical data instead, they say.

I might have been able to believe that if it weren't for a 2017 invitation I received from a couple of clergy friends, Seth Wispelwey and Tracy Howe Wispelwey. Their city, they told me, was becoming an epicenter for white supremacist activity. A huge rally of white supremacists and neo-Nazis was coming up in August, and my clergy friends were helping organize a multi-faith religious response. "For all the Jews, Muslims, and people of color in our area, we want to have a united public voice that says we care and we won't let hateful ideologies go unchallenged here," they said. They were getting a lot of courageous support from black clergy and surprisingly strong support from white female clergy. But so far, too few white male clergy were willing to come. Since most of the demonstrators would be white and male, they felt it was important to have white male faith leaders present in significant numbers too. Would I come, even though it would probably be somewhat dangerous?

---

* Sometimes, I've seen the reverse happen: zealous young Stage One purists can root out their Stage Three and Four elders who seem to them soft on the fundamentals. The Stage Two pragmatists usually side with whichever group offers them more opportunities for advancement.
† See "The Future of World Religions: Population Growth Projections, 2010–2050," April 2, 2015, https://www.pewforum.org/2015/04/02/religious-projections-2010-2050/.

So I found myself in Charlottesville on August 10, 2017. I came face to face with realities I never thought I'd see in the United States: hundreds of young white men (and a few women) carrying Confederate and Nazi flags, chanting hateful slogans as they marched, some with baseball bats in hand, looking for a fight. I saw angry men with homemade shields throwing punches, lobbing Coke cans filled with cement and bottles filled with urine, and hurling curses, insults, and threats. The "Unite the Right" rally ended with one woman dead, many injured, and the country more divided than ever.

I normally don't wear clergy garb, but that day, I joined my colleagues in a collar and stole. We felt it was important to be visible as a sign of spiritual resistance to demonstrators, as a sign of support for counter-demonstrators, and as a sign of solidarity with the people the rally was meant to intimidate. Throughout the day, counter-demonstrators thanked us for being there at every turn. Late in the day, a group of us heard shouting and screaming a half-block away. We ran down the sidewalk toward a crowd, arriving just after a car had plowed through it as a terrorist act. We found ourselves kneeling on the street, holding victims, caring for their friends and relatives, and doing what we could to restore calm, even before ambulances arrived. (The police were eerily absent for a surprisingly long time.) The echoes of screams, shouts, and sobs, and the memories of tear-streaked, terrified faces are with me even now, as I write these words.

In the days after the event, I was given access to screenshots of the private communications among the fascist and white supremacist groups who organized the event (and who were called "very fine people" by the president). These communications convinced me that when people leave traditional religious identity behind, or subordinate it to a political or racial ideology, they don't advance to a blissful secular harmony. No: we humans just as easily shift the sense of identity we once found in a passionate Stage One or Stage Two religious faith into what we might call quasi-secular religions like racism, nationalism, fascism, classism, and other -isms.

With the vicious chants, hateful insults, obscene flags, and vitriolic communications of "Unite the Right" fresh in my mind, I started doing research on hate groups, not a pleasant subject, I assure you. I came across articles by and about several former white supremacist leaders who had defected from the movement. In one interview, a defector was asked why anyone would join a hateful extremist movement like the one he once helped lead. He answered with three words I'll never forget: *meaning, belonging,* and *purpose.** Exactly what religious faith is supposed to provide,* I thought. If we humans don't find meaning, belonging, and purpose in healthy forms of spirituality, we'll seek them in unhealthy forms of ideology, as Tara Isabella Burton explains:

> online communities of incels, white supremacists and anti-Semitic conspiracy theorists make no metaphysical truth claims, do not focus on God and offer no promise of an afterlife or reward. But they fulfill the functions that sociologists generally attribute to a religion: They give their members a meaningful account of why the world is the way it is. They provide them with a sense of purpose and the possibility of sainthood. They offer a sense of community. And they establish clear roles and rituals that allow adherents to feel and act as part of a whole. These aren't just subcultures; they are churches. And until we recognize the religious hunger alongside the destructive hatred, we have little chance of stopping these terrorists.
>
> Now more than ever, the promises religion has traditionally made—a meaningful world, a viable place within it, a community to share it with, rituals to render ordinary life sacred—are absent from the public sphere. More and more Americans are joining the ranks of the religiously unaffiliated. There are more religious "nones" than Catholics or Evangelicals, and 36 percent of those born after 1981 don't identify with any religion. These new reactionary movements, with their power to offer answers at once mollifying and vituperative to the chaos of existence, [are] one of many ways that Americans are filling that gap. . . . When we ignore the religious aspect of extremist groups, we allow them to claim the monopoly on meaning. That's not ground I, at least, am willing to cede.[†]

---

* See "A Former Neo-Nazi Explains Why Hate Drew Him In—and How He Got Out," *Fresh Air,* NPR.org, January 18, 2018, https://www.npr.org/templates/transcript/transcript.php?storyId =578745514/.

† Tara Isabella Burton, "The Religious Hunger of the Radical Right," *New York Times,* August 13, 2019, https://www.nytimes.com/2019/08/13/opinion/sunday/religion-extremism-white -supremacy.html/.

That's one reason I can't give up on faith, even though I know its discontents all too well.

John Lennon asked us to imagine a world without religion, so "the world will be as one." As a lifetime insider in the world of religion, I have seen its weaknesses as well as strengths, so I feel deeply the appeal of Lennon's proposal. But in the absence of religion, we fractious humans will simply unite and divide around other things: ideologies, dictators, demagogues, racial identities, wealth, weaponry, rumors, patriotism, conspiracy theories, revenge, threats.

I've watched as several of my friends, all former clergy, have left not only professional ministry but explicitly religious identity. And here's what they've found: the same kinds of bigotry, closed-mindedness, hostility, anger, and arrogance they associated with religion kept turning up in atheist and secular communities. The problem, they realized, wasn't simply with faith: it was with human nature, or more precisely, human nature at early stages of human development. We have not just a religious problem but a *human* problem.

I don't doubt that my friends had good personal reasons to give up on the "religious industrial complex," but ultimately, whether in or out of faith communities, we need to help more people mature toward Harmony. If we don't, antagonistic individuals and nations will sooner or later press the red button and nuclear weapons will fly. And they will quickly discover that radiation does not discriminate between Christian, Muslim, atheist, or humanist flesh. Whether the bombs fall in the name of God, race, nation, revenge, or economic ideology, there will be no winners when civilization self-destructs, except perhaps carrion flies.

Less dramatic but no less catastrophic: ego- and money-driven individuals and corporations will keep plundering the earth, risking the long-term health of all life on earth for short-term returns for their corporate investors, so blinded by their quest for success that they fail the test of survival. Rising sea levels, hurricanes, wildfires, and droughts won't discriminate between black or white lives, Christian or Muslim lives, rich or poor lives, socialist or capitalist lives. None of them will matter to a destabilized ecosystem.

That's why I take the risk of saying something that sounds outrageous to some people, blasphemous and unpatriotic even, but is necessary, I think, to help them wake up: *only doubt can save the world.* Only doubt will open a doorway out of hostile orthodoxies—whether religious, cultural, economic, or political.* Only through the difficult passage of doubt can we emerge into a new stage of faith and a new regenerative way of life. Everything depends on making this passage. To slightly paraphrase Dr. King, either we will learn to live together in harmony, or we will die together in misery.

Some people are betting their lives on the possibility that secular sectors like business, the academy, the arts, politics, or technology will lead the way into Harmony, because religion, they feel, is hopelessly regressive. I agree with them that we desperately need movement forward in each of these sectors, but I honestly can't imagine any one single sector (including religion) leading the way. Ultimately, we need radical change in each sector of life, flowing from a new set of values and deeper spiritual narratives. And we need forward-leaning faith communities to nourish those values and narratives in the context of a new kind of faith, a faith after doubt, a faith characterized by humility rather than arrogance, solidarity with the other rather than exclusion and antagonism, courage rather than fear, collaboration rather than competition, and love rather than self-interest.

Yes, of course, most religious communities these days are known by their vocal absolutist/dualist gatekeepers and their power-hungry/pragmatic spokespeople. (The same is true for many political parties and economic ideologies.) But remember that for every loud and regressive Jerry Falwell (Sr. or Jr.) or Franklin Graham, there have been dozens of lesser-known St. Teresas of Avila or Mother Teresas of Calcutta. For every Pope Nicholas V or Juan Ginés de Sepúlveda in history, there have been a hundred lesser-known St. Francises and Claires, Bartolomé de las Casas, Rev. Dr. Martin Luther King, Jrs., or Desmond Tutus. Thank God, there are saintly sages and activists who renounce faith entirely and work from a completely secular posture as agents of Harmony too, including the former-clergy friends I mentioned earlier.

---

* David Korten powerfully addresses the power and rigidity of economic orthodoxies and dares to doubt their hallowed dogma: "Most university economics courses currently promote societal psychopathology as a human ideal and give legitimacy to institutions that serve only to make money, without regard for the common good," he explains in a *Yes!* magazine article (July 2019), https://www.yesmagazine.org/opinion/2019/07/03/how-to-radical-economy/). See also Korten's *When Corporations Rule the World* (Berrett-Koehler, 1995, rev. 2015), *Change the Story, Change the Future* (Berrett-Koehler, 2015), and *Agenda for a New Economy* (Berrett-Koehler, 2010).

Based on my experience, I would venture to say that there are more Stage Four people on earth today than most people realize, and more inside religious traditions than outside them.

Here's why: apart from a religious tradition or some community of faith and spirituality, doubt often becomes a dead end, a hamster wheel from which there is no escape. Just as you can assume that the *being right* of dualism is all there is, or that the *being successful* of pragmatism is all there is, you can conclude that the *being suspicious* of relativism and skepticism is all there is.* You can find no exit ramp, unless you have mentors who welcome you into their community and show you how to relativize your relativism, become skeptical of your skepticism, think critically about your critical thinking, and doubt your doubt. Then, a way appears where there appeared to be no way: a way to embrace your doubt while transcending it, a way to nurture and embody a new kind of faith, a fourth stage of faith, faith that expresses itself in love.

Reflection and Action

1. This chapter is a pause to catch our breath and handle some objections and concerns. What objections or concerns did you feel before reading this chapter, and did the responses satisfy you?
2. *Life is messy and difficult*, this chapter explains, so all schemas (like the four stages) have to acknowledge that messiness. Can you think of ways in which your life doesn't fit neatly in the four stages?
3. *The lines between stages are somewhat arbitrary*, and theorists have posited from two to nine stages. How do you feel about the four given in this book?
4. *There really is no top or bottom or best or worst*, this chapter says, but schemas like the four stages can easily be abused for purposes of judgment. How do you recommend we avoid abusing them?

---

* One of my mentors defined an "-ism" as a way of thinking that claims it sees all there is(m). I should add that I see hopeful signs in non-religious communities that are seeking to nurture Stage Four consciousness. For example, consultants in the business sector are teaching contemplative mindfulness, as are some leaders in primary, secondary, and public education. It is my hope that faith communities across religious traditions and these not explicitly religious groups can share gifts and collaborate as respectful allies in the years to come.

5. How do you respond to the idea that *the stages are iterative*, that Harmony becomes the new Simplicity, and the stages repeat like four seasons across many years?

6. I describe a process of excommunication in this chapter. Have you seen this process operate in your own experience?

7. I recount my experience in Charlottesville, Virginia, to emphasize the importance of keeping some form of evolving religion alive. How did you respond to that story and to the conclusions I drew from it?

8. How do you respond to my conviction that, in spite of all their problems, faith communities still have a vital role to play in our world?

❧

10

FAITH, BELIEFS,
AND REVOLUTIONARY LOVE

Love is more than a feeling. Love is a form of sweet labor: fierce, bloody, imperfect, and life giving—a choice we make over and over again. If love is sweet labor, love can be taught, modeled, and practiced. This labor engages all our emotions: Joy is the gift of love. Grief is the price of love. Anger is the force that protects that which is loved. And when we think we have reached our limit, wonder is the act that returns us to love.

—Valarie Kaur,
See No Stranger: A Memoir and Manifesto of Revolutionary Love

I have all kinds of mixed feelings about slogans. They often oversimplify and therefore mislead. But they're pithy and memorable and therefore have some value. So, acknowledging my mixed feelings, I'd like to offer this pair of slogans to summarize the heart of our message so far:

Faith before doubt: it's about correct beliefs.
Faith after doubt: it's about revolutionary love.

In other words, the journey of faith through Simplicity and Complexity involves learning and perfecting beliefs. The journey of doubt through Perplexity involves questioning not only specific beliefs but the whole belief system approach to faith. Then, the journey into Harmony is a journey beyond beliefs into revolutionary love.

By revolutionary love, I mean *love beyond*: love that goes beyond myself to my neighbor, beyond my neighbor to the stranger, alien, other, outcast, and outsider; beyond the outsider to the critic, antagonist, opponent, and enemy; and even beyond the human to my non-human fellow creatures. In short, revolutionary love means loving as God would love: infinitely, graciously, extravagantly. To put it in more mystical terms, it means loving *with* God, letting divine love fill me and flow through me, without discrimination or limit, as an expression of the heart of the lover, not the merit of the beloved, including the correctness of the beloved's beliefs.

Now I need at this point to make clear that I am not against beliefs. Beliefs are necessary. They are interesting. They are unavoidable. But *belief*, the act of holding a set or system of beliefs, is not the same thing as *faith*, even though we often use the words imprecisely and interchangeably. To explore the difference, let's consider the insight of Alan Watts, a twentieth-century philosopher of Eastern religions who tried to capture the difference between *faith* and *belief* like this:

> We must here make a clear distinction between belief and faith, because, in general practice, belief has come to mean a state of mind which is almost the opposite of faith. Belief, as I use the word here, is the insistence that the truth is what one would "lief" or wish it to be. The believer will open his mind to the truth on the condition that it fits in with his preconceived ideas and wishes. Faith, on the other hand, is an unreserved opening of the mind to the truth, whatever it may turn out to be. Faith has no preconceptions; it is a plunge into the unknown. Belief clings, but faith lets go. In this sense of the word, faith is the essential virtue of science, and likewise of any religion that is not self-deception.*

For Watts, then, while faith is unreserved openness to the truth—a refusal to reduce truth to what we already understand, *beliefs are ideas we cling to because we wish they were true or want them to be true.* Faith is like looking at the sky through a clear or open window, he says, with an openness to accepting it as it is: blue or gray, light or dark, starry or sunny, rainy or fair. But beliefs are like blue paint that people decide to apply

---

* From *The Wisdom of Insecurity* (Vintage Books, 1951), quoted here: https://www.brainpickings .org/2014/06/27/alan-watts-belief-vs-faith/. I should add that there are other accounts of the etymology of the word *belief*. The English word seems to have been derived in the twelfth century from the German verb *louben*, meaning "to love" or "hold dear."

to the window glass to be sure it will always be the color they wish it to be. He compares doubt to the "scraping of the paint from the glass" and laments that many religious people resist doubt and "confuse faith with clinging to certain ideas."*

In *Zero Theology* John Tucker creates a similar analogy, based on an old tale told by Hans Christian Andersen. In the fable, a prince searches around the world for a true princess to be his bride.† But something about each potential princess seems inauthentic. One night in a torrential rainstorm, a soggy woman knocks at the gate seeking shelter and claiming to be a princess. Could she be the one for the prince to wed, or is she another impostor? The queen devises a plan to test whether this young woman is in fact a true princess fit for her son. She puts a pea underneath twenty mattresses and puts twenty thick blankets on top of the mattresses. The next morning, the queen asks the young woman how she slept, and she answers, "Oh, very badly! I have scarcely closed my eyes all night. Heaven only knows what was in the bed, but I was lying on something hard, so that I am black and blue all over my body. It's horrible!"

Everyone then knows this is a true princess, for "nobody but a real princess could be as sensitive as that," so the prince takes her as his bride. Tucker uses the story to suggest that the truest part of us is sensitive to the deep uncertainty of life (the pea), and we use comforting beliefs like mattresses and blankets to try to shield ourselves from that painful reality. To the degree we remain sensitive to life's uncertainty and pain in spite of all our layers of self-protection and all our attempts at self-delusion, we reveal our true nobility and authenticity.

Watts's blue paint and Tucker's mattresses help explain why, for example, people might believe in an afterlife; or in promises of divine healing, protection, or prosperity; or maybe even in divine vengeance on one's enemies. We humans find it very natural to wish to circumvent death; escape sickness, stress, and poverty; or see our enemies get what we feel they deserve.

---

* The term psychologists use for clinging to desired beliefs is "confirmation bias." Interestingly, for Watts, then, belief means surrendering to confirmation bias, while faith means resisting it. For more on bias, see my short e-book, *Why Don't They Get It? Overcoming Bias in Others (and Yourself)*, available here: https://brianmclaren.net/store/.

† See *Zero Theology* (Cascade, 2019).

However, some people raised in conservative religious backgrounds like mine might object and say that we hold or have held many beliefs we actually wish were *not* true. They didn't reduce our pain; they increased it.

For example, as a boy, I never wished for people I loved to be tortured in hell forever if they didn't join my religion. Against my wishes, the gatekeepers of my religious community agreed that this belief was required by our Scriptures. So they taught the absolute necessity of this belief, and for many years, I gave my consent, against my own wishes. Similarly, as a teenager, I never wished to see sex as dirty and shameful. But the gatekeepers of my religious community found that a steady feeling of sexual shame renders followers perpetually in need of the forgiveness and absolution the gatekeepers offer, which tends to keep followers consistently compliant and gatekeepers gainfully employed. So they continued to require it and I continued to consent, against my wishes and even my common sense, for a surprisingly long time.

Likewise, I never wished for the huge body of scientific evidence that supports the theory of evolution to be massive hoax. But the gatekeepers of my religious community justified their religious authority based on a literalistic reading of the Bible, and they saw science as a challenge to their authority. So they required me to deny science as proof of my loyalty to their authority, and for a while, I complied, against my own wishes and better judgment.

In each of these cases, my beliefs were less a matter of my personal, conscious wishes and more a matter of my unconscious wish, need, or desire for belonging. My wish to belong to a certain group led me to consent to beliefs I neither wished nor thought, personally, in my heart of hearts, to be true. I painted the blue paint on the windows and piled up the mattresses not only because I wished to do so for my personal comfort but also because groups I depended on required me to do so.

That's why I'm now convinced that religious beliefs have as much to do with group dynamics as individual wishes, and that's why I define religious beliefs as *statements or judgments that a group of religious people agrees to hold as true or correct.* They often do so, as Watts and Tucker said, because they wish their beliefs were true and hope to shield themselves from the uncertainties of life. But even when that's not the case, they "resist scraping the paint from the glass" or removing the mattresses because they wish, in a more general sense, for their group to at least to stick together. Their need, desire, or wish to belong to a group requires them to defend their group's beliefs at great cost. Some will claim them to be good, true, and beautiful in public even if the most genuine "true princess" part of themselves suspects in private that some of those beliefs are in fact bad, false, and ugly.

In this light, my religious gatekeepers didn't need me to wish our required beliefs were true, nor did they need me to sincerely believe them to be true, nor did they even need me to understand those beliefs enough to have an opinion! But they did need me to *say I believe them* and *act as though I believe them*, regardless of my level of understanding or certainty. Why, you might ask, would I ever agree to say I believe something and act as though I believe something that I don't understand, haven't really thought much about, have no way of knowing, find morally abhorrent, or am pretty sure is not actually true?

To answer this question, I return to an insight from Chapter 2: *we are hive or herd creatures*. For tens if not hundreds of millennia, we have survived by being part of groups. Given how interdependent we are on one another, and given how easily we can fragment and turn on one another, for scores of millennia we have found it advantageous to our survival to use public statements as pledges of agreement and allegiance, indicating our commitment to co-exist peacefully and collaborate effectively in groups. In many religious settings—and especially Christian settings—beliefs lie at the center of these agreements.* Clearly, in this context, beliefs don't function as a simple matter of honest personal intellectual commitment but as a more complex matter of personal social affiliation.

Whether they're true or not, then, belief agreements help us fractious human beings get on with surviving and thriving together. Practically speaking, people who share our beliefs, or at least say they do, have given consent to our group's leaders. They have agreed to cooperate with our group's norms, which makes them inherently more safe to be around.

---

* In *The Future of Faith* (HarperOne, 2009, especially Chapters 5–7 and 10), Harvey Cox explores some of the reasons behind the intense focus of Western Christians on beliefs since the fourth century.

Every time people affirm or recite what our gatekeepers require, they pass a loyalty test that makes them more worthy of our continuing trust. People who are bound together in mutual trust by shared agreements like these have all kinds of competitive advantages, especially when they compete against other groups that constantly fragment, squabble, and turn on each other. Required beliefs, we might say, are the secret weapons of competitive advantage, and they have proven their usefulness for thousands of years.

Of course, along the way, religious and political demagogues have learned to manipulate this secret weapon with great skill. One can imagine a gang of unscrupulous authoritarians toasting one another behind a curtain somewhere, gleefully boasting, "If we can get these gullible idiots to believe what we tell them to, whether it makes sense to them or not, we have them in the palms of our hands! If they are afraid to question what we label unquestionable, if they are afraid to think what we label unthinkable, we control their thoughts, which means we also control their words and their actions! At that moment, they trust us more than they trust themselves!"

It's even better (from the perspective of demagogues) if they can compel compliant people to perjure themselves, to say they believe something they do not actually believe. Whether group members do so to curry favor or to avoid punishment, once they sell their integrity, the demagogue holds exquisite power over them. Each time members willingly exchange their integrity to gain belonging and other benefits or to avoid exclusion and other punishments, a religious cult or political dictatorship grows a little stronger.

When religious gatekeepers today demand compliance with beliefs, many people (especially people in Stage Three) smell that stale cologne of con-artistry and sweaty authoritarianism and become suspicious. Once these suspicious members dare to voice their doubts, gatekeepers discover that their authority is like a bar of soap: the more they use it, the less they have. They're forced to capitulate on one belief and demote another belief from required to optional status, only to fall back and double down on others even more desperately. But each time leaders get their followers to affirm the group's required beliefs, the leaders' grip on authority remains strong, and the group reasserts its commitment to stick together.

In times of instability and change, many people (especially people in Simplicity and Complexity) become especially anxious. They need somewhere to belong. They feel nostalgic for the certainty, clarity, and belonging that authoritarian groups provide. These days, they quickly discover they don't need to leave their homes and go to a church building or cult compound to gain the desired benefits of cult membership. From the convenience and comfort of their own homes, they can tune into mass and social media channels that will reinforce their group's beliefs 24/7, creating the perfect self-reinforcing bubble of confirmation bias, blurring the line between being a free consumer of media and a willing victim of brainwashing. In these media bubbles, all windows show blue skies all the time, and all uncomfortable peas are cushioned with piles of mattresses.

These media bubbles allow the nostalgic to enter a time warp and experience the same sense of homogeneity that many of our ancestors shared centuries ago, when few people traveled to encounter others who thought differently and when homegrown dissenters were quickly silenced, imprisoned, banished, or otherwise dispatched.

Of course, in today's context, doubters and dissenters don't need to be silenced by inquisitions; they only need to be denied air time or page views by mass media programming executives or social media algorithms.

For me, the more I stepped outside of the bubble of my religious heritage, the more my inherited beliefs were challenged on every side. In university, I got to know people whose beliefs radically differed from mine. True, I had been trained to befriend them and listen to them, but only as a prelude to witnessing to them and converting them to my group's beliefs. But when I listened, really listened, I began to see why their beliefs made sense to them and mine didn't.

My beliefs were further challenged by scientific and historical information that was readily available in libraries and is even more readily available today online. Such information is still easy to ignore, but it's harder than ever to suppress. My beliefs were further challenged by journalism that exposed the moral failures, corruption, and hypocrisy of the contemporary religious leaders and gatekeepers who demanded my belief compliance. My beliefs were most directly challenged by a few outspoken individuals who first dared to doubt privately and then dared to dissent publicly because they no longer feared (or respected) the religious gatekeepers.

I was a very loyal person, respectful of authority and always ready to give the benefit of the doubt to my tradition and its spokespeople. But over time, I not only lost confidence in many of the beliefs that gatekeepers required: I lost faith in the gatekeepers themselves and their whole system of using beliefs as markers of belonging. If I was going to be a person of faith, it couldn't be in a community that was obsessed with policing my beliefs. I needed a different understanding of faith entirely, as something beyond beliefs.

To my surprise, I discovered that at the heart of my own tradition, in the Bible I had been reading my whole life, and especially in the life and teachings of Jesus, Mary, Paul, James, and John, the fresh understanding of faith my heart was thirsty for had been waiting like a hidden spring all along.

Rather than recounting the unfolding of this discovery here (since I have written in detail about it elsewhere), I can illustrate it by contrasting biblical misquotations with what we actually find in the biblical text.

While people don't often think of Mary as a teacher in the Bible, her short prayer known as the Magnificat is powerfully informative. She *doesn't* say:

> *My soul magnifies the Lord,*
> *and my spirit rejoices in God my Savior,*
> *for he has looked with favor on the correct beliefs of his servant.*
> *Surely, from now on all generations will call me blessed;*
> *for the Mighty One has done great things for me,*
> *and holy is his name.*
> *His mercy is for those who hold correct beliefs about him*
> *from generation to generation.*
> *He has shown strength with his arm;*
> *he has scattered the doctrinally incorrect in the thoughts of their hearts.*
> *He has brought down the heretical from their thrones,*
> *and lifted up the orthodox;*
> *he has filled those with correct beliefs with good things,*
> *and sent the incorrect away empty.*

Instead, her prayer is a manifesto of God's loving concern for the poor, the hungry, the lowly, and the powerless. (You can read her actual words in Luke 1:46 ff.) Similarly, her son Jesus never said, when asked what is the greatest commandment:

> *"You shall hold correct beliefs about the Lord your God with all your heart, and with all your soul, and with all your mind." This is the greatest and first commandment. And a second is like it: "You shall convert your neighbors who do not hold correct beliefs, and if they will not convert, you shall defeat them in a culture war." On these two commandments hang all the law and the prophets.*

Instead, he said something truly revolutionary: first, he said to love God with our whole being. Second, and *equally important* (which is the meaning of "the second is like it"), he said to love our neighbors as ourselves (Matthew 22:36–40). In Luke's version (Luke 10:25 ff.), Jesus tells a parable that makes it clear that one's neighbor includes the stranger, the other, the outsider, the outcast, and the unclean.

In the Sermon on the Mount, Jesus doesn't teach a list of beliefs to be memorized and recited. Instead, he teaches a way of life that culminates in a call to revolutionary love. This revolutionary love goes far beyond conventional love, the love that distinguishes between us and them, brother and other, or friend and enemy (Matthew 5:43). Instead, we need to love as God loves, with non-discriminatory love that includes even the enemy.

If that weren't revolutionary enough, we could turn to Paul, the originator of the phrase "faith expressing itself in love" (Galatians 4:6).* According to many of our leading religious gatekeepers today, Paul didn't get it quite right. He should have said, "For in Christ Jesus correct beliefs about circumcision and uncircumcision are still very important; the only thing that counts is faith expressing itself through correct beliefs."

When he tries to summarize what God requires and desires, Paul does not say: "For the whole law is summed up in a single commandment,

---

* In light of the original Greek, the phrase could be rendered, "the only thing with power or value or worth is faith energizing through love" or "faith working through love."

'You shall have the correct beliefs.'" Rather, he declares, "For the whole law is summed up in a single commandment, 'You shall love your neighbor as yourself'" (Galatians 5:14). It appears that, for Paul, if you love your neighbor, the love of God is implied, assumed, included, or experienced as a byproduct, which, of course, echoes Jesus' words, that those who love the "least of these" actually love him (Matthew 25).

Of course, I haven't even mentioned Paul's famous love poem in 1 Corinthians 13 (where he does *not* say, "These three things remain: liturgy, polity, and correct beliefs, and the greatest of these is correct beliefs"), or his fine-tuned argument in Romans that culminates in a call to self-sacrificing love (12:9, 13:10, where he does *not* say, "Correct beliefs must be held sincerely. . . . Correct beliefs fulfill the law").

We find this theme carried on later in the New Testament. For example, James does *not* say this:

> *Religion that is pure and undefiled before God, the Father, is this: to have correct beliefs, and to affirm liturgies, hierarchies, and creeds that reflect those beliefs.*

Instead, he says this:

> *Religion that is pure and undefiled before God, the Father, is this: to care for orphans and widows in their distress, and to keep oneself unstained by the world.*

What matters to James centers in caring for people, not confessing beliefs. That's why he goes on to say that "faith without works is dead." Real faith is found not simply in words that express compliance but in actions that express care.

We find the same in the Epistles of John. In 1 John 4:7 ff., John doesn't say:

> *Beloved, let us hold to correct beliefs, because correctness is from God; everyone who believes the required statements is born of God and knows God. Whoever does not confess the right beliefs does not know God, for God is correctness.*

Rather, John says this:

> *Beloved, let us love one another, because love is from God; everyone*
> *who loves is born of God and knows God. Whoever does not love does*
> *not know God, for God is love.*

Then, echoing Jesus' words about the greatest commandment, John continues:

> *Those who say, "I love God," and hate their brothers or sisters, are*
> *liars; for those who do not love a brother or sister whom they have seen,*
> *cannot love God whom they have not seen. The commandment we*
> *have from him is this: those who love God must love their brothers and*
> *sisters also.*

Again, he doesn't come anywhere close to saying,

> *Those who say, "I love God," and hold incorrect beliefs are liars; for*
> *those who do not express correct beliefs that they can capture in words,*
> *cannot love God whom they cannot capture in words. The command-*
> *ment we have from him is this: those who love God must have the*
> *correct beliefs about God.*

This emphasis on love isn't unique to the Christian Scriptures, of course. When the Torah repeatedly calls for compassionate treatment of aliens, refugees, widows, orphans, the poor, and the vulnerable, it calls Jews to make love central.* The prophet Hosea echoes this emphasis when he proclaims the word of the Lord (6:6): "I desire compassion, not sacrifice." The other prophets make similar statements in passage after passage (see Isaiah 1 and 58, or Micah 6, for example).

When the Quran says that no one is a believer until they desire for their brother or sister what they desire for themselves, and that God made

---

* In Proverbs, for example, the way we treat the poor is the way we treat God: see Proverbs 17:5 and 19:17, along with 14:21, 21:13, 22:2, 22:9, 22:16, 22:22–23, 28:7, 29:7, and 31:19.

us different so that we would seek to understand and know one another, it is calling on humanity to put love first.

When the gurus of Sikhism say to value others as you value yourself, and to avoid creating enmity with anyone because God is within everyone, when Taoists say to regard your neighbor's gain or loss as your own, when Buddhists and Hindus say do not hurt others in ways you would find hurtful, and when secular humanists advocate the principle of reciprocity, they are calling on humanity to put love first.

We're used to thinking of the real differences in the world as among religions: *you are Buddhist, I am Christian, she is Jewish, he is atheist.* But I wonder if that way of thinking is becoming irrelevant and perhaps even counter-productive. What if the deeper question is not whether you are a Christian, Buddhist, or atheist, but rather, *what kind of Christian, Buddhist, or atheist are you?* Are you a believer who puts your distinct beliefs first, or are you a person of faith who puts love first? Are you a believer whose beliefs put you in competition and conflict with people of differing beliefs, or are you a person of faith whose faith moves you toward the other with love?

That phrase I just used, *person of faith*, in one sense makes a simple generalization. It serves as a description that makes room for Christians, Muslims, Jews, and so on. But I am coming to see that *person of faith* is not just a generalization. It is also a differentiation, in contrast to a *person of beliefs*. It reflects a shared desire among people in all these diverse traditions to be identified not by lists of beliefs that exclude one another but by something deeper, by faith in a universal, non-discriminatory love that calls us all together.

In that light, the word *doubt* can mean two very different things. When it is applied to faith that expresses itself in beliefs, it means one thing. When it is applied to faith that expresses itself in revolutionary love, it means something very different. Sometimes, it is only by doubting a religion that expresses itself in beliefs that we can discover a faith that expresses itself in revolutionary love.

That is what I mean by faith after doubt.

To some, that will sound like heresy. To others, it sounds like liberation.

Reflection and Action

1. Respond to the pair of slogans at the beginning of the chapter.
2. How would you explain the difference between faith and beliefs in your own words? Summarize the window and mattress analogies.
3. Gatekeepers, I suggest in this chapter, are more interested in their adherents saying they affirm required beliefs than in whether or not those adherents actually believe or understand those beliefs. That may have been an overstatement. What do you think?
4. Describe the relationship between beliefs and demagoguery.
5. Read the actual Magnificat poem that begins in Luke 1:46 and contrast it line by line with the altered version in this chapter.
6. Respond to this rhetorical question: "What if the deeper question is not whether you are a Christian, Buddhist, or atheist, but rather, *what kind of Christian, Buddhist, or atheist are you?*"
7. Share your emotional response to this chapter. What emotions did it stir? What feeling stays with you after reading it?

PART THREE

LIFE AFTER
(AND WITH)
DOUBT

꙳

11

COMMUNITIES
OF HARMONY

> Imagine joining a knitting group. Does anyone go to a knitting group
> and ask if the knitters believe in knitting or what they hold to be true
> about knitting? Do people ask for a knitting doctrinal statement? In-
> deed, if you start knitting by reading a book about knitting or a history
> of knitting or a theory of knitting, you will very likely never knit.
>
> —Diana Butler Bass, *Christianity After Religion*

I had just given a lecture on the four stages of faith at a conference in
North Carolina, and I was asked to do a book signing. I noticed a woman
waiting not in the line but off to the side, over near the door. As soon as I
signed the last book, she quickly approached me and introduced herself.
"My name is Charis. Kind of like a mix between Karen and Lois," she
said. "Any chance I could buy you a cup of coffee as a bribe to answer a
personal question?"

We found a coffee shop just a block away. We ordered and sat down
at a little table near the door, and her story poured out.

Charis was raised in a Southern Baptist church that expected her to
affirm beliefs about women being submissive to men and gay marriage
being an "abomination," because the inerrant Bible told her so. During
her teenage years, she began doubting these beliefs, and by her senior year
of high school, she thought these beliefs were not only false and ridiculous
but also dangerous. "I felt morally compromised every time I went to
church," she told me. "I felt that my presence showed support for beliefs
I found appalling."

She got a scholarship to an Evangelical college, where she continued to struggle with her religious identity. "Like a lot of students, I stopped going to church on Sundays, but we had required chapel, and I would say three out of every four chapel speakers made me feel furious, livid, or even physically ill," she explained. "The arrogance, the fear tactics, the cheap shots, the us versus them mentality . . . it was straight from the Simplicity/dualism script you shared this morning."

In one of her required religion courses, she studied American church history, and it grieved her to learn that her denomination formed in 1845 to defend the rights of slaveholders to keep slaves, basing all their arguments on the Bible: "My professor then made a big deal about how our denomination later repudiated slavery and racism, but that wasn't until 2009! Talk about being late for the party! And don't even get me started on what happened in 2016 with the election of Trump."

"Since graduation from college," she continued, "I've stayed away from church, religiously, you might say. But when I'm driving somewhere, I do still listen to Christian radio in my car occasionally, even though usually, it just makes things worse. Every time I hear some preacher complaining about how the federal government is taking away their 'religious liberty,' I realize they mean their liberty to control women's bodies and discriminate against gay people's bodies, and I feel like I've been sucked into a time machine and transported back to 1845, when it was black bodies that were in question. Why be part of a group like that?"

She was pretty amped up, and her volume was causing a few people around the coffee shop to look in our direction. She noticed, laughed, took a deep breath, leaned forward, and lowered her voice: "So, Brian, here's my question: I've been up to my neck in doubt all through my twenties, and I'm ready to move on. But where in the hell do I find a church that fosters the faith after doubt you talked about? If there are any of those Stage Four churches here in North Carolina, they sure are doing a good job of hiding, because believe me, I've been looking!"

I started to respond, but she wasn't finished: "Look, I'm almost thirty and I'm dating someone and it's getting pretty serious. And eventually, we want to have children. And I know what I *don't* want to teach my hypothetical future children, but I have no idea what I *do* want to teach them . . . and I guess, more personally, I wish I could find some group of people who have sifted through all the best from the past and use it to help people like me get a little more of that harmony in our lives that you talked about this morning. For all the problems I have with what I was taught growing up, I do feel that having a faith community was worth a lot to me. And I think the world will *not* be a better place unless we can find a way to have healthy faith communities without all the _____." She used a vivid barnyard noun to complete the sentence.

Everywhere I go, I meet people like Charis who ask me their version of this same question: where can I find a faith community that welcomes doubters like me and my friends, a good place in which to raise children, a fellowship that helps us move toward "faith expressing itself in love"? I generally answer by telling them I have good news and bad news. I offer the bad news first but warn them that the bad news is really, really bad. That's what I said to Charis, and she asked, "How bad?"

"It's not just that the supply of faith communities for doubters is far below the demand. It's that the demand is still pretty low too."

"I don't believe that," she countered. "There are so many people like me. I know they're out there."

"You're right, people like you are out there in growing numbers," I replied, "but here's the problem. On the one hand, we have faith communities that are quite progressive in their methodology. They've got rock and roll music, online streaming, apps, the whole shebang. But under the paint, they're rigidly conservative, even regressive, in their theology. Then, on the other hand, we have faith communities that are more progressive in their theology, but they tend to be rigidly institutional in their methodology."

She interrupted. "Been there. I tried a couple churches like that. Big on committees. Big on vestments and keeping the liturgy just so. A *little* low on action and energy. Really nice people . . . of my grandparents' generation. So you're saying those are my two options, both less than satisfactory: young, hip, and regressive or old, institutional, and progressive."

"It's even a little worse than that," I said. "A lot of these non-regressive faith communities have gone from Stage One into a kind of twilight zone with a little Stage Two pragmatism and a little Stage Three perplexity mixed in. When angsty post-conservatives like you show up with all your questions, these faith communities don't know what to do with you. They aren't Stage One, which is a relief, but they aren't Stage Four either.

They've debugged their software of fundamentalist belief systems, but they haven't installed a love-driven program in its place. They're like a bicycle that runs on a front wheel of ambiguity and a rear wheel of institutional momentum. Meanwhile, a lot of these faith communities are aging and declining numerically. It's been a long time since they've had experience with younger people. They want you, and they need you, but . . ."

She interrupted again. "I get it. I get it. They want the 'millennials' like me to come and save them. But really, they want us less as members or partners and more as fuel to keep their operation going. So people like me give up on church entirely and join the 'nones,' which means that the demand stays low for faith communities that welcome people with questions and doubts and want to focus on love instead. It's a self-perpetuating downward spiral."

I nodded. I still had some good news, but I wanted to wait until she asked for it.

She looked pensive and started to say something a few times but kept stopping herself. Finally, she said, "Look, I do all the nones stuff. I do yoga. I go to therapy. I do these online self-awareness-unleash-your-inner-goddess courses and stuff like that. But I'm not an idiot. I know about climate change and nuclear war and economic inequality and all that. And the world is in such a mess, I don't just want to be a good, happy, fulfilled, spiritual consumer while it all goes down the toilet. I want to be part of a group, a movement, that's trying to . . . you know, *save it*. There. I said it. I want to be part of a community that isn't obsessed with saving their own damned souls, but that actually wants to try to save this world that we're on the verge of destroying. So you've got to tell me what a Stage Four church would look like and where I can find one. That's what I'm asking for in exchange for the tall decaf skim mocha I just bought you (which, by the way, does *not* say good things about you). You travel around. You see what's out there. I need you to be my informant. Or maybe my matchmaker, to help me find what you call a Stage Four faith community that I can fall in love with."

Then, suddenly, unexpectedly, her eyes brimmed: "Brian, let me tell you something. It's not easy out here, out here in nones-land, I mean. I'm working my backside off in my profession, and corporate America is draining my soul like a vampire. And all it offers me by way of compensation is more stuff and more rat-race. Here's the thing: if people like you don't find some way to fix this fast, I think the whole religious system is going to collapse, because people like me aren't going back to the options you just outlined for me, at least, not many of us. So I hope your good news is really good, because you're killing me with this bad news, Brian. So how about it? Can you show me at least one glimmer of hope?"

"We're it," I said.

She gave me a half eye-roll, half-frown.

I continued, "Really. You, and me, and people like you and me: doubters in the old way but believers in a new way. We've doubted enough of the belief systems we inherited that we can help embody faith after doubt, the faith that's trying to be born, the faith of harmony that expresses itself in love. There's nothing to stop us from being the solution instead of just complaining about the problem. I don't think we have a full-blown movement or revolution yet, but things are getting bad enough that more and more people are getting ready to make a leap to the better."

"Oh, please," she said with a full eye-roll and frown this time. "Please don't give me the 'we're the ones we've been waiting for' line. You've got to give me more hope than that."

Then I told her about the signs of hope that I saw: "People are already doing amazing things. There are courageous, creative pastors, rabbis, and other faith community leaders who are stepping into the gap, and new experiments are springing up all over, including here in North Carolina. Meanwhile, normal people are gathering spontaneously to learn all over the place, but instead of gathering exclusively in buildings with stained-glass windows, they're learning together through podcasts and TED Talks. They're starting reading groups in living rooms and pub theology groups in bars and restaurants. Instead of gathering fifty-two times a year for one hour, I see people gathering once a year or twice a year for fifty-two hours, in festivals and retreats, in excursions into the wilderness and intense conferences. We have growing numbers of brilliant scholars and gifted artists who offer amazing resources to the conversation without needing to control it or monetize it, with daily email devotionals, weekly podcasts, and all kinds of on-demand online resources. There's this amazing sense of sharing that's happening . . . it's like an open-source revolution and multi-source revelation. More and more of us are ruthlessly honest about what's not working, and we're absolutely unwilling to invest our best energies in ambiguous institutions that, for all their good intentions, aren't radical enough to make the transition that's needed."

I took the last sip of my coffee and continued, "There are a few folks of my generation who have worked our whole lives to build an exit ramp off the old religious superhighway before it runs us off a cliff, and now, more and more people of your generation are coming together to build a new way forward from that exit ramp. Of course, I imagine that this process will take more than a generation to complete, so it's probably your hypothetical children who will really see what it can look like."

"No. No way," she said, literally slapping her hand on the table and shaking the silverware and coffee mugs. "We don't have time for that. We need it now. The sea levels are rising, man. The oligarchs, kleptocrats, and demagogues are consolidating power."

"I agree," I replied. "As Bill McKibben says, when your ice caps are melting fast, winning very slowly is another way of losing. So you're right: this is a genuine emergency and there's no time to waste. To get there, we need first dozens, then hundreds, then thousands, then tens of thousands of people talking honestly about our doubts and our dreams and desires, just as we're doing right here, right now, at this table."

"Yes, but . . ." she began.

Then she caught herself. "I guess that's the problem, isn't it, way too many *yes, buts?*"

We sat in silence for maybe half a minute. I wished I could offer her better news, but I was giving her the best I could honestly give.

Then she continued, "I guess that's my dissatisfaction with Stage Three. We've always got a million *yes, buts*. As if we'll only be able to spring into action when the last argument or objection or concern is answered. There will always be another objection, but we need action and we need it now. So we need faith communities that are big on action, and big on love, but small on beliefs and bureaucracy. We need faith communities we can say *yes* to, yes, without so many *buts*."

I looked at my watch and realized I had a plane to catch, so we exchanged email addresses. As I traveled to the airport and boarded my flight, I felt a renewed commitment, inspired by Charis, to intensify my efforts to help people in Perplexity move beyond their *yes, buts*, and to focus on the *yes*. In fact, it was during that flight that this book began taking shape.

For people weary of belonging to the "church of the last detail," the church that claims it has perfected its list of beliefs, this possibility of a community of faith that expresses itself in love rather than beliefs may seem too good to be true. But actually, I think it is the only possibility good enough to be true. With years of practice behind me, I find that I can say *yes, but* to just about everything. But "faith expressing itself in love"—that evokes my wholehearted *yes*.

It's *faith expressing itself in love* that beckons children to do the work of Simplicity, learning to habitually choose goodness and generosity and reject meanness and self-centeredness so they can become vibrant, healthy adolescents. It's *faith expressing itself in love* that beckons those adolescents to grapple with Complexity and master the skills needed to succeed as young adults, so they can become loving friends, partners, parents, workers, neighbors, and citizens. It's *faith expressing itself in love* that summons thoughtful young adults to pass into and through Perplexity, seeing through hypocrisy, rejecting ignorance, and challenging injustice, even when doing so is costly, all in the pursuit of love. And it's *faith expressing itself in love* that welcomes the passionate young seeker into a deep adult lifestyle of empathy, kindness, and compassion, where love is the prime directive, the greatest thing, the most excellent way, the Harmony way.*

We currently have about 330,000 Christian *communities of beliefs* in North America, where I live, plus thousands of non-Christian communities, with millions more around the world. But too few of these communities are all in as *communities of faith expressing themselves in love*. True, within many if not most of those communities, you can find a little core of people who have made their way through Simplicity, Complexity, and Perplexity and into Harmony. But centuries of obsession with accumulated beliefs are hard to overcome, and so are the worries associated with

---

* Indigenous theologian Randy Woodley describes the Cherokee idea of the Harmony Way here: Ben Katt, "Randy Woodley on the Harmony Way," replacingchurch.org, September 12, 2017, https://replacingchurch.org/77-randy-woodley-on-the-harmony-way/; and here: "Modeling the Harmony Way," *Prism Magazine*, April 1, 2014, https://prismmagazine.org/modeling-the -harmony-way/. This Cherokee concept is one of the best articulations of Stage Four faith that I've come across anywhere. See Woodley's book, *Shalom and the Community of Creation* (Eerdmans, 2012).

aging buildings, aging members, dwindling numbers, and shrinking bank accounts. So faith expressing itself in love still lies hidden like a treasure buried in a field, and too few ever find it.

As a result, tired of belief systems and weary from religious adventures in missing the point, more and more people are simply dropping out. Their departure leaves religious institutions edgy and anxious, with some doubling down on the old ways, others holding on until retirement, and at least a few opening up to new possibilities. In that foment, in that fragility and blessed unrest, there is an opportunity. Something is trying to be born. This new kind of faith, faith expressing itself in love, may, if we dare to nurture it, have a bright future, as promising as an acorn that is breaking out of its husk, as full of promise as a baby crying out for her first breath.

My fellow author and friend Diana Butler Bass and I are always on the lookout for those cries of new life. We're probably in the top ten people who speak to the most clergy across the most denominations from year to year in North America, maybe even in the top three. Our concerns, vision, and passion resonate deeply. We get on the phone every few months to share what we're seeing, where we're discouraged, and where we see those signs of something trying to be born. Sometimes, we're both feeling pretty grim. Sometimes one of us feels more upbeat and the other more beaten down. Occasionally, both of us are hopeful at the same time.

Of course, Diana literally wrote the book on forward-leaning congregations with *The Practicing Congregation*.* Anyone can trace through her books how she has been grappling with the question of how a new kind of faith can be expressed in a new kind of faith community, and my books show a parallel trajectory. One question still remains open for both of us: will denominations and congregations in decline keep their heads down, obsessed with saving themselves and micro-managing their own decline (to use the language of Lutheran pastor Wolfgang Herz-Lane)? Or will they seize the destabilizations of their current systems as opportunities to give birth to something fresh, needed, and new?

In other words, will the faith communities of the future, communities of *faith after (and with) doubt* and *faith expressing itself in love*, grow

---

* Diana Butler Bass, *The Practicing Congregation* (Rowman & Littlefield, 2004).

naturally from collaborations across current denominations . . . or will they arise from the ashes of current denominations after they dwindle, crash, and burn in a desperate attempt to save themselves in isolation?

If I were to write a five-step plan to help us give birth to the communities we need, communities that are centered on faith expressing itself in love, it would look like this:

1. We should help willing churches (and other faith communities) that are declining to do more than manage their decline, namely, to put everything on the table for change on the one hand or, on the other, divest of their assets as soon as is practical and invest most or all of those assets in a "church of the future" fund.*

2. This church of the future fund would be a joint venture across denominations, so that these future churches will have denominational roots (if they want them) and support (if they need it) while remaining free of the control and politics of any single denomination. (Our Jewish friends have already created at least one network of this sort, as have some Muslim friends.†) In other words, Methodists, Episcopalians, Lutherans, and others would be giving birth to churches that were no longer merely outposts of their denomination.‡ Instead, the new congregations would be hybrids, drawing together strengths from across denominations, without being entangled in the internal politics and bureaucracies of any single denomination in its current form. Freed in this new way, they would have the opportunity to "rebrand" and announce themselves to the world.

3. These faith communities of the future would develop new norms for financial independence and interdependence, quality control, and collective action, using existing structures whenever possible and creating new ones when necessary.

4. These congregations would develop parameters for collaboration and inclusion to keep faith expressing itself in love as the primary

---

* I'm grateful for organizations like Convergence (https://convergenceus.org/consultants/), the FaithX Project (https://faithx.net/), and others that are helping congregations in these ways.
† See the Jewish Emergent Network, http://www.jewishemergentnetwork.org/, and Muslims for Progressive Values, http://www.mpvusa.org/.
‡ One such network bringing together non-denominational Christian church leaders, the W/ Collective, can be found here: https://withcollective.org/about/.

focus. They would organize one or more minimalist institutions to support their multi-generational movement of revolutionary love, shifting governance responsibility to congregations themselves and maximizing shared vision and mission. They would draw inspiration from models as diverse as Alcoholics Anonymous, environmental organizations, Black Lives Matter, labor unions, yoga studios, activist movements, and franchises. The result would be some form of connected congregationalism, meaning that each congregation would be responsible for its own governance while participating in the larger movement of shared vision and mission for the common good.

5. This movement or movement of movements would have intra-faith and multi-faith dimensions. In other words, there would be specifically Christian, Jewish, Muslim, and other movements within each faith tradition, and there would also be intentional collaboration among and across traditions.

Diana and I, along with many others, have devoted much of our adult lives to this kind of movement building. And although the movement we continue to strive for still hasn't reached critical mass, each year there are more prototypes, more creative local faith communities that people like Charis are desperate for.

I'd like to describe just four of them: one Jewish, one Muslim, one mainline Protestant, and one post-Evangelical.

If you go to the website of IKAR, you'll see a photograph of my dear friend Rabbi Sharon Brous, followed by photographs of children and adults singing and praying at the beach.* Over these photographs, a series of statements appear, each beginning with the words "We are . . ."

> We are dreamers . . . We are seekers . . . We are doers . . . We are
> activists . . . We are thinkers . . . We are hell-raisers . . . We are
> irreverently pious . . . We are piously irreverent . . . We are
> die-hards . . . We are newbies . . . We are skeptics.

---

* https://ikar-la.org/, accessed October 2019. Websites of innovative congregations change quickly, so when you access this and other sites noted in this chapter, they may be even more interesting.

At the bottom of the landing page, you'll find links to photographs of members of IKAR, all young or young-ish, each with a self-descriptive moniker like *awake, mindful wanderer, bearded rebel, skeptical activist, soul on fire, lover and fighter, searching, Reconstructionist Bu-Jew, enthusiastic pray-er, feminist mother, Jew-ish.* If that isn't enough to convince you that this isn't your typical synagogue, you'll find this description in a recent article about IKAR:

> The Los Angeles congregation Ikar likes to break the unspoken rules of American Judaism. It does not call itself Conservative, Orthodox or Reform. It doesn't even call itself a synagogue, because it has no permanent home. It holds services—known for their drum circles and packs of roaming children—in rented auditoriums and classrooms.*

Also in Los Angeles, you'll find Muslims for Progressive Values (MPV), a faith community led by another friend, Ani Zonneveld. On MPV's website, you'll see these words in bold: *Be Yourself. Be Muslim.*† An article describes Ani, the mosque's founding imam, like this:

> Ani Zonneveld is an imam, and yes, also a woman. She qualifies that she is "an imam with a small 'i'"—though her reluctance to go with a capital "I" says more about her democratic approach to worship than any deference to Islamic tradition, one that has been and still is very male-dominated. She has no patience for that Islam.
>
> . . . [S]he founded a Muslim community—Muslims for Progressive Values—that embraces gender equality, gay rights and interfaith marriage. And although it is based in Los Angeles, it has spread—often quietly—across the world. . . . Zonneveld is not shy of challenging the rules of her religion, most of which she insists are cultural accretions. She happily takes turns with others in her L.A.-based community to lead Friday prayers. She also sings during worship—anathema to the

---

* Ari Feldman, "Ikar Is Building Something. Just Don't Call It a Synagogue," Forward.com, June 2, 2018, https://forward.com/news/national/402306/ikar-is-building-something-just-dont-call -it-a-synagogue/.
† http://www.mpvusa.org/, accessed October 2019.

traditionalists—and she created Muslims for Progressive Values as an alternative model of community.

Her group has spread beyond North America, and counts more than 10,000 members, though many have joined or sympathize in secret. Her open embrace of LGBTQ rights, now culturally acceptable in America, is still radical in many Islamic contexts.*

Ani describes MPV as "a way for us to bring together Muslims of like minds" to work for "gender parity, human rights for everyone, freedom of expression, freedom of and from religion, separation of religion and state, all (those) good values that have been side-lined and instead have been replaced by blind ritual and orthodoxy that is very stiff and very harsh in its interpretation." The movement has spread to fourteen countries.

If you zip east across North America to New York, there you'll find Middle Collegiate Church, led by another woman and dear friend, Rev. Dr. Jacqui Lewis. Like many churches, its website has a "What We Believe" page, but notice what that page says:

We believe in the power of Love. Period. Through Love, we are each created in God's image and filled with the Divine Spark. No matter whom we love, no matter how we look, no matter where we are on our journey, God's imprint is in every person of every race/ethnicity, every gender, and every sexual orientation.

Worship at Middle Church is a joyous celebration of the transformative power of love. In worship, we rehearse the Reign of God on earth. We celebrate the sacraments in our sanctuary and outside on the streets as activism. We express our faith in music and the arts; the arts are an active prayer connecting us with the Holy Spirit.

Following in the way of Jesus, who taught us to love God with everything we have, and to love our neighbor as we love [ourselves], we do love out loud as we work for justice. At Black Lives Matter protests, LGBQTIA+ rallies, the Women's March, Climate Change events, and

---

* Jane Little, "She's an Imam in LA and Doesn't Have Patience for a Strict Interpretation of Islam," BBC News, July 17, 2015, updated July 18, 2015, https://www.pri.org/stories/2015-07-17/shes -imam-la-and-doesnt-have-patience-strict-interpretation-islam.

activism around gun violence, prison reform and a living wage, we are there.

There's little doubt that faith expressing itself in love is the focus of a congregation like Middle Collegiate.

Head west about 1,800 miles and you'll come to Highlands Church, a post-Evangelical church in Denver led by a team of three: Jenny Morgan, Rachael McClair, and Mark Tidd.* You'll find the Apostle's Creed on their website (the creed is a much more inclusive statement of beliefs than most Evangelical churches require), and here's how the creed is introduced: "People who call Highlands Church home find themselves on a wide spectrum of beliefs. While making plenty of room for that, the teachings of HC are grounded in the beliefs about God consistent with the early followers of Jesus as expressed in the Apostle's Creed." You'll also find this ethos statement, written by Mark Tidd:

> Married, divorced and single here, it's one family that mingles here.
> Conservative and liberal here, we've all gotta give a little here.
> Big and small here, there's room for us all here.
> Doubt and believe here, we all can receive here.
> LGBTQ and straight here, there's no hate here
> Woman and man here, everyone can here.
> Whatever your race here, for all of us grace here.
> In imitation of the ridiculous love Almighty God has for each of us and all of us, let us live and love without labels!

As I explained to Charis, in addition to organized congregations like these, many informal groups are springing up all around the world. They might call themselves a study group, a pub theology group, a festival, a retreat, a school, a yoga studio, an online community, or some other kind of organization, and they are fulfilling for one another some or all of the functions that traditional congregations have provided in the past.

---

* http://www.hchurchdenver.com/. The term *post-Evangelical* is mine, not theirs. I use it to indicate that the church has its roots in Evangelical Christianity. Because the term *Evangelical* is so highly contested and increasingly associated with the Religious Right and Donald Trump, many people and congregations of Evangelical heritage can no longer use the term without a differentiating prefix, if at all.

I am for all of these informal communities that seek to build meaning, belonging, and purpose among individuals and families, whether they are Christian, Muslim, Jewish, Hindu, Sikh, Buddhist, or whatever.

I am also for non-religious humanist communities who draw their primary inspiration from non-religious sources and multi-religious or multi-faith communities that draw their inspiration from a variety of religious sources. I am for any community that seeks the common good in a spirit of love. In fact, as a Christian, I dare to believe that the Spirit of God is the inspiration and guide for groups like this, whatever their label, because God, as I have come to understand God through Jesus, is happy to remain anonymous or to be named in a wide variety of ways or even to go incognito. In a world that desperately needs a sense of meaning, belonging, and purpose beyond individual, religious, national, economic, or political self-interest, the responses we need are not *either/or* but *both/ and* and *all of the above.*

Sadly, in thousands of cities and regions, there are still no communities of faith with the spirit of IKAR, MPV, Middle Collegiate, or Highlands. Yes, there are thousands of congregations where people in Simplicity and Complexity will feel at home, but millions of people in Perplexity and Harmony—people like Charis—still feel spiritually homeless. As thankful as I am for the growing number of prototypes like these, I have to acknowledge that at this moment, when most people think *religion* or *church* or *synagogue* or *mosque*, they still think of conventional communities carrying on their traditional beliefs, liturgies, and hierarchies and not these new prototypes of faith expressing itself in love. They don't even know that such alternatives exist or could exist.

Religious groups pay people like Diana and me to come bring them hope. I empathize. They see declining numbers. They see their aging congregations. They see young people moving away. They see their denominational leaders squabbling over lesser matters and micro-managing their decline. Meanwhile, they're working their hearts out in thousands of labors of love, and they want to know they're not wasting their efforts. I want to encourage them with all my heart.

But I have to admit that I am much less eager to dispense hope than I once was.

Young Greta Thunberg helped me understand why. When I think

about our need for Stage Four faith communities, communities of faith after (and with) doubt, and when I think of the lack of urgency or creativity or boldness among so many of our leaders, I recall what Greta says about our looming environmental catastrophe: "I don't want you to be hopeful," she says. "I want you to panic. I want you to feel the fear I feel every day, and then I want you to act. I want you to act as you would in a crisis. I want you to act as if our house is on fire. Because it is."

When will a critical mass of innovative leaders come together to design, fund, and launch the new collaborative structures that will support the new communities of Stage Four faith so needed by people like Charis? We don't have time to waste. We need these new kinds of faith communities now. As Charis so aptly said: "The sea levels are rising, man. The oligarchs, kleptocrats, and demagogues are consolidating power."

Charis is right. Greta is right. The house is on fire. The time for "Yes" has come.

Reflection and Action

1. Charis spoke of feeling that she had been sucked into a time machine and transported back to 1845. Have you ever felt something similar?

2. Have you struggled to find a congregation that has room for your doubts? Describe your experience in this regard. If you have children or friends who share this struggle, tell their stories too.

3. Charis was concerned that older congregations want to use the "millennials" as "fuel to keep their operation going." Comments?

4. "I don't just want to be a good, happy, fulfilled, spiritual consumer" while the world "goes down the toilet," Charis said, and then expressed her desire to be part of a community that is trying to "save the world." Does that sound grandiose to you? How do you respond to her desire?

5. "It's not easy out here . . . in nones-land," Charis said. If you are or have been a none, or if you know some nones well, talk about the difficulties of not having a faith community.

6. This chapter mentions ways that people are meeting their spiritual needs outside of stained-glass windows: through "podcasts and

TED Talks . . . in reading groups in living rooms and pub theology groups in bars and restaurants." Share any experiences you've had with resources like these.

7. How do you respond to the five-step plan I sketched out in this chapter? Perhaps this will be the outline of a future book. If so, what questions would you want me to answer?

8. What struck you most about IKAR, MPV, Middle Collegiate, and Highlands?

9. What were your *yes, buts* in relation to this chapter? Can you imagine a faith community that elicited *yes*, without so many buts?

10. Respond to the final two paragraphs about hope and fire.

❧

12

THEOLOGIES OF HARMONY

Unfortunately, the notion of faith that emerged in the West was much more a rational assent to the truth of certain mental beliefs rather than a calm and hopeful trust that God is inherent in all things, and that this whole thing is going somewhere good.

—Richard Rohr,
"Jesus, Christ, and the Beloved Community," *The Mendicant*

We need thousands of communities of harmony to be born, and we need them soon. For that to happen, we need to have some serious theological breakthroughs. And to help us in that quest, I would like to recommend an unlikely resource.

I know many think of Paul the Apostle as a stodgy traditionalist who hated women, feared sex, and basically ruined the beautiful thing that Jesus started. But I see him differently. I see him as a midwife who devoted his life to helping a new kind of faith, faith expressing itself in love, to be born.

Sure, he had his faults like the rest of us; in fact, he described himself as a superlative sinner and a violent man (according to 1 Timothy 1:13–15). But I also see him as a revolutionary who took Jesus' core message and explored its radical implications in new cultural settings. Inspired by the nonviolent story of Jesus and set afire by a mystical encounter with him, Paul envisioned not simply a new religion but a new way of life. This way of life would challenge people of all religions to leave behind their old understandings and to open their minds and hearts to something radically new, a new testament or covenant or agreement, a "Religious New Deal," if you will, not just a new way of being religious but a new way of being human. I agree with Paul's contemporary critics that what we call Christianity today often has very little to do with the beautiful movement Jesus started. I just don't blame Paul for getting us in the mess we're in. In fact, I would say we Christians through the centuries all have a share in ruining the beautiful thing Jesus started and Paul developed.

I picture Paul as a wiry old bald guy who squints. I imagine him in Galatia, in a crowded house, leaning forward, elbows on knees, almost vibrating with intensity as he speaks to a couple dozen people in the flickering lamplight. He's trying to tell them in person what we have recorded in one of his letters, written about twenty years after Jesus' death: "The only thing that matters," he whisper-shouts, "is faith expressing itself in love." Then he leans forward even farther and repeats himself, louder now, his bony hands wildly gesticulating for emphasis: "The *only* thing that matters is faith expressing itself in *love*!"

Immediately, I imagine people getting restless. First one, then three, then five hands shoot up with questions and objections.

"What about circumcision? Moses commanded that!" one says.

"Circumcision or uncircumcision . . . it's utterly insignificant," he says. "The *only* thing that matters is faith expressing itself in love."

"What about our dietary restrictions? You're not giving up on that biblical absolute, I hope!" another asks.

"The only thing that matters is *faith* expressing itself in *love*," Paul says, a little louder.

"What about Gentiles? You're not talking about granting them equality in our community, are you?" another asks tensely. "That's just not right!"

The *what abouts* continue . . . observing certain holidays, avoiding meat that had been sacrificed to idols, not fraternizing with people of other religions . . . and each time, Paul responds with the same words, finally ending in a voice so gentle it is barely more than a whisper: "The *only* thing that matters is faith expressing itself in *love*." I see his eyes brim with tears.

Finally, I see about a third of the people stand up and walk out in exasperation, muttering among themselves, "That's too simple. It's just too simple. The man is a heretic, a liberal, a revisionist, a rebel."

Harmony, it turns out, is radically simple, offensively so to some

people, especially people who have zealously worked for years, even decades, perfecting their Stage One belief project, polishing their Stage Two
piety project, and sharpening their Stage Three critical thinking project.
As we've seen, Harmony marks a return to Simplicity, but a deeper and
wider Simplicity, a bottomless second simplicity characterized not by
two but by one, not by dualism (categorizing everything in binaries of
good/evil, us/them, insiders/outsiders) but by holism, seeing all of humanity, even all of creation, as held in one love as one creative project,
full of beloved diversity. That's why many of us call Harmony *non-dual
consciousness*, although a slightly more accurate term might be *post-dual
consciousness*, since a unity after duality is far richer and stronger than a
unity before duality, just as a faith after doubt is far richer and stronger
than a faith before doubt.

This emerging way of thinking and seeing and being aware includes the
ability to hold or embrace opposites in what Ken Howard calls *paradoxy*.*
Frank Schaeffer describes it with stark clarity: "These days I hold two ideas
about God simultaneously: he, she or it *exists* and he, she or it *doesn't exist*. I don't seesaw between these opposites; I embrace them. . . . You will
always be more than one person. You will always embody contradiction.
You—like some sort of quantum mechanical physics experiment—will
always be in two places at once."†

For people who have invested so much energy and effort in constructing rigid dualisms, complex systems of beliefs, elaborate schemes for
success, and rigorous habits of deconstruction, the second simplicity of
Harmony might seem like a step backward, maybe even a step of infidel-
ity. But for those of us who have been struggling to keep our heads above
dark waves of despair in the depths of Perplexity, the second simplicity
of Harmony feels like salvation, like a rebirth. It integrates all we have
learned and enlists all our capacities in the service of love.

But what to do with all those systems of beliefs? What to do with all
the rules and requirements, the projects and programs of religious communities? I don't think there's any way to avoid facing this fact: most
Western Christian theologies were created by and for minds steeped
in Simplicity. And truth be told, they were created by powerful men

---

* *Paradoxy* (Paraclete Press, 2010).
† *Why I Am an Atheist Who Believes in God* (Createspace, 2014), 13, 19.

(in Christianity, almost always privileged white men) who used those systems to give advantage to people like them, while exploiting, excluding, and controlling people unlike them, always protecting their own power. In fact, when we use adjectives like orthodox, historic, or traditional to modify our religions, we're almost always referring to the versions of our religions rooted and grounded in Simplicity, and then enhanced by Complexity, usually with powerful, rich, older straight white males serving as their authority figures and gatekeepers.*

These historic versions of faith competed and fragmented, argued and mutually excommunicated, aligned and realigned, and often went to war. Some of those wars raged or smoldered on for centuries with tragic, almost unbelievable death tolls. Their trauma still lingers today. Meanwhile, people here and there kept doubting their way into Perplexity, asking why the whole thing couldn't be torn down and reconstructed in some new, less violent way. And as you would predict, periodically, gatekeepers purged those troublesome doubters and dissenters, using the tools of vilification, sanction, excommunication, banishment, imprisonment, torture, and execution.

In the middle of all this, and in spite of it, surprising numbers of people penetrated through Perplexity and arrived at Harmony, moving beyond faith expressing itself in beliefs to faith expressing itself in love.

Some of them moved to the desert or wilderness, seeking to create monastic communities where faith expressing itself in love could be experimented with as the norm. Others formed schools and missions or launched new congregations, orders, and movements, translating their spiritual breakthrough into compassionate organizing and action. Others created art, poetry or novels, essays or plays, paintings or sculptures, seeking in some way to communicate their vision of faith expressing itself in love. Still others quietly expressed their faith in love wherever they were, and through their acts of kindness, wisdom, and generosity, they

---

* In times like these, when older straight white privileged men are seeking to reassert their privilege and dominance in what I hope is their last (pathetic) stand, I am tempted to just shut up and get out of the way, because these adjectives apply to me. But so far, I have come to feel that to do so would be an abdication of my responsibility. For that reason, I have sought to use my older straight white privileged male voice to help deconstruct older straight white male privilege, and I have sought to lift up the voices and leadership of colleagues who are younger, LGBTQ, female, nonwhite, and poor whenever possible. Of course, there is still much more to do in this regard.

earned a reputation for being either odd or saintly or both. Gradually, a new generation would apprentice themselves to these mystics and saints and "catch" from them a deeper kind of faith, what many of us call an alternate orthodoxy, a generous orthodoxy, or a Stage Four faith.

I have Jewish friends who went through their version of this process. At some point in their lives, they were super Sabbath-observant, faithful in synagogue attendance, and diligently kosher. They studied the history of Israel, both ancient and modern. They felt responsible for the well-being of Jews around the world, especially in Israel, and they became politically involved, guided by Jewish organizations. Gradually, they grappled with the epic texts of their tradition, wrestling with the Tanakh, Mishnah, and Talmud, following the arguments of the rabbis from generation to generation.

At some point, they became sensitive to tensions and divisions in the Jewish community and found the actions of some of their fellow Jews (including some leaders of the nation of Israel) deeply offensive and embarrassing, which ushered them through Complexity into Perplexity. Eventually, they found a way forward, learning to delight in the never-ending give-and-take of conversation, in the willingness to say, "I don't know. I'm still seeking." (Some of them, having deconstructed some old taboos, occasionally ate bacon just for fun.) Eventually, they perceived the wisdom at the heart of the Torah, and the love at the heart of the prophets, and the feeling of union that led the mystics into ecstasy. They heard Hosea speak for God: "I desire compassion, not sacrifice." They heard Micah speak for God, "What does God require of humanity, but to do justice, love kindness, and walk humbly with God?" And they came to know that most Jewish of treasures: faith expressing itself in mercy, compassion, kindness, love.

Many of my Muslim friends have had their parallel journeys. They immersed themselves in the Quran, some in Arabic, some in translation, savoring every word for its simple truth and beauty. They cherished being a member of the *ummah*, the Muslim community, and they explored the rich and complex treasures of Muslim history and civilization, choosing sides in theological arguments and standing up for Islam in public. They pursued growth and goodness with fervor, the true jihad of the soul. But then, through one obstacle or another, their spirituality grew beyond complex to perplexing. They saw how fundamentalists took what was beautiful and made it ugly, what was peaceful and made it violent, what was sweetly merciful and made it bitter. They questioned, doubted, struggled, waging *ijtihad*, or radical rethinking. Then, perhaps in the sublime poetry of the Muslim mystics, they discovered some of the clearest expressions of Stage Four faith to be found in any literature anywhere, like this:

> *My heart can take on any form:*
> *A meadow for gazelles,*
> *A cloister for monks,*
> *Ka'ba for the circling pilgrim,*
> *The tables of the Torah,*
> *The scrolls of the Quran.*
> *My creed is Love;*
> *Wherever its caravan turns along the way,*
> *That is my belief,*
> *My faith.* *

Or like this:

> *Out beyond ideas of wrongdoing and rightdoing,*
> *there is a field. I'll meet you there.*
> *When the soul lies down in that grass,*
> *the world is too full to talk about.*
> *Ideas, language, even the phrase "each other"*
> *doesn't make any sense.*
> *The breeze at dawn has secrets to tell you.*
> *Don't go back to sleep.*
> *You must ask for what you really want.*
> *Don't go back to sleep.*
> *People are going back and forth across the doorsill*
> *where the two worlds touch.*

---

* From "Gentle Now, Doves," by Ibn al-Arabi (1165–1240), a Sufi mystic, poet, and philosopher who lived in Spain. This translation is widely available on the internet, of uncertain origin. For another translation, see https://sufiway.org/teaching/notes-from-the-open-path/14-teachings/113 -a-garden-among-the-flames.

The door is round and open.
Don't go back to sleep. *

Many of my Sikh, Hindu, Buddhist, Baha'i, and Turtle Island indigenous friends have had their own journey on the same caravan, or through this same round, open door, even though each of our traditions is unique, with its own irreducible story.

For me as a Christian, my caravan led me through doors of Simplicity, Complexity, and Perplexity, toward faith expressing itself in love. I discovered my first portals in literature, initially with Protestant writers like Lewis and Tolkien, for whom imagination transcended the complexities of argument and analysis. Then came Catholic writers like Walker Percy, in whose writings I first encountered the word *postmodern*. The idea of postmodernity opened to me the possibility that maybe my problems weren't with Christianity but with the modern version of Christianity, and maybe, just maybe, there could be a postmodern version that I could live with. I gradually came to see that *postmodern* meant *postcolonial*, which led me to the liberation theologians; the black, Latinx, feminist, womanist, and ecofeminist theologians; and, later still, to queer and indigenous and other theologians as well.

As a young and zealous fundamentalist boy, I had memorized a lot of Bible verses, verses that proved I was a sinner who needed a personal savior, verses that proved our savior was supreme and all others were satanic, verses that kept me on the path of Simplicity. But over time, I kept bumping into all these other verses in between the ones I memorized, verses I had been tacitly taught to ignore. Those verses talked about what sin was, and its meaning was clear: it was social and systemic as well as personal. Once I acknowledged that, suddenly this life, this world, this moment mattered again, not just for their effect on my life after death but for their own sakes and for God's sake. The flattened, figured-out, formulaic Bible of my inherited so-called orthodoxy unfolded from two dimensions into three, and from black and white first into shades of gray and then into full color. And before long, it became clear to me that through all the duality, all the complexity, all the perplexity, one message was emerging in the

---

* From the poem "The Wagon," in *The Essential Rumi*, translated by Coleman Barks (HarperOne, 2004). For a musical treatment of this poem and others, see David Wilcox and Nance Pettis's beautiful album *Out Beyond Ideas* (Songs for the Peace Project, 2015).

Bible, emerging like the real world as one awakens from dreams and sleep, and that message was as clear as it was revolutionary: *the only thing that matters is faith expressing itself in love.*

Along the way, I learned that Eastern Christianity, which called itself Orthodoxy, had taken some very different paths from the familiar Western version that also called itself orthodox. When I started reading Eastern writers and meeting Eastern Christians, I discovered deep treasures of mysticism and a message of God's deep solidarity with all humanity and all creation. I discovered this same message in the Roman Catholic mystical tradition as well, captured so beautifully by the English mystic Lady Julian of Norwich (c. 1342–1416), author of the earliest surviving book written by a woman in the English language:

> The all-powerful truth of the Trinity is the Father, who created us and keeps us within him. The deep wisdom of the Trinity is our Mother, in whom we all are enfolded. The exalted goodness of the Trinity is our beloved Lord: we are held in him and he is held in us. We are enclosed in the Father, we are enclosed in the Son, and we are enclosed in the Holy Spirit. The Father, the Son, and the Holy Spirit are enclosed in us. All Power. All Goodness. All Wisdom. One God. One Love.*

More recently, Catholic feminist theologian Catherine LaCugna (1952–1997) echoed the same insight, concluding her theological masterpiece *God for Us* with these majestic, all-encompassing words: "The very nature of God, therefore, is to seek out the deepest possible communion and friendship with every last creature on this earth."† I discovered the same primacy of universal, non-discriminatory love in mainline Protestant mystics, theologians, poets, and activists; in Quakers and others in the Radical Reformation tradition; and in some Evangelical Protestants as well.‡

---

* Julian of Norwich, Fourteenth Revelation, Chapter 54, in *The Showings of Julian of Norwich*, trans. Mirabai Starr (Hampton Roads, 2013), 149–150.
† Catherine Mowry LaCugna, *God for Us: The Trinity and Christian Life* (HarperSanFrancisco: 1993), 411, quoted by Richard Rohr in *Daily Meditation*, May 13, 2019.
‡ Among mainline Protestants, I discovered theologians and writers like Walter Rauschenbusch, Jürgen Moltmann, Howard Thurman, Rowan Williams, Barbara Brown Taylor, and Fred Buechner, and poets like Mary Oliver and Wendell Berry; among Quakers, most notably Philip Clayton, Parker Palmer, and songwriter/poet Carrie Newcomer; among Evangelicals, most notably Dallas Willard and Ruth Haley Barton, and of course, many more.

Through these influences and more, a new center was emerging for me, a center that didn't require agreement to long lists of beliefs but rather that required my heart to grow deeper in faith expressing itself in love. First, there was love for my neighbor, love with no exceptions and no discrimination: theist or atheist, Muslim or Jew, liberal or conservative, male or female or nonbinary, gay, straight, or other. Interestingly, this new center involved not only love for my neighbor, but also love from my neighbor, because love, like electricity and light, is a flow, an alternating current of connection and mutuality.

This new center also invited me to grow deeper in love for myself, a self that my inherited theology had taught me to assess with a strange mixture of shame and fear. Love for the earth was also part of the invitation. This love had always come naturally to me, but I had suppressed it, once again, because of agreements required by my religious community.

And what about love for God? My old belief agreements about God were deconstructing through Stage Three, but even in Stage Four, they continued to decompose. But like a fallen tree in the forest, or like last year's composting leaves, what was dying was becoming soil, fertile soil. I felt that in the decomposition of failed or failing ideas, concepts, or beliefs about God, a deeper faith was taking root. And from that soil, a new sense of God was emerging and arising as well. There was a beautiful surprise in this: I more honestly and sincerely loved the emerging God than I had ever loved the one I tried so hard to understand, believe in, satisfy, and prop up for many years. And to my surprise, the God that was rising or emerging didn't even require me to use the word *God* to name it.

I gradually came to see that the love of God, however God was understood or described, was not separate from the other loves of neighbor, self, and creation but was, in fact, the love I encountered and experienced in all of these other loves. Love for God and love from God were equally present in the love I gave and in the love I received in my relationships with neighbor, self, and my fellow creations. It was love all the way down, love all the way up, love all the way out, and love all the way in.

I became more comfortable with God being a mystery, a mystery too holy for words. I realized that when people were asking me to agree with (or deny) this or that belief about God, this or that set of words about God, they were only acting out of their scripts as members of Stage One,

Two, or Three groups. They were trying to be good people, good soldiers, and they were trying to help me as best they were able. I could respect that, even though some of their well-intended actions actually hurt me. I realized that their acceptance of me was highly conditional, based on my agreement with their beliefs about God. But I became increasingly confident that God's acceptance of me (and them) was different: unconditional, preemptive, non-discriminatory, free. And that felt, and feels even now, like truly good news, like liberation.

Ironically, these new insights only made me love the Bible more, because once I could see them, they were there on every page, sometimes in black and white, sometimes in between the lines, sometimes in a new insight that only became visible against the backdrop of an old argument. Even old beliefs began to shine again, but in fresh ways:

Trinity, not as a math problem or orthodoxy test but as divine interbeing, divine one-another-ness, and divine relationality at the source and center of the universe.

Jesus' death, not as a blood sacrifice necessary to assuage the infinite fury of a hot-tempered supreme being but as a revelation of self-giving love facing down imperial cruelty with death-defying nonviolence.

The incarnation, not as a one-time exceptional event but as a window into God's inter-being with all of us and even all of creation.

Sin, not as a legal infraction for which I fear punishment from an angry cosmic police force but as a relational disconnection, a broken solidarity, a harm inflicted upon the common good when I fail to live in love.

Salvation, not as an evacuation plan to get souls into heaven after death but as a transformation plan to bring justice and peace for the earth and all its creatures.

The Bible, not as a constitution or law code by which I argue my cases, justifying *us* and condemning *them*, but as a library containing a treasury of poetry, arguments, insights, stories, models, and more, useful to inspire and equip us to be positive protagonists in our mutual liberation today, just as our ancestors in the faith were in their day.

The resurrection, not as a single resuscitation alone but as the uprising of a whole new humanity, filled with the Spirit of the risen Christ, to be the ongoing embodiment of God-with-us.

The gospel, not as information about how to avoid hell but as good news of great joy for all people, that there is a better way to live, a better path to walk, and that if we are willing to rethink everything, we can start walking that path of love right now, just as we are.

As I write these words, I wonder how they strike you . . . Nonsense? Obvious? Beautiful? Dangerous? Too late? Too soon? Just in time? I wonder if you can see what I only see faintly but see nonetheless: there can be rich and vital theologies of Harmony, just as there were theologies of Simplicity, Complexity, and Perplexity. There can be deeply Christian, Jewish, Muslim, and other theologies in which faith expresses itself not just in Stage One beliefs, Stage Two organizations, and Stage Three critical scholarship but also in Stage Four love. Without that love, nothing else matters. And with that love, everything has its place. Everything belongs.

Isn't that the simple but profound original vision old squinty-eyed Paul saw inside that old, bald, beloved head of his? And isn't that what Jesus was pointing to when he said the single greatest old commandment and the only new commandment was love?

Let's be frank: Stage One and Stage Two gatekeepers are not going to give us permission to explore this territory. To be faithful and to maintain their own personal integrity, they must dutifully oppose us at every turn, by all moral means necessary (and sometimes, no doubt, they'll slip beyond moral means in their zeal and desperation). Don't expect to receive an award from them for doing what needs to be done at this critical moment. No, expect the gatekeepers to do their best to make you suffer for doing what they sincerely see as disloyal, evil, and wrong. Don't take it personally. It's not about you. It's how change happens.

Please let me encourage you, as someone engaged with this struggle for many decades now: all, or nearly all, the pieces are in place for the theological revolution we need. If you need permission to start putting those pieces together, don't expect Stage One and Stage Two gatekeepers to give it, for again, they never will because they simply can't. Pull away into solitude, open your heart to the Spirit, and listen. You will receive all the permission you need. From that point on, it will not be permission you require but courage and creativity.

If you need an example of courage and creativity to inspire you, you need look no further than Paul.

Reflection and Action

1. Respond to my description of Paul. How does that compare to your impression of him, if you have one?
2. Do your best to put the ideas of dualism and non-dual or post-dual consciousness into your own words.
3. This chapter offers a critical view of what is often called *orthodoxy*. How do you respond to it? If you disagreed in general, was there anything you could agree with? If you agreed with it in general, was there any detail that you weren't sure about?
4. How did you respond to the example of a Jewish theological quest for faith expressing itself in love? How did you respond to the example of a Muslim theological question for faith expressing itself in love? If you are a Christian, how did these examples help you think of your own theological quest? Consider researching a Sikh, Bahá'í, Hindu, Buddhist, or Turtle Island indigenous expression of faith expressing itself in love and sharing with others what you learn.
5. What from my telling of my own theological journey resonated with you?
6. Respond to the "new sense of God" that I describe in the chapter, especially to the idea that God doesn't require us to use the word *God* to name God.
7. The chapter ends with an invitation to solitude and a call to courage. Why do you think those two need to be held together at this point in the book?

❧

13

SPIRITUALITIES OF HARMONY
FOR THE RISING GENERATION

> The art of loving each other well is letting people be where they are and
> not trying to convince them to be where I am.
>
> —Kathy Escobar, *Faith Shift*

Allie and Jake approached me not long ago at a five-day gathering at
the Center for Action and Contemplation (CAC) in New Mexico. The
center has a tremendous impact through conferences, a two-year educational program called the Living School, a daily email delivered to the
inboxes of nearly half a million people, and other resources too. It invites
people across traditions to discover a deeper faith beyond doubt. I had
just given a lecture that provided an overview of the four stages and the
role of spiritual practices in helping people in each stage. (You'll find a
short summary of what I shared in Appendix V.)

Allie and Jake told me how much they love the CAC and how it
helped them move through their Stage Three doubts and discover some
life-giving and soul-sustaining Stage Four practices. "If it weren't for
the CAC and writers like you, we wouldn't be Christians anymore,"
Jake said. "But that brings up our question." Jake put his hand gently on
his wife's rounded abdomen. "Allie's pregnant with our first child, a little
girl, and . . ."

Jake couldn't finish his sentence because Allie broke in. "I can't imagine putting our daughter through what I went through in church. I was
raised Catholic, and I would never want our little girl to be brought up in
an all-male religious hierarchy, especially one that tries to tell women and
LGBTQ people what they can and can't do with their bodies while the

male hierarchy is covering up its own pedophilia scandals. And I certainly don't want our child to be subjected to all the guilt and shame that I'm only now beginning to recover from."

Jake picked up from there. "I was brought up Lutheran, and overall, I have positive memories of my church growing up. There wasn't any other place in my life where I interacted with people across generations, and the kids and youth programs were amazing, especially the summer camps, retreats, and mission trips. But even though my religious upbringing was more healthy than Allie's, still, I dropped out before I graduated from high school and haven't been back in ten years. Really, in about middle school I got the feeling that I had learned all they had to teach me, and that from then on, it would basically be a lifetime of reruns going over the same few ideas. That's why we're so thrilled with what we're learning here. We're going deeper and being challenged and stretched. The CAC is giving us what we both wish our religious upbringing had given us. I guess that's what we're curious about. How do you think we should raise our child, in terms of spirituality? We need some sort of framework for introducing our little one to contemplative spirituality, or what you're calling Stage Four spirituality, but we don't know where to start."

Allie had the last word: "If we have to make a choice between raising our child with no religion and raising our child with harmful religion, we'll choose no religion in a second. But we know there should be a better option."

Allie and Jake's question is now the most common question I'm asked in my travels. How can a family, church, or other faith community provide the simple Stage One moral training that children need and then lead them into the more complex Stage Two practical training that adolescents need? Then, how can that same family or faith community give teenagers and young adults not only permission but also encouragement to ask tough questions and develop a grown-up, Stage Three faith in a grown-up God, as my friend Jacqui Lewis likes to say? And no less important, how can families and other faith communities lead children, youth, and young adults into the more mystical, contemplative, and integrative Stage Four spirituality of Harmony? How can we make growth through the four stages less traumatic and less accidental and more natural and more intentional?

I told Jake and Allie that their question brought to mind some sage advice from Stephen Covey's classic *The Seven Habits of Highly Effective People* (a largely Stage Four resource disguised as a Stage Two self-help book). "Begin with the end in mind," Covey said. What would it look like if we led people through a process of spiritual formation that from the beginning anticipated as its end or goal *faith expressing itself in love*?

Allie perked up. "That's what Father Richard does with the three boxes, right?" Allie asked. "You'd do all the small-box work inside the big-box space of harmony and love?"

Allie was referring to a visual metaphor Richard Rohr frequently uses in the CAC, drawing from the work of Walter Brueggemann.* Richard puts three boxes—small, medium, and large—on a table. The small box is labeled *ORDER*. That represents the childhood spirituality we often receive in Stages One and Two, characterized by orderly doctrines and orderly steps to success. Many people feel comfortable in those boxes through their whole lifetimes, so they never bump up against the lid. But for many of us, through great pain and great love (and, I would add, through a great education and cross-cultural travel), that box begins to feel way too small.

So we break out of our childhood order and find ourselves in the bigger box labeled *DISORDER*. That box gives us more space to ask our questions, deconstruct our inherited assumptions, be suspicious of authority figures, subject every belief or truth-claim to scrutiny, and doubt anything and everything we want and need to doubt . . . all the important work of Stage Three. Again, many of us either feel comfortable in this box for the rest of our lives, or we have no place to go from there, since we can't return to the small box of order, and we have been shown no bigger space of reorder. Many of us eventually find the box of disorder to be its own sort of prison, bigger than our previous cell but confining nonetheless. So we dream of growing beyond deconstruction to reconstruction, beyond doubt to faith after doubt, and that's when we move into the big box labeled *REORDER*.

"I love how you put that, Allie," I said. "Instead of thinking of the boxes in succession, as if we climb out of one and then climb into the

---

* See https://cac.org/order-disorder-reorder-2016-02-23/, https://cac.org/the-invitation-of-grace-2016-03-21/, and Fr. Richard Rohr, "Human Development in Scripture," cac.org, March 26, 2019, https://cac.org/human-development-in-scripture-2019-03-26/.

next, we need to think of the bigger boxes as containing the smaller boxes. When we're inside the littlest box, we think it's all there is. Then we break out of it and think the medium-sized box is all there is. And then we break out of that and think our REORDER box is all there is. Eventually, we realize that the universe, life, and God are the limitless mystery no box can ever contain, and we begin to understand that even the big box of REORDER takes place inside of the larger mystery of divine love, that God is always bigger than our biggest box."

"So maybe," Allie said, "the key is for the REORDER box to have no lid on it."

"I like that," I said, "because even after you create that REORDER box, you'll eventually encounter some new data that it can't contain. We'll always have a box of some kind simply because of the way our minds work, but if we're wise, we'll learn to keep the lid off, just as you said, and we'll remember from the beginning that love is our ultimate goal. If you two do that for yourselves and your daughter, I have no doubt that she's going to do just fine, and so will you."

Our conversation ended, but I haven't stopped thinking about it, or about Jake and Allie's little girl, who by now has been born and is getting used to this big, beautiful, lidless world from the safety and comfort of her parents' arms. I keep wondering: How can parents and faith communities help rising generations to grow in faith without getting trapped in small boxes? What would spiritual formation look like if we more intentionally thought of the end from the beginning?

Returning to the image of a tree cross-section, our children can't skip the small inner rings, because each has lessons to teach and each contributes to the structure of the adult person. But we can guide our children through each inner ring or smaller box, always remembering that it's not the end in itself, not the goal, not the destination. In fact, each stage is valuable for its own sake, and more: each stage matters because it develops and enlarges our capacity to receive and give more love, and then more love, and then more love still. That's the end we keep in mind from the beginning.

As I reflect on this growth in love, I recall Paul's words in Ephesians 3:16–19, where he prays that "you may be strengthened in your inner being with power through God's Spirit, and that Christ may dwell in your hearts through faith, as you are being rooted and grounded in love . . .

that you may have the power to comprehend, with all the saints, what is the breadth and length and height and depth, and to know the love of Christ that surpasses knowledge, so that you may be filled with all the fullness of God." The infinite love of God is there at the beginning, there at the middle, there at the end, always inviting us to expand our capacities to "comprehend" and "know" it even though it overflows all boxes and surpasses all comprehension and knowledge.

So yes, we still need to introduce children to the Stage One skills of Simplicity. For example, we will lead them into the essential work of caring deeply about right and wrong, truth and falsehood, fairness and injustice, helpful and harmful, selfish and unselfish. But we will also remind them that even if people do wrong, they are still worthy of love, and that there is no such thing as being truly right without being truly loving. In fact, since without love Stage One Simplicity is worth nothing (to paraphrase Paul once more, in 1 Corinthians 13), we will teach that Simplicity's rules only have value insofar as they help us love. With this in mind, we might explain to a small child that we say *please* and *thank you* and practice other acts of courtesy as ways of showing love to our neighbors. Later, we might teach an adolescent that our rules about drugs, alcohol, and sex are intended not to keep us from joy but rather to help us love ourselves and others by protecting us from addiction, sexual harm, and other unhealthy behaviors. We might explain that our rules for recycling, reducing our consumption, and conserving energy are expressions of our love for the earth. Rules and love, we would help them see, are not enemies. In fact, rules only make sense in service of love.

Similarly, we will help our children and students do the Stage One work of learning respect for authority. But we will also try to model a Stage Four style of authority characterized by service rather than domination, motivated by love rather than fear, and determined to empower others rather than hoard power. We will help them see that it's not only our right but our duty to refuse to comply with authority figures who abuse their power, even if doing so means we have to suffer.

In the same way, we will try to give our children a strong sense of identity, as individuals and as members of families, faith communities, cultures, and nations. But we will also warn them of the danger of building identity among *us* through hostility toward *them*. We will invite them to hold "small-box identities" within a more powerful, transcendent, inclusive "big-box identity" in which everyone and everything are our relations.

Likewise, we will introduce them to the Scriptures, beliefs, rituals, heroes, and other treasures of our faith tradition. But we will also remind them that the box of our tradition could never contain all of the goodness and wisdom in humanity, nor could it ever contain all of God. Our tradition is a starting line, not the finish line. It's a runway from which we launch, not the sky into which we soar. Each tradition, we will teach them, has treasures to share, and the more deeply we understand our tradition, the greater our spiritual literacy to understand the traditions of others.

In all these ways and more, the ultimate goal of *faith expressing itself in love* will color and flavor all our Stage One spiritual work. In that larger (lidless) box, framework, or context of love, we will introduce our children to the values and competencies of Stage One, not as ends in themselves but as a foundation for Stages Two, Three, Four, and beyond, in the iterative, never-ending process of growth in love.

The same would be true for Stage Two. We will help our children and adolescents to master the complex bodies of knowledge and skill sets necessary to survive in our modern world. But we will never let pride, fame, power, or money be the ultimate goal of survival. Instead, we will teach again and again that we develop our knowledge and skill so that we have more capacity to receive and give love. Similarly, we will teach our children and young people to practice spiritual disciplines or practices such as *lectio divina* and meditation, silent contemplation and solitude, soul friendship and spiritual direction, journaling and self-examination. But we will make clear from the start that the purpose of spiritual self-development is not to earn anything or merit anything. Rather, it equips us for spiritual self-giving as an expression of love for God, self, others, and our fellow creatures. Along the same lines, we will instill in young people the Stage Two values of excellence, of pride in doing one's best, even (in a carefully curated sense) the value of competition and winning. But we will simultaneously warn them of the dangers of pride and superiority and of the dangerously addictive power of winning, and we will teach them about the painful but precious lessons that often come through loss, defeat, failure, and even humiliation.

In the same spirit, we will teach the value of study and learning as an expression of love for ourselves, because if we love ourselves, we want the best for ourselves, including developing our minds and other capacities to their highest and best potential.

The greatest possible success, we will teach our children in Stage Two, is not popularity or power or profit or pleasure, but service, connection, community, and love. So we will challenge them to set their Stage Two ambition on the goal of becoming the most loving version of themselves possible. In these ways and others, as in Stage One, we will help future generations explore pragmatic Stage Two spirituality with the end in mind, the goal of non-discriminatory, universal love.

It will be the same for the holy work of Stage Three: we will help our children develop critical thinking, honest questioning, doubt, skepticism, the ability to challenge and critique, and other related skills. But we will remind them that these tools, like a scalpel, can be used to heal or to harm. So we will help them critique and challenge authority figures and authority structures without hate or disrespect, driven instead by love for the truth and love for the common good. We will instill in them a healthy skepticism toward advertising, toward political propaganda, and toward religious communication as well, remembering how business, political, and religious leaders often distort the truth to achieve their agendas. Love for self and others requires this kind of critical thinking.

We will guide them to turn their critical and suspicious eye inward, to face their own hypocrisies, their own shadows, their own blind spots and mixed motives, not to foster self-hatred but as an expression of healthy love for self. In this way, our children can learn to critique both others and themselves with the same graciousness and loving gentleness, recalling Jesus' teaching about taking the boards out of our own eyes before trying to remove the splinters out of the eyes of others (Luke 6:42). It's easy to see how this approach to Stage Three skills naturally leads people into Stage Four.

What would the skills and spiritual competencies of Stage Four be, and how would a parent, pastor, teacher, or other spiritual presence in a child or young person's life help guide that person into the spirituality of Stage Four? As I sit with that question, an image keeps coming to mind: a camera with a zoom lens. With the lens zoomed in, I can see within a small frame, but as I zoom out, the frame grows wider. Stage

Four, it seems to me, involves widening my frame, seeing more and more within the frame of connection, solidarity, and love. In Stage One, I widen the frame beyond myself to include my group. In Stage Two, I widen the frame to include other groups, other cultures who are playing the same game of life but with slightly different rules. In Stage Three, I widen the frame still more, seeing the strengths and weaknesses of all these different groups. And in Stage Four, I zoom out as far as possible, daring to see everything—and every single thing—bathed in the same light of infinite, universal, non-discriminatory love.

With that end in mind, here's what I see more clearly than before: *we can't wait until people reach the end of Stage Three to introduce them to the ultimate end of love.* We need to infuse Stage Four Harmony as the desired goal of each earlier stage. Love isn't like calculus, which can't be taught until after one learns geometry and advanced algebra. No, love is more like music. We expose the youngest musicians to the most sublime music so that, as they learn the basics of scales, keys, tone, tempo, and timing, they know why the basics matter and what they can produce. Again, in Covey's words, we are mindful of the end from the beginning.

How can we, from the beginning, help people keep in mind the ultimate desired end of *faith expressing itself in love?* Obviously, we have to start not with children but with ourselves, their parents and teachers. We will reproduce what we actually are, not simply what we say or wish. It's ridiculous to think that children are like empty bowls, and if we pour into them a recipe of Bible stories, doctrinal knowledge, songs, lectures, and other religious activities, then stir and bake, we will magically help them become loving people. Deep personal formation of the next generation depends on close-at-hand mentors and models who authentically embody the way of life we hope the children will "catch" through imitation. The loving hearts of parents, teachers, and other significant adult models in a child's life are the primary sacred texts from which the child will learn faith expressing itself in love.

That fact, in all likelihood, explains the catastrophe that is unfolding in organized religion these days. Because organized religion has remained largely a Stage One and Stage Two affair, seeing moralism and pragmatism as ends in themselves, relatively few parents and teachers are able to embody and exemplify the essential qualities of Harmony, the qualities of non-dual, non-discriminatory, revolutionary love. They can only give what they have received; they can only teach what they have learned. So Stage One parents can only introduce their children to Stage One spirituality, and so on. This is the crisis in religion today: not that children fall short of their parents' faith, but that they grow beyond it.

Perhaps, in this light, the much-lamented decline in organized religion is simply a consequence of churches' refusal to stay mindful of the goal of love. As C. S. Lewis quipped in *Mere Christianity*, "It may be hard for an egg to turn into a bird: it would be a jolly sight harder for a bird to learn to fly while remaining an egg. . . . And you cannot go on indefinitely being just an ordinary, decent egg. We must be hatched or go bad." Of course Stage One religion will go bad if it doesn't hatch into Stage Two, and Stage Two into Stage Three, and so on. When faith expressing itself in beliefs (Simplicity) and faith expressing itself in activity (Complexity) and faith expressing itself in doubt (Perplexity) start to stink, perhaps only then we will be ready to rethink everything, risk everything, and in fact give everything up to let religion hatch into faith that expresses itself in love.

I wince as I ponder this. Grace and I were so dedicated to being good parents when we started this adventure of parenting back in our twenties. We had four children in six years, and we gave our all to our kids. Now we are humbled, grateful, and delighted to see what amazing adults our children have grown into. But I have to be honest: the religious training I received in parenting was, as I look back, maybe thirty percent helpful and seventy percent harmful. It was so rooted in Stages One and Two, and so oblivious to Stages Three and Four, that to the degree I followed it, I'm afraid I became a worse parent than I would have been otherwise. Yes, of course, I was taught by books, radio programs, sermons, and other resources that I should be loving. But the expansive dimensions of love were, to use Lewis's imagery, stuck inside the egg, and the eggshell was made of titanium.

In the framework many of us were taught, parenting was all about discipline (which, in that context, meant punishment). Parenting was all about instilling in our children unquestioned submission and obedience to authority (which, in that context, meant our children agreeing to be dominated). It was all about conformity (which, in that context, meant conforming to the norms of patriarchy). It was all about a certain kind of purity (which, in that context, meant an inability to understand, much less cope with, much less enjoy, one's own body, one's own sexuality, and the full range of one's humanity).

I've often told my kids, "I did the best I knew how as your father, but you deserved so much better." Thankfully, I think my grandchildren have better parents than their parents did, and I suppose that's the best we can hope for: that each generation will build on the previous ones and take their children farther than their parents took them . . . in the caravan of love across generations.

Assuming, then, that we are helping parents mature to the point where they can model non-discriminatory, unconditional, revolutionary love and see it as the desired end from the beginning, what else can parents and other caring adults do to help children grow through the stages of faith?

You may be surprised to hear me say that I think it will be an absolute spiritual necessity to expose children to nature and to build in them, from the youngest age possible, a lifelong sensitivity to the patterns of the natural world. If we think of God as both the creator of the cosmos and the source of love, then it sounds ludicrous to think we could encounter God and divine love apart from God's creative project. Yes, I love a beautiful cathedral or Bach cantata or stained-glass window, but if we think a manmade creation is more effective at communicating the heart of the divine than the original creation, I worry that we would rather see a reflection of ourselves than a reflection of our creator.

A painter signs his or her painting, but in a sense, every touch of the brush on the canvas is a more important signature. As an author who has signed many a book, I can also say that my heart comes through the words on all the other pages much more than through my signature on the title page. Similarly, in faith after doubt, in faith that expresses itself through love, in Stage Four faith, we encounter God first and foremost through God's original self-expression, in aspen trees and the waters that gush out of mountain springs, in swirling galaxies and the green-gray lichen that adorns a rock, in the wood thrush and orangutan, in a shimmering brown trout or the power of a summer thunderstorm. This divine glory is found not just in the individual creations but, even more, in their inter-relations in habitats and ecosystems, solar systems and galaxy clusters. In this dynamic and constantly evolving cosmic art gallery or library, we discern the logos, or embodied logic, and music of God, an ever-emergent theology that constantly breaks out of eggs and blows the lid off human language and limitations.

As a human being who has loved and contemplated my little corner of the universe across six decades now, I can say that creation has led me ever deeper into contact and communion with its creator, source, companion, and animator. Along the way, creation has also been the source of many of the doubts that unsettled the Stage One and Stage Two beliefs that my religion taught me; she was too big, too fertile, too dynamic, too wild to be domesticated by my inherited theological boxes. If my only option was an indoor religion, a faith that fits with man-made structures but withers in the open air, I would have become an atheist long ago. But because I could never deny the transcendent wisdom and wildness I found outdoors in creation, I could never walk away from faith, even though my path led me through the valley of the shadow of doubt and blew my little belief boxes to smithereens.

Frankly, the natural world was largely irrelevant to my inherited system of beliefs in Simplicity and Complexity. My entire Stage One and Stage Two religion could have been conducted under artificial light while I breathed heated, cooled, and filtered air; moved from one little box to another; saw nothing except through glass or screens or in black and white on pages; and heard nothing but human voices and human words.

It makes sense, then, that when I was deep in Perplexity, I found myself drawn irresistibly outdoors. I would walk along the Potomac River on my days off, sensing that the questions and doubts I felt surging within me could only be answered by the wordless flow of the river, the rhythm of seasons, the richness of forest loam, the trill of toads and tree frogs, the whisper of wind in pine needles, the arc of a hawk circling overhead in the wind, the branching patterns that run through trees and river deltas and circulatory systems and taxonomy charts.

I know that emphasizing the role of the natural world will sound privileged to some, because the industrial economy has domesticated and caged so many of us so thoroughly, some in urban ghettoes, some in shopping malls, some in a digital unreality, and some in literal prisons. For many, going to the wilderness feels like a luxury that only the well-off can afford, and even then, precious few of the well-off have time or interest to do so, busy as they are getting and staying well off. As a result, many children and adults today find the natural world unfamiliar, frightening, and even annoying with all its pesky bugs and unpredictable weather. It speaks a language that is more remote to them than Klingon, and they just don't get it.

They feel like foreigners in their actual home, walking as aliens through this world of wonders, utterly disconnected from the soil, water, air, and other elements of which we humans are made and which we share with all our fellow creatures. I understand this alienation, and find it sad beyond words. I certainly don't want to make anyone feel bad or guilty for not enjoying nature. But if we want to raise a new generation for whom progression toward Harmony will be natural, we must raise them differently than most of us were raised. We will, as some friends of mine say, re-wild God, spirituality, and ourselves, from our earliest childhood until our final days.* We will understand from the start that the language of nature actually is the language of God, as the Psalmist told us long ago (in Psalm 19), and as the Fourth Gospel reiterated (the Greek word *logos* in John 1 could be defined as *the pattern of meaning inherent in the universe*). There is so much more I would like to say about this, but realize that I already said much of it in my most recent book, *The Galapagos Islands: A Spiritual Journey.*†

In addition to instilling in children a lifelong practice of listening and looking for God in nature, we will help children understand that we encounter the love of God in others. Most obviously, we do so in moments of intimacy and kindness, when God flows like an alternating current among us. But we also encounter divine love in times of conflict, as our hearts break, as we feel wound and absence, and as we weep and work for reconciliation and peace. Beyond intimacy and conflict among those closest to us, we humans encounter and experience divine love in the experience of the other, the stranger, the outsider, the outcast, and even the enemy. In Scripture, for example, Abraham and Sarah receive their promise through strange visitors (Genesis 18); two disciples meet Christ in

---

* See https://www.seminaryofthewild.com/.
† *The Galapagos Islands: A Spiritual Journey* (Fortress, 2019). In the UK, it is entitled *God Unbound: Theology in the Wild* (Canterbury, 2019).

a stranger on the road to Emmaus (Luke 24); people welcoming strangers have encountered "angels unawares" (Hebrews 13); those who were kind to a homeless stranger or a prisoner discover that they were loving Christ in a distressing disguise (Matthew 25). Story after story in the Bible makes this clear, but our Stage One and Stage Two eyes have been terribly slow to see it.

Beyond discovering divine love in the natural universe and in relationships with others, we will help our children and students learn to encounter divine, transcendent, universal love in themselves, in the depths of their own being. This, I believe, is what contemplation means. We often say that contemplation involves stilling our thoughts and finding God in silence, and that is true. But there is nothing magic about silence itself. The magic comes as we experience our deepest selves in and with God, beneath our chattering thoughts, obsessive analysis, and noisy commentary.

When we are able to encounter our own vitality on a level deeper than all our internal noise, even imperfectly and for the briefest moment, we find in our own consciousness the presence of a deeper consciousness, so bottomlessly deep and wide that we might call it Consciousness itself. Similarly, as we accept ourselves as we are, we experience the presence of a deeper acceptance, so unlimited in its love that we can call it Acceptance itself. As we listen to ourselves, we find a Listener; as we behold ourselves, we find a Beholder; as we rest with ourselves, we find a Companion also at rest; as we feel at home in ourselves, we find a divine Host who welcomes us home; as we encounter our own creativity, we recognize the Creative Spirit; as we allow ourselves simply to be, we find holy Being. As Moses encountered God in the bush that burned and was not consumed, we encounter God in the unconsumed life-ember that glows deep in our own heart.

Children, I believe, would find it as natural as breathing to recognize and love God in creation, in their companions, and in themselves, if only faith communities would help them do so. But sadly, so many faith communities immerse children in books and doctrines rather than in life, as if God were more present in a man-made medium than in God's original media of matter and energy, of time and space, of joy and sorrow and life itself.

Spiritual communities that create this kind of spiritual space will offer themselves as travel guides, not as the destination itself, helping all of us, young and old alike, wake up and slow down, so we can see the holy mysteries that hide in plain sight in nature, in one another, and in ourselves. Our faith communities will also encourage us to share our divine encounters with one another, so that the capacity for spiritual insight spreads and intensifies from person to person and generation to generation. In the Hebrew Scriptures (Numbers 11:29), Moses muses, "Would that all the Lord's people could be prophets," and in the New Testament, Paul similarly urges people to desire the ability to prophesy (1 Corinthians 14:1) as a way of expressing love. Perhaps in the broadest sense, when we share the stories of our encounters with God in nature, in community, and in our own personhood, we are being prophets to one another.

I hope you feel as I do: that we need these multi-generational four-stage spiritual communities right now. We need them desperately, for people like Allie, Jake, and me, for their little girl and for my grandchildren. Meanwhile, the vast majority of our current faith communities have been designed to keep us warehoused in Simplicity and Complexity, with little to offer beyond, and they are functioning according to design.

I do not know how many of our current congregations and denominations will be willing to be redesigned around the ultimate end or goal of faith expressing itself in love. I do not know to what degree these four-stage faith communities will have to arise separately and independently of our current structures, as new wine in new wineskins. Nor do I know how long this transition will take. But here is what I do know: the development of four-stage faith communities is not simply a matter of interest. It is a matter of survival, as we shall see in the next chapter.

Reflection and Action

1. How do you respond to Jake and Allie's story about their religious upbringings at the beginning of this chapter?
2. Summarize the three-box metaphor in your own words. How are our first stages, Simplicity and Complexity, contained in the first box of ORDER?
3. Contrast teaching Stage One spirituality (Simplicity) as an end in itself versus as a means toward love.

4. Do the same for Stage Two spirituality (Complexity) and Stage Three spirituality (Perplexity).
5. I offer five essentials for Stage Four spiritual formation: parents and other adults who model it, deep engagement with the natural world, deep encounter with others, deep encounter with one's own person or soul, and the support of a faith community. Reflect on these elements and how they might interact.
6. Contrast seeing a faith community as a destination and as a travel guide.
7. Re-read the last two paragraphs and offer your opinions on what I say I do not know.
8. How do you respond to the claim in the last paragraph that developing four-stage faith communities is a matter of survival?

14

HARMONY AS A
SURVIVAL STRATEGY

They are not crazy. They are part of this spiritual revolution—people
discovering God in the world and a world that is holy, a reality that en-
folds what we used to call heaven and earth into one. These people are
not secular, even though their main concern is the world; they are not
particularly religious (in the old-fashioned understanding of the term),
even though they are deeply aware of God. They are fashioning a way
of faith between conventional theism and any kind of secularism devoid
of the divine. . . . The future of faith would be an earthy spirituality, a
brilliant awareness of the spirit that vivifies the world.

—Diana Butler Bass, *Grounded*

How would you feel if you sat down on a plane next to a bald, bespecta-
cled fellow in his sixties who was reading a book called *On Killing*?

You'll understand why I always did my best to keep the cover hidden
as I read this fascinating book a few years ago.

Lt. Col. Dave Grossman wrote *On Killing* to explore a surprising finding: in World War II, a significant percentage of soldiers in the thick of
combat chose not to fire their rifles at the enemy, even when their own
lives were in danger.* Research done on battlefields of the American Civil
War, that most intimate and brutal of wars, indicated a similar pattern:
a shockingly high percentage of bullets were found shot deep into the
soil, suggesting that once again, many soldiers, even when their own lives
were at risk, aimed into the ground to avoid taking a life. (It is easier,

---

* Lt. Col. Dave Grossman, *On Killing* (Back Bay Books, 2009).

Grossman's research indicated, to take life at a distance, whether through bombing, artillery, or drones.)

We have an inborn moral resistance to killing, Grossman said, but that resistance can be overcome through desensitization training. Military leaders picked up on this, of course, and have adapted accordingly, creating a new long-term danger for soldiers, one that may follow them home and stay with them for many years, called *moral injury*. Its symptoms are similar to post-traumatic stress disorder, but while PTSD is a psychological condition that arises after living in intense conditions of danger and fear, moral injury results from violating one's own moral code.

Grossman raised concerns that our culture at large may be desensitizing us to violence, through movies and video games, through hate speech, through political demagogues whose tough-guy bravado and us-them rhetoric easily fire up a certain belligerent sector of the electorate. His book left me with a sense of hope mixed with foreboding: hope that our instinct for intra-species solidarity could be strengthened, foreboding that we remain vulnerable to desensitization.

That foreboding intensified a few months ago, when I picked up an article written by emeritus social sciences professor and peace activist Brian Martin. Martin put *On Killing* into conversation with *The Pathology of Man: A Study of Human Evil*, a work by psychologist-philosopher Steven Jay Bartlett.[*] Bartlett delved deep into the historical records of the Holocaust, hate crimes, terrorism, and other acts of cruelty, and he concluded that people who participate in horrific violence are not uniquely evil monsters or sociopaths, as many claim.[†] No, Bartlett said, most people who participate in the horrors of collective and individual violence are "psychologically normal" people, people like you and me. For that reason, Bartlett described violence as a "functional pathology," meaning that it resembles a disease that people don't want to cure because "when it flares up, it provides great psychological satisfactions."

Those "satisfactions" range from the close bonding shared by soldiers on the front lines to the sense of excitement shared by citizens at home who find in war headlines and video footage an invigorating escape from

---

[*] Brian Martin, "What If Most People Love Violence?" wagingnonviolence.org, May 3, 2019, https://wagingnonviolence.org/2019/05/what-if-most-people-love-violence/.

[†] Charles C. Thomas Publishing, 2005.

their tedious, day-to-day lives. Echoing insights from anthropologist René Girard and war correspondent Chris Hedges, Bartlett paid special attention to the psychological usefulness of having an enemy or out-group.* For example, when an in-group projects its own fears and shame on an out-group, it simultaneously renders *them* as deserving of harm and *us* as worthy of inflicting that harm. In this way, outbreaks of violence help in-group members actually feel better about themselves, not worse . . . more zealous, innocent, and righteous, not less. In fact, their violent purging of the out-group reinforces their self-perception as purifiers and therefore pure.

As further evidence for his assessment, Bartlett noted that in the aftermath of war, most people simply carry on with their lives, doing nothing to decrease the likelihood of another war: "If men and women were desirous of peace, they would invest significant resources to further the causes of peace, but hardly a country in the world reserves a significant part of its national budget to study ways to foster peace." Bartlett concluded that because of our pathological thirst for violence and our resistance to being cured from it, we humans are ourselves "pathogenic," meaning that we are like a disease that decreases health both in human society and for the whole planet.

Bartlett's work struck me as both depressing and interesting, but even more interesting (and less depressing) were Martin's reflections, especially those on religion and morality:

> War provides an escape from everyday morality. Religious leaders preach about the sanctity of life, but few do much to resist the war system, revealing how moral principles can be compromised to enable preparation for mass violence.

I couldn't help but think of the ways that dualistic Stage One and pragmatic Stage Two faith communities could be seen as exacerbating the violent "pathology of humanity." It's not hard to foresee the outcome of rendering *us* as God's pure and holy in-group under siege by or at war with *them*, the Devil's dirty and evil out-group. Add to that dualistic

---

* See Chris Hedges, *War Is a Force That Gives Us Meaning* (PublicAffairs, 2014); and for a good overview of René Girard's body of work, see James Warren, *Compassion or Apocalypse?* (Christian Alternative, 2013).

judgment of Stage One moral Simplicity the ingenuity and energy of Stage Two pragmatic complexity, and you're sure to contrive more and more war strategies and weapons with greater and greater kill-power.

Less obvious, but more insidious, conventional religions often increase people's sense of shame and fear: shame about their sin, their lack of piety, their sexuality, and so on; and fear of falling into the hands of an angry God, an angry Devil, angry unbelievers, or (perhaps most terrifying of all) their angry fellow believers. People whose inner angst is constantly activated by conventional religion would likely have a bigger reservoir of shame and fear to project on an out-group. In this way, guilt-focused and fear-oriented piety would keep the embers of anxiety burning so they could at any moment be stirred into warrior flames.*

In this light, the Stage Three mindset could be seen as an attempt to undermine this pathological process by raising doubts about the authority and legitimacy of violence-prone Stage One and Stage Two leaders and systems. By "perplexifying" and deconstructing conventional systems of religion and politics, Stage Three thinkers could be calling the rest of us, very literally, to repentance, to turn away from old violent ways of thinking and to open ourselves to new nonviolent ones.

But what then? It's not enough to stop the "functional pathology" of violence without replacing it with more robust habits of well-being; otherwise, the human petri dish will soon be filled with some new infection. But how do we turn the tide on this human proclivity to violence?

Martin suggests a number of alternatives, including a "different media environment, one that counters nationalism, domination over nature, enemy-creation and violence." But that would only be a start, he says. We would still face the immense "challenge of creating full-scale alternatives—from child rearing to rituals honoring contributions to society." But even then, he acknowledges, "Persuading people that war and violence are bad is inadequate. . . . Knowledge and logic are not enough."

If they were, the horrors of war, and the devastation of a future nuclear war, would be more than adequate to impel masses of people to join

---

* For a detailed study of how Christian piety has been stirred for violent ends via the image of the cross, see Rebecca Ann Parker and Rita Nakashima Brock, *Saving Paradise: How Christianity Traded Love of This World for Crucifixion and Empire* (Beacon, 2008).

peace movements. Warning people that nuclear war could annihilate much of the world's population should be all it takes. However, despite warnings since the early 1980s that nuclear war could trigger a globally devastating "nuclear winter," most people take no special action against nuclear arsenals.

Martin concludes, "Awareness of the damaging effects of violence is not enough to turn more than a few people towards a rejection of violence." The only option, he argues, is to help more people become "different from the norm via greater moral intelligence." First, we would have to help people go beyond "distinguishing right from wrong" (conventional Stage One morality, in our terms). Next, we would have to help people develop "the capacity to link reason and emotion to enable doing good," skills that we could naturally develop in Stage Two. Then, we would need to help people develop the moral courage to "act against oppressive authorities rather than going along with the crowd," and "stand up to persecution," characteristics that we would associate with Stage Three dissent. Who could take on this task? Who could lead people through the first three stages into a fourth stage in which nonviolence is normal and habitual?

Schools promote intellectual development, but *there is no institution systematically helping people to achieve the most advanced forms of moral development*—ones that involve seeing beyond self-interest, attachments to organizations and countries and our species. The challenge for nonviolence supporters is to help develop *forms of learning through practice* that foster moral development. [Italics mine.]

As I read those words, my conversation with Allie and Jake came back to me like a body slam. What Allie and Jake are seeking on behalf of their daughter is exactly what Brian Martin describes as being so desperately needed by human civilization at this moment of history: *institutions that systematically help people to achieve the most advanced forms of moral development . . . learning through practice.*

That's why I can't give up on faith and faith communities. That's why I can't give up on the potential of a new generation of four-stage faith communities to teach a new kind of spirituality to a new generation of people. That's why I must doubt that religion in its current form is good enough, and that's why I reach forward into the unknown toward something better that I trust can become real.

Imagine this: what if even a portion of the religious infrastructure of the world could be made available for this kind of spiritual formation in love? In the United States alone, for example, houses of worship are valued at over $600 billion in real estate.* Each year, U.S. religious institutions bring in about $125 billion in donations.† If we add the volunteer hours and the social services provided by the faith sector, its net economic contribution has been estimated at $1.2 trillion annually, more than Apple and Google combined.‡ What might happen if more people who evolve through Simplicity, Complexity, and Perplexity, instead of leaving religion entirely, stayed and occupied it? What if these change agents worked wherever they could find a little foothold to transform their faith communities from belief factories to schools of "moral intelligence" or studios of love? What if these studios of love helped people learn the spiritual lessons of each stage, and then guided them into the next? And where existing institutions are hostile and unresponsive, what might happen if a new generation of spiritual entrepreneurs created new kinds of spaces, communities, and institutions to fill the void?

Then imagine if these religiously connected people join with their nonreligious counterparts, not simply to become happy consumers in the suicidal economy but rather to see "beyond self-interest, attachments to organizations and countries and our species." Imagine that they integrate the best resources they can find from religious traditions, brain science, education, sociology, psychology, anthropology, and art, gleaning anything of value from anywhere they can find it, *systematically helping people to achieve the most advanced forms of moral development possible.*

---

* See Dylan Matthews, "You Give Religions More Than $82.5 Billion a Year," *Washington Post*, August 22, 2013, https://www.washingtonpost.com/news/wonk/wp/2013/08/22/you-give-religions-more-than-82-5-billion-a-year/?utm_term=.374610d6e22c.

† "Americans Donated $125 Billion to Religion in 2018 – 29% of All Charitable Giving," Evangelical Council for Financial Accountability, https://www.ecfa.org/Content/Americans-Donated-125-Billion-to-Religion-in-2018-29-of-All-Charitable-Giving.

‡ Harriet Sherwood, "Religion in US 'Worth More Than Google and Apple Combined,'" *The Guardian*, September 15, 2016, https://www.theguardian.com/world/2016/sep/15/us-religion-worth-1-trillion-study-economy-apple-google.

Speaking as a Christian, I can attest: it's not that my religious tradition has devoted itself to this endeavor and failed. No: it has largely devoted itself to other things, including 1) keeping 384,000 buildings staffed, repaired, and open*; 2) training pastors and priests to teach required beliefs and perform required liturgy in those buildings; and 3) raising money to do 1 and 2. Obviously, along the way some amount of energy is spent in teaching people the moral and spiritual intelligence of love, but often, too often, it's only the skinny leftovers, if even that, and it's done within the little boxes of Simplicity and Complexity, with the lids bolted on tight.

And sadly, as any number of scandals and political misadventures make clear, often, too often, our religious institutions are not simply wasting time and resources and failing to do needed good: instead, they are doing real, measurable harm.†

That's why doubt is so necessary these days: doubt that refuses to settle for religion as it is, doubt that deconstructs the systems of beliefs that uphold authoritarian structures. But even though it's necessary, doubt is not sufficient. We need to imagine a spiritual movement that goes beyond doubt to support what may be humanity's greatest challenge: helping human nature and society mature in their moral and spiritual development, evolving in the direction of nonviolence and love before it's too late.

This movement for moral and spiritual development must begin with inner work, because we won't change our behavior in a lasting way until we change our consciousness. (Or perhaps more memorably, we won't change our way of being until we change our way of seeing.‡) We invest so much during our years in Simplicity and Complexity developing dualistic minds, dividing the world into good and bad, us and them, sinners and saints, winners and losers. It takes hard, often agonizing work in Perplexity to challenge those rigid categories. And then it takes a different kind of work, more like the labor of giving birth, to bring a new consciousness into the world, a consciousness that is able to hold our dualism in a bigger

---

* See Rebecca Randall, "How Many Churches Does America Have? More Than Expected," chris tianitytoday.com, September 14, 2017, https://www.christianitytoday.com/news/2017/september /how-many-churches-in-america-us-nones-nondenominational.html.
† See, for example, this powerful indictment by former priest James Carroll: "Abolish the Priesthood," *The Atlantic*, June 2019, https://www.theatlantic.com/magazine/archive/2019/06/to-save -the-church-dismantle-the-priesthood/588073/.
‡ This emphasis on seeing evokes insights of both Jesus and Paul. See Matthew 6:22 and Ephesians 1:18, 3:19.

Harmony, a harmony that doesn't dissolve difference but rather holds it in an expansive, universal, unitive love. Many of us have a name for this vital inner labor: *contemplation*.

"Contemplation is work," Richard Rohr says, "so much so that most people give up after their first futile attempts."* He continues, "Contemplation is an entirely different way of knowing reality that has the power to move us beyond mere ideology and dualistic thinking. . . . Believe me, it is major surgery, and we must practice it for years to begin to rewire our egocentric responses." He says that "it is the job of elders" of one generation to pass on the capacity for contemplation to the next generation, "so we need not start at zero." Then he offers this fascinating definition of contemplation:

> Contemplation is meeting as much reality as we can handle in its most simple and immediate form—without filters, judgments, or commentaries. The ego doesn't trust this way of seeing, which is why it is so rare, "a narrow gate and a hard road that leads to life, and only a few find it" (Matthew 7:14, New Jerusalem Bible). The only way we can contemplate is by recognizing and relativizing our own compulsive mental grids—our practiced ways of judging, critiquing, blocking, filtering, and computing everything. But we first have to catch ourselves in the act and recognize how habitual our egoic, dualistic thinking is. Each person must do this homework for themselves. It cannot be achieved by reading someone else's conclusions.
>
> When our judgmental mind and all its commentaries are placed aside, God finally has a chance to get through to us, because our pettiness and self-protective filters are at last out of the way. Then Truth stands revealed on its own—quite simply—and we will experience a rebirth of the soul.

I remember what it felt like for me as a young fundamentalist, emerging out of Simplicity and into Complexity, not yet ready for Perplexity. I had learned the dualisms of my tribe well: Christians good/non-Christians bad, conservatives good/liberals evil, and so on. When I met a Muslim,

---

* Fr. Richard Rohr, "Doing the Homework," cac.org, October 13, 2019, https://cac.org/doing-the-homework-2019-10-13/.

atheist, or Buddhist who appeared to be better than Christians I knew, or when I met a liberal who appeared to be better than the conservatives I knew, I didn't immediately respond with a humble admission, such as, "Wow, I guess I was wrong in my previous judgment." No, I couldn't handle that much reality. So I assumed their goodness was deceptive. I doubted what I saw with my physical eyes so I could maintain my long-practiced "filters, judgments, or commentaries." It was indeed hard inner labor, like major surgery, to move into contemplation.

And to the degree I did that inner work, I was thrust into outer work too. As I progressed through faith into doubt, and then through doubt into Stage Four faith on the other side, I could not be satisfied with inner work alone. To the degree I descended into deep communion with God, I was led, through God, into deep solidarity with other people and with all living and non-living creations.

What we said about faith communities turns out to be true of God as well: God is not a destination. Like a river, like a road, God takes us somewhere. For that reason, the authentic experience of communion with God leads into communion with all God's creations. The deeper we go into the love of God, the deeper we are led into all that God loves. In contemplation, the beloved and the lover are one, and love is all in all.

Contemplation, in this way, is the gateway to the most profound practice of activism. In one of my early presentations at the Center for Action and Contemplation, I reminded the audience that the organization was not the Center for Contemplation and Contemplation, nor was it the Center for Action and Action. Then I quoted the organization's founder, who regularly reminds us that the most important word in the name is *and*.

James, of course, made the same point (2:14): faith without works is dead. John agreed (1 John 4:20): How can you say you love God whom you haven't seen when you don't love your brother whom you have seen? And they were both echoing Jesus, who in his great commandment (Matthew 22:39) said that love for neighbor is absolutely inseparable from love for God, himself echoing an insight expressed frequently in the Hebrew Scriptures. For example, Proverbs 19:17 said that whoever is generous to the poor lends to the Lord, and Proverbs 14:31 said that whoever is cruel to the poor insults God. Similarly, Jeremiah delivered the word of the Lord to King Jehoikim, who was eager to build a first-rate royal palace but did not share his father, King Josiah's, concern for social justice (22:13–17):

> *Woe to him who builds his house by unrighteousness, and his upper rooms by injustice; who makes his neighbors work for nothing, and does not give them their wages; who says, "I will build myself a spacious house with large upper rooms," and who cuts out windows for it, paneling it with cedar, and painting it with vermilion. Are you a king because you compete in cedar? Did not your father eat and drink and do justice and righteousness? Then it was well with him. He judged the cause of the poor and needy; then it was well. Is not this to know me? says the Lord.*

A striking message indeed: to know God is to make things right for the poor and needy.

For reasons that are easy to guess, Stage One and Stage Two religion today seems happy to divorce spirituality from social justice, contemplation from activism, private and personal beliefs from public and political behavior.* But Stage Three sees through that facade and exposes that hypocrisy as Jeremiah did, clearing the way for Stage Four visionaries to integrate contemplative spirituality and activism in all its dimensions: social, economic, and ecological.

We see this integration powerfully in Thomas Merton. The deeper he was drawn into monastic silence and contemplative communion with God, the more outspoken he became about war, poverty, and other expressions of injustice. The more alive he became in God, the less he could remain a guilty but silent bystander.

Through the inner work of contemplation, we no longer see love for God and love for neighbor as separate things. They become inseparable dimensions of the same thing: we encounter and love God in our neighbors, and we are loved by God through our neighbors. (Similarly, we encounter and love God in creation, and we are loved by

---

* Among those reasons: churches find it hard to bite the hand that feeds them, major donors often have made their wealth through industries that exploit workers or the earth, and both churches and their donors have bought into ideologies that justify exploitation.

God through creation. The same is true of our own innermost being. It is the organ through which we simultaneously give and receive the love of God.)

Our conventional faith communities in Simplicity and Complexity produce adherents to beliefs, many of whom are indistinguishable from religious customers who make transactions with religious professionals to receive an array of religious goods and services. But four-stage communities produce spiritual activists, harmony activists, whose faith expresses itself in socially transforming love, politically liberating love, and ecologically restoring love.

What this vision means for organized religion, as I see it, is both unsettling and exciting. It invites individuals and congregations into a radical conversion from organized religion (religion organized institutionally for the self-interest of its staff and members) to organizing religion (religion organizing its staff and members as a spiritual-social-economic-political-ecological movement for the common good of all). But this kind of transformation can never happen when a faith community's leaders all remain in Simplicity, Complexity, and even Perplexity. Just as an apple branch can't be grafted onto a walnut tree, a social justice program can't be grafted onto a faith community whose theology and spirituality don't support it. We need leaders in Harmony who have done the hard inner work of contemplation, so that the needed integration is natural. These leaders can nurture the development of four-stage communities, the kind we described in the previous chapter, where the important work of Simplicity, Complexity, and Perplexity all takes place in the context of Harmony.

These Stage Four leaders and four-stage communities exist, thanks be to God. But they are still too rare, and their powerful yet quiet work is often drowned out by arrogant preachers and mega-institutions with big budgets, unacknowledged bigotries, and loud bullhorns. Even so, I can imagine a time in the not-too-distant future when people tire of their noise and polarizing rhetoric and start migrating toward something better. They will no longer be content to be adherents of systems of beliefs but will aspire to be genuine disciples, contemplative spiritual activists in the growing movement of revolutionary love.*

---

* For more on spiritual activism, see Matt Carmichael and Alastair McIntosh's brilliant "bible" on the subject: *Spiritual Activism: Leadership as Service* (Greenbooks, 2015).

If such a spirituality were to become more widely available, and if growing numbers of congregations embodied it, we could deploy a vast, nonviolent peace-army of joyful evangelists for this good and beautiful way of life. For them, Harmony would be a survival strategy. They would not bear the old colonialist message of "join my religion or be tortured forever in hell," the religious equivalent of "Resistance is futile; you will be assimilated." No: they would bear good news indeed, good news of great joy for all people and all creation at this dangerous moment in history when, as Greta Thunberg says, the house is on fire. *You can join the Spirit-inspired movement for the healing of the world*, they would say. *You can bring and embody good news for the poor, comfort for the brokenhearted, recovery of sight for the blind, and liberation for the oppressed and imprisoned. You are needed, you are wanted, just as you are, with all your questions and doubts. In fact, your questions and doubts are among your greatest assets.*

Reflection and Action

1. "We have an inborn moral resistance to killing," but "most people who participate in the horrors of collective and individual violence are 'psychologically normal' people." How can you reconcile these two claims?

2. How do you respond to the idea that human beings are "pathogenic"?

3. Brian Martin said, "There is no institution systematically helping people to achieve the most advanced forms of moral development. . . . The challenge for nonviolence supporters is to help develop forms of learning through practice that foster moral development." How has your experience with religion been in this regard? Where have you seen other institutions filling the gap by helping people become more morally and spiritually mature and learn moral development through practice?

4. In this chapter, I hold out hope that our religious institutions can take on this mission of moral and spiritual development. But I have to admit that sometimes I feel I am hitting my head against a closed box. How do you feel about the possibility of some significant sector of organized religion taking on this vital task? If religious institutions don't do so, who will?

5. Respond to this statement: *Doubt is necessary, but not sufficient.*
6. Describe in your own words the difference between organized religion and organizing religion.
7. Name some Stage Four leaders and four-stage faith communities you are aware of in your area. What kind of spiritual activism are they involved in? Where are they making a difference?
8. Where are you already involved as a spiritual activist as described in this chapter? Where do you hope to get more involved?

⚘

15

A Civilization in Doubt

My perversity is to think that Mother Teresa's finest moment is found in the doubts she expresses about whether she "believed" any of the teachings of the Church, whether she even "believed" in "God," which is what she called this spectral solicitation emanating from the faces looking back at her on the streets of Calcutta, a solicitation she had been answering all her life. What she never doubts is her work, because her work is the Kingdom of God; her answer to the call is the only reality enjoyed by that call. In her moments of doubt, of "incredulity toward big stories," I think, the name of God is purified of existence and the sheer insistence of God, the call to make the name of God come true, is disclosed. The sheer purity of that inexistent solicitation shook a very strong woman to the bones and, while it rattled her "beliefs," it did not lay a glove on her deeper "faith" in the event, under whatever name it addressed her.

—John Caputo, *What Would Jesus Deconstruct?*

I took a long walk on the beach near my home the other day. I was accompanied by an old friend I hadn't seen in over a decade. His religious upbringing was similar to mine, conservative Evangelical. Rob described how he felt his path had led him out of our childhood faith into a long, long stretch of doubt. He left one belief after another along the uphill trail, like extra weight in a backpack. His loss of easy answers and inherited comforts felt terrifying one moment and liberating the next.

Rob said the process continues. His notion of God today is a far cry from the bearded white Almighty sitting on a throne and controlling everything, as he pictured in childhood. These days he's also rethinking his inherited beliefs about death and the afterlife, pondering his own mortality and the mortality of the whole human race—whether through a human-induced suicidal catastrophe in the short term, or through some more cosmic termination millions or billions of years from now, in a big freeze or big crunch.

"It's strange," he said. "But to the degree I stare into the abyss and accept the inevitability that I will someday die and the possibility that humanity will eventually go extinct and our little human DNA story will be over forever, to the degree I face this without trying to suppress it, candy-coat it with some beliefs, or fix it with some dogma, something happens. I stop trying to explain away all the pain in the universe and my life. I stop having some ironclad explanation for everything, and I admit that I don't know. I feel less and less like I'm trying to play God and have all the answers, and I feel more and more like the tiny human being I actually am."

He told me that this experience of surrendering to not-knowing felt like a death and resurrection. "The more I face this stunning fragility of life and the tiny scope of what I can actually figure out," he said, "the more I find myself looking around and thinking, 'Wow, I'm still alive now.' And that strikes me as a pretty wonderful thing. A gift. A wonder. A miracle, even. It's like waking up after a catastrophe and realizing that you've lost everything, but you're still alive. And then you realize that when you had everything, you didn't feel half this alive."

Then Rob raised his hands and turned around in a complete circle. "I get to enjoy this. To witness this sand strewn with shells, these waves and white surf, these pelicans plunging into the water, this breeze, those clouds towering above us. With a good friend beside me." Then he closed his eyes, took a deep breath, and exhaled: "Right now." Then another breath. "And still now." And then another: "And still now."

We started walking again, silent except for the crunch, crunch, crunch rhythm of our feet on the sand and crushed shell. Rob mused, "I used to think that if I didn't have answers, I would only be left with questions. But now I'm starting to realize that if I live into the questions, if I don't have to fix or solve every problem, then I can welcome all the unknowns with wonder and innocence and—I don't know what to call it, a kind of meditative awareness maybe, or even reverence. In the midst of all my questions, I keep finding gratitude. And wonder. And joy. And this feeling of companionship and freedom. I'm less sure of what God is, and more sure that whatever God is, God is with me in all this." A few moments later, he added this: "That's not such a bad thing, living in a world of wonders rather than a world of answers," he said. "It's actually very, very good."

My friend Hannah is on a similar journey. She grew up Catholic, "super-Catholic," she says, with all her education in Catholic schools. She works as an environmental scientist and weekend activist, and she wakes up every morning feeling the weight of the world on her shoulders. I marched with her recently at a climate change protest, and we talked about how we're surviving in these strange and chaotic times.

"I feel like I've lost faith," she said, protest sign raised high. "Faith in God, faith in humanity, faith in government, faith in markets . . . it's all gone." She made a gesture with her free hand to indicate her faith had vanished in a puff of smoke. "I've even lost faith that my research will make any difference, or that marching and protesting will make any difference. I've reached the depressing conclusion that the world runs on money, not wisdom or common sense or justice."

Her words were grim, but somehow, her tone was more defiant than defeated. "Money is like crack," she continued. "It's even more addictive and even more deadly in the long run. So Exxon and Chevron will keep pumping oil out of the ground for money even though they know it will destroy the earth. And people will keep buying Exxon and Chevron stock as long as they think it will pump money into their retirement accounts, even though it decreases the chance that their grandchildren will live until retirement. For the sake of money they'll keep voting for politicians who are as corrupt as hell, as long as they promise lower taxes and accelerating economic growth, as if their economic systems will be left standing when the ecosystem collapses. Meanwhile, you religious leaders are so afraid of offending the people who love money so passionately that you'll never muster the guts to tell the truest truth of all: that money lies, that it's a false value, and that to put money first is to commit suicide."

"You may have lost your faith," I said, "but you sure haven't lost your fire."

She laughed, then said, "Yeah, even though I've lost any confidence that my efforts will make a difference . . . I've come to realize that I can't give up trying. So I'm going to keep marching and researching and working and telling the truth. I'll keep pushing forward because I couldn't live with myself otherwise. I'll keep living this way and fighting this losing battle because this is the only way it makes sense to live my one and only little life, fighting for the earth to my very last breath. I guess I can't help it. It's just who I've become."

"That strikes me as the greatest kind of faith of all," I said. "Faith that goes on when every reason for hope is gone."

"It sure doesn't feel like faith," she said. "It feels like hell. But maybe it's love. It's love for the earth. Love for life. Love for the whole 13.7 billion–year story that brought us here, and that is too beautiful to end so prematurely."

I interrupted, not telling her who I was paraphrasing: "Well, as far as I'm concerned, the only kind of faith that means anything is faith that expresses itself in love."

"I guess that's all I've got left, then," she replied. "Loving what's left with the time I have left."

"Sure beats living for money," I said.

"Yeah. It beats the hell out of that," she replied.

I can't stop thinking about Hannah and Rob. Their journeys of doubt have left them with less than many of my other friends. But then again, I think they've gained more than they've lost. I love the way Rob's faith after doubt allows him to cherish each moment without minimizing its pain and unknowing, and I think that Hannah's motto of "loving what's left with the time I have left" is about as good a life mission as I've heard of lately. In spite of all they've lost, what they've retained and gained strikes me as pure gold: wonder, fire, gratitude, a feeling of being awakened to the fragility and preciousness of the moment, courage, and insight into what really matters: love.

Like them, I often grieve the losses that have come through the stages of faith. But other times, it dawns on me that what I have left are the best things, and even though I'm not always sure if I'm miserable or ecstatic, I know I'm alive.

I know you have already experienced that aliveness. It may have been for a fleeting moment at the birth of a child, the death of a parent, an experience of profound sexual intimacy, a sublime turn in a symphony or poem or film, or an act of self-giving. It may have come as you looked out the window of a train or airplane, as you walked along a hiking trail, when you bodysurfed a curling wave at the beach, or as you held or nursed your newborn child. You may have hardly even acknowledged that little moment because it was so foreign and odd on the one hand or so personal and intimate on the other. It may have even scared you a little bit, or embarrassed you, even made you feel guilty because it didn't fit in the small boxes of Simplicity, Complexity, or even Perplexity. But whenever it came and however it felt, you knew you were alive and you knew life was precious, holy, sacred. You knew more than you could put into words. You felt in your marrow that every single thing was priceless and profound and beloved.

In the absence of that aliveness, in the absence of that faith after doubt that expresses itself in love, people settle for less. They settle for easy answers that candy-coat reality, as Rob says. They settle for measuring all things by money, as Hannah realizes, and when asked, "Your money or your life?" they clutch their wad of money even tighter. Along with their money, they elevate their religion, race, ideology, or nation to the status of an absolute, as if it alone matters. Or they shrink their aspirations to the circumference of their ego and decide that their personal pride, power, and pleasure are all that matters. One way or another, in refusing to doubt their assumptions, they deteriorate.

Among all the other things doubt is—loss, loneliness, crisis, doorway, descent, dissent—it is also this: a *crossroads*. At the crossroads of doubt, we either become better or bitter. We either break down or break through. We become cynics or sages, hollow or holy. We choose love or despair.

And I wonder if what is true of individuals is also true of civilizations. The old theory you may have learned in high school, *ontogeny recapitulates phylogeny*, has been debunked. But even so, the pattern of the whole may be reflected in the parts, and vice versa. Individuals may pass through the same stages in a single lifetime that their ancestors did over many generations. If that's possible, we might propose with all due humility and nuance that Stage One Simplicity represents what we might call the pre-modern world, with societies oriented around absolute truths revealed (and enforced) by divinely appointed authority figures (usually powerful men, or patriarchs). This arrangement dominated human societies in the West until around 1500, when the medieval framework began to fragment and the modern world began to take root in its cracks.

Since then, the modern world of the last five hundred years has given us trains, planes, and automobiles; aspirin and penicillin and vaccines; skyscrapers and space stations; mass media and social media; credit cards and voting booths; public schools and online courses; and screens of all shapes and sizes. This complex and ambitious world looks like the perfect embodiment of Stage Two pragmatism. It was and is driven by gaining knowledge, acquiring power over nature and other people, and making as much money as possible as fast as possible.

In recent decades, we see a global cultural phenomenon emerging that has much in common with Stage Three Perplexity. Postmodernity (or post-colonialism) isn't simply an attempt to throw out morality and order, as its modern critics erroneously say. Rather, it is (at its best, anyway) a moral critique of the unacknowledged costs of modern profit and the unacknowledged failures of modern success.

Postmodern protesters point out how the heroes of the modern project have, over the last five hundred years, exploited human life and the health of the planet to increase their personal and national wealth and power. Yes, postmodern critics say, modern-era planes, trains, and automobiles were great for convenience and the human economy. But they've had disastrous results for the planet's ecology. Yes, they say, modern-era technology produced spaceflight and smartphones, heart transplants and chemotherapy, but along the way, it also unleashed the slave trade, colonization, and the unaccountable multi-national corporation, along with world wars, the Holocaust, weapons of unprecedented killing power, and a raging global climate catastrophe. Yes, they say, modernity has increased our knowledge measured in information and our wealth measured in money. But has our moral wisdom kept pace with our intellectual exploits? Have we mortgaged our long-term planetary well-being for short-term monetary profits?

Modernist elites, predictably, respond defensively and derisively to this critical assessment. Utterly unable to imagine anything beyond their current stage, they presume the status quo is their only option, so they deny its unsustainability with all the intensity of a desperate addict.

The postmodern critique is powerful, profound, and persistent, and its volume and passion are growing. But the corporate titans and their corporate-sponsored politicians still aren't listening. In fact, they have lost their capacity for listening. At this moment, they seem so afraid of the self-examination and self-doubt of Stage Three Perplexity that they are choosing to double down, often reverting to authoritarian Simplicity, circling their wagons behind demagogues and their Stage One fundamentalisms, whether nationalistic, economic, religious, or, worse still, a fusion of the three.

The doubt of Stage Three postmodernity may defeat the arrogant confidence of Stage Two modernity, but modernity may actually defeat itself first. Sooner than it thinks, it may expand until it self-destructs, overshooting and collapsing on itself like the economic bubbles it habitually creates and pops, exemplifying the ancient Hebrew proverb *pride goes before destruction*. That fall may come suddenly through the next hot war with nuclear bombs, or it may come in stages through global warming, rising sea levels, intensifying storms, droughts, fire, pandemics, and the social havoc they create.

Speaking of pandemics, I completed this book in the early stages of the COVID-19 pandemic. At this point, nobody knows whether our current human systems will be resilient enough to recover quickly from the economic and social effects of the virus. The pandemic provides a powerful opportunity for contemporary societies to learn: about our connectedness to the environment, about our connectedness to each other, about our need for long-range global planning and preparedness that go far beyond typical short-term economic and political strategies, about the fragility of the current global economy, and about the need for intelligent national and global leadership. So far, however, many global leaders seem desperately determined not to learn the lessons this moment can teach, because learning would require thinking, and thinking would lead to doubting, and doubting would challenge any number of political, economic, and religious orthodoxies that our global elites simply do not want to challenge.

So for now, many of our leaders do the only thing they know how to do: they press their foot down harder on the accelerator of Stage One absolutism and Stage Two pragmatism. (Remember that each stage includes its predecessors.) They will swallow almost any fake news cocktail that allows them to maintain their current course. Desperate to make reality conform to their assumptions, they monitor

their progress only by measurements that make them appear successful (like GDP or stock market averages).* Meanwhile, they studiously
avoid any measures that might raise questions or doubts about their
project (like the tonnage of carbon they're pumping in the atmosphere
every second, the acreage of forests they're slashing and burning, the
size of the swirling plastic garbage patches in our oceans, the number
of species facing extinction, or the misery and anxiety of their own
children).†

So our modern global elites, whether they be secular or religious, forge
ahead with furious zeal, absolutely confident in their own exceptional
goodness and rightness and absolutely certain about the folly of their
postmodern critics, who keep telling them to listen to the cries of the
poor and the cries of the earth and to rethink everything. To the *Homo
colossus* of Stage Two, however, these postmodern prophets sound like
crazed doomsday preachers. *They couldn't possibly be right.*‡

Even the postmodern intellectuals who have moved into Perplexity face a challenge at this moment. Because every new day gives them
more data on the cluelessness of those they critique, they are tempted to
become as addicted to critique as their modernist counterparts were to
profit.§ At this moment, I fear that people in the early and middle stages

---

* As someone raised fundamentalist/Evangelical, I'm struck by the similarities among the ways
  that modernist economists selectively quote and interpret statistics, the ways that modernist
  politicians selectively quote and interpret their legal codes and precedents, and the ways that
  modernist religious leaders selectively quote and interpret their sacred texts.
† Religion has been telling us for millennia that even though we humans are special and rare, we
  are also flawed and sinful, foolish and arrogant. We have gone astray, lost our way, and need to
  be rescued, found, saved, redeemed, transformed, healed. Now science is giving us a number
  every day to quantify our folly. Today, as I write, that number is 414.5. That's the measurement of
  carbon dioxide in our atmosphere, a number that we never should have allowed to rise beyond
  350. Along with this telling number, there are plenty of other indicators: recent news that a
  million species are threatened with extinction; the resurgence of racist and neo-Nazi organizations around the world; the shocking proliferation of weapons, including nuclear weapons; the
  shocking rise in addiction and suicide rates at a time when corporate profits and national GDPs
  say we're thriving.
‡ For more on the fall of *Homo colossus*, see William Catton, *Overshoot* (University of Illinois Press,
  1982). Also see the brilliant and needed work of Michael Dowd: http://michaeldowd.org/.
§ The two dominant pragmatic economic ideologies of the modern era, capitalism and Marxism,
  are seen as bitter enemies, but really, they are rival brothers, two ways of functioning in a modern
  framework. One promotes unregulated markets, and the other promotes centralized planning,
  but both models have proven unsustainable. In addition, while they differ on who owns the
  means of production, they both are based on an extractive industrial economy, and neither is
  sustainable with over seven billion humans living at current standards of living. For more on

of Perplexity will be unwilling to move into the deep end of the pool, so to speak, to face the depths of late Perplexity that will open and prepare them for Harmony. As a result, I fear that too many will keep pounding the minor chords of moral outrage, and too few will learn to play the inspiring chords of moral imagination so we can envision and create a new and better way of life for the world after overshoot and collapse.

Those familiar with the biblical tradition will recall how the biblical prophets did indeed play the minor chords of scathing critique, complete with grim warnings of woe and doom. But they also played the major chords of prophetic imagination, with bright and fertile images of deserts blooming, virgins conceiving, swords and spears being melted down into farm tools, and nations studying war no more.

So, we might say, just as individuals move from Simplicity and Complexity into Perplexity, our global civilization stands in late Complexity, with some of us leaning forward into critical Perplexity and others leaning backward into pre-critical, authoritarian Simplicity. If you judge my superbrief and super-general analysis here to be even partially valid, then you'll see that at this crossroads moment, we simultaneously need two things.

First, just as individuals have important work to do in Stage Three, so do civilizations. For that reason, at this moment we need to help more people move into Perplexity, to do the critical work that our global civilization needs. If we aren't critical enough, we'll carry through toxic elements of earlier stages that will limit our future. If we're overcritical and reactionary, we may leave behind treasures of true value that we will need in the future. This is delicate work, fraught with perplexing challenges (as we would expect), with everything at stake.

Second, just as individuals can get stuck, polarized, and paralyzed in Stage Three, so can civilizations. The acid of critique and deconstruction can eat away everything and hollow out everything. For that reason we need a growing movement of intrepid moral and spiritual pioneers to move beyond critical Perplexity into post-critical Harmony. We need, in the terms of this book's title, not naive, untested faith without doubt, and not merely doubt upon doubt upon doubt, but a new kind of faith after (and with) doubt.

---

this subject, see Philip Clayton and John Heinzekehr, *Organic Marxism* (Process Century Press, 2014); and Chapters 9–14 of my *The Galapagos Islands: A Spiritual Journey* (Fortress, 2019).

Sensitive readers, I'm sure, are already asking the essential and urgent question: How can we cross that threshold into Harmony as a civilization?

We spoke earlier of doubt as dissent and descent. A sister word for *dissent* is *protest* and a sister word for *descent* is *humility*. We protest when we see the faults of others; we experience humility when we see the faults in ourselves. When we develop the ability to see and protest the faults in others *and* in ourselves, when we become both critical *and* self-critical, when we realize that *we* are no better than *they* are and that both *we* and *they* are all in this together, then we pass through the portal from Stage Three postmodernity to what lies beyond.

When I say *we are no better*, I don't mean that our ideas are no better. Obviously, people who face the scientific facts of climate change, the economic facts of growing inequality, and the practical facts of weapons proliferation have better ideas than those who deny those facts. But we face a peculiar challenge in this postmodern moment, this moment of Perplexity, this moment when we de-absolutize both pre-modern authority structures and modern economic structures: we must also de-absolutize our own critical thinking. We must come to terms with the reality that the problem is not *them*, it is *us*, *all* of us, the *big* us of humanity that includes both us and them. Our problems are shared human problems.

We got into this mess together, and we will only get through it together, or as Dr. King put it, "We may have all come on different ships, but we're in the same boat now." That applies to us as individuals, and, as Dr. King was saying, it applies to us as races. But it also applies to us as religions.

A black-and-white photograph sits on my desk, a gift from a friend. Inside the picture frame, it's 1968, and a young Thomas Merton stands beside a young Dalai Lama, two monks in the garb of their faith communities, two contemplatives from two ancient traditions, one Christian, one Buddhist, trying to figure out how to live in the twentieth century.

Merton visited the Dalai Lama's monastery for eight days, during which they had three extended meetings. At the end of those meetings, Merton said, "It was a warm and cordial discussion and at the end I felt we had become very good friends. . . . I feel a great respect and fondness for him as a person and believe, too, that there is a real spiritual bond between us." A month later, Merton died, but years later, the Dalai Lama said that meeting Merton was one of the happiest memories of that period in his life. Merton introduced him "to the real meaning of the word 'Christian'" and became one of the three most influential people in his life. During a visit to Merton's monastery nearly thirty years later, he said:

> I always consider myself as one of [Thomas Merton's] Buddhist brothers. So . . . I always remember him, and I always admire his activities and his life-style. Since my meeting with him . . . I really follow some of his examples. . . . So for the rest of my life, the impact of meeting him will remain until my last breath. I really want to state that I make this commitment, and this will remain until my last breath.*

I love this photograph. It brings to mind deep connections I have enjoyed . . . with Muslims, with Jews, with Sikhs, with Hindus, with Buddhists, and many others, including non-religious people. Yes, I have been surprised and disappointed at times by the fury and vitriol of my fellow Christians (mostly in Stage One) who see people like my friends and me as enemies and condemn us to hell.

But I have been even more profoundly surprised and delighted by the love of people from other traditions who have found their way to the Harmony at the very heart of their tradition. Interestingly, their entry into Stage Four faith didn't make them less wholeheartedly Christian or Muslim or Buddhist or Jewish, but more. When they discovered the sound of the genuine at the heart of their faith tradition, they were able to recognize it in other faith traditions. The deeper they went in their own tradition, the deeper their love for all people, whatever their tradition, and simultaneously, the deeper their love for their own tradition. They found they could go down through the deepest center of their tradition and come up in another.

I borrowed that language of going down and coming up from a commencement speech given in 1980 by one of my favorite theologians, Howard Thurman. I was twenty-four when he gave the speech, and I wonder if the twenty-four-year-old, Stage Two me of 1980 had been there, whether I would have sensed the sparkling magic and deep brilliance I sense now. He begins by inviting us to listen for the "sound of the genuine" in ourselves:

---

* To see the photograph, go to http://www.merton.org/dalailama/. To see a similar photograph of the Dalai Lama and Desmond Tutu, see their joint book, *The Book of Joy* (Avery, 2016).

There is something in every one of you that waits, listens for the sound of the genuine in yourself and if you cannot hear it, you will never find whatever it is for which you are searching and if you hear it and then do not follow it, it was better that you had never been born. . . . You are the only you that has ever lived; your idiom is the only idiom of its kind in all of existence and if you cannot hear the sound of the genuine in you, you will all of your life spend your days on the ends of strings that somebody else pulls. . . .

The sound of the genuine is flowing through you. Don't be deceived and thrown off by all the noises that are a part even of your dreams, your ambitions, so that you don't hear the sound of the genuine in you, because that is the only true guide that you will ever have, and if you don't have that you don't have a thing. You may be famous. You may be whatever the other ideals are which are a part of this generation, but you know you don't have the foggiest notion of who you are, where you are going, what you want. Cultivate the discipline of listening to the sound of the genuine in yourself. . . .

There is in you something that waits and listens for the sound of the genuine in yourself and sometimes there is so much traffic going on in your mind, so many different kinds of signals, so many vast impulses floating through your organism that go back thousands of generations, long before you were even a thought in the mind of creation, and you are buffeted by these, and in the midst of all of this you have got to find out what your name is. Who are you? How does the sound of the genuine come through to you . . . ?

Listening for the sound of the genuine is, I think, one of the finest translations of *love* to be found anywhere. *The sound of the genuine* is Thurman's term for what Merton called *the true self,* and I suspect it's equivalent to what the Quakers referred to as *that of God in everyone.*** To listen for that true

---

* For more on Merton's use of *true self,* see Richard Rohr, *Immortal Diamond: The Search for Our True Self* (Jossey-Bass, 2013), 38–39. The Quaker phrase comes from George Fox: "Be patterns, be examples in all countries, places, islands, nations wherever you come; that your carriage and life may preach among all sorts of people, and to them; then you will come to walk cheerfully over the world, answering that of God in everyone; whereby in them you may be a blessing, and make the witness of God in them to bless you." "Statement of 1656," from *The Works of George Fox* (1831), available here: https://books.google.com/books?id=BU5mGfV-XD8C&hl=en.

sound or true song in themselves, Thurman tells the college graduates, is the best and truest way for them to know and love themselves. But Thurman doesn't stop there, of course. He applies his metaphor to our interactions with one another, following the same pattern found in the great commandment of Jesus, to love one's neighbor as oneself. Just as we listen for the sound of the genuine in ourselves as individuals, we listen for it in others:

> Now there is something in everybody that waits and listens for the sound of the genuine in other people. . . . I must wait and listen for the sound of the genuine in you. I must wait. For if I cannot hear it, then in my scheme of things, you are not even present. And everybody wants to feel that everybody else knows that she is there.

But we are beckoned farther still, beyond just listening for the sound of the genuine in others: we want others to listen for that sound of the genuine in us, so there is a mutuality of respectful, reverent encounter:

> I want to feel that I am thoroughly and completely understood so that now and then I can take my guard down and look out around me and not feel that I will be destroyed with my defenses down. I want to feel completely vulnerable, completely naked, completely exposed and absolutely secure . . . that I can run the risk of radical exposure and know that the eye that beholds my vulnerability will not step on me. That I can feel secure in my awareness of the active presence of my own idiom in me.
>
> So as I live my life then, this is what I am trying to fulfill. It doesn't matter whether I become a doctor, lawyer, housewife. I'm secure because I hear the sound of the genuine in myself and having learned to listen to that, I can become quiet enough, still enough, to hear the sound of the genuine in you.

Then Thurman leans in even deeper still: this encounter with the genuine in *myself* prepares me for an encounter with *another*, which in turn prepares both of us for a mutual encounter among *one another*, a form of communication that is better called *communion*, where "the wall that separates and divides will disappear and we will become one":

Now if I hear the sound of the genuine in me, and if you hear the sound of the genuine in you, it is possible for me to go down in me and come up in you. So that when I look at myself through your eyes having made that pilgrimage, I see in me what you see in me and the wall that separates and divides will disappear and we will become one because the sound of the genuine makes the same music.

Elsewhere, Thurman makes it clear that for him, this coming-into-union, this encounter-without-judgment, this knowing-without-control goes from me to you to us and beyond, to plants and animals and all of the created world.* We come to hear the "same music," the sound of the genuine, flowing through *everything, every* thing, every *thing.*†

And this, I propose, is the core of spiritual experience shared by all or nearly all religions. It is the pearl of great price and the great treasure buried in the field, to use Jesus' terminology.‡ Unfortunately, that treasure is often made inaccessible to insiders and outsiders alike because the gatekeepers of our traditions have never themselves explored the field and are unaware of its greatest treasure, or else they have experienced it but forgotten it, so now they neglect it. Some of them even built razor-wire fences around the part of the field where it is hidden, and they distract us with lesser things that are of more use or interest to them: beliefs, rules, policies, controversies, budgets, programs, activities, rituals, offerings, inquisitions.

---

* For example, in *Disciplines of the Spirit* (Friends United Press, 1963), Thurman wrote, "As a child I was accustomed to spending many hours alone in my rowboat, fishing along the river, when there was no sound save the lapping of the waves against the boat. There were times when it seemed as if the earth and the river and the sky and I were one beat of the same pulse. It was a time of watching and waiting for what I did not know—yet I always knew. There would come a moment when beyond the single pulse beat there was a sense of Presence which seemed always to speak to me. My response to the sense of Presence always had the quality of personal communion. There was no voice. There was no image. There was no vision. There was God. . . . [For Jesus] God breathed through all that is: the sparrow overcome by sudden death in its flight; the lily blossoming on the rocky hillside; the grass of the field and the clouds, light and burdenless or weighted down with unshed waters; the madman in chains or wandering among the barren rocks in the wastelands; the little baby in his mother's arms."

† This is a central theme of Richard Rohr's *The Universal Christ* (Convergent, 2019).

‡ See Matthew 13. I think Thurman's metaphor is, in this way, an expression of Jesus' central metaphor, *the kingdom of God.* When we are in the same kingdom, we recognize one another as belonging to the same whole, which means we belong together and to one another. The kingdom of God, then, is the ultimate sphere of belonging, where all creations are beloved and belong, where all are safe to be themselves, "to feel completely vulnerable, completely naked, completely exposed and absolutely secure," where all creations "can run the risk of radical exposure and know that the eye that beholds [their] vulnerability will not step on [them]."

The good news, however, is that this treasure is not the wholly owned subsidiary of any religious entity. The gatekeepers do not have an exclusive license to distribute it. The good news is that this Stage Four spirituality is available to everyone, like wind, rain, and sun, because it is, in my Christian vocabulary, the presence of grace and the creative current of the Holy Spirit that flows like a song through all of creation.

It is here. Available. At hand. Within reach. Right now. If those of us who have found this treasure in our religious traditions can begin to sing it, speak it, pray it, celebrate it, and live it out loud, perhaps together we can lean into Harmony as a civilization. Perhaps we can sing the song of Harmony in genuine harmony as a multi-faith visionary choir.

Right now, much work waits to be done. In politics, we've been studying war for centuries. We must now study how to create the conditions for deep and lasting peace. In many sectors of religion, we've been obsessed for centuries with escaping this day-to-day life on earth for an afterlife in heaven (or an experience of personal bliss). We must now cherish life on earth and engage with it by focusing our best energies on learning to love neighbor, self, earth, and God, who is Love. In education, for centuries we've been focused on basic morality, technology, and critical thinking. Now we must learn how to teach our children not just to know right from wrong, and not just to be able to make a living, and not just to be able to think critically, but also to live well with ourselves, one another, and the earth, discovering and cherishing the "sound of the genuine" in all things.

I don't know how bad things will have to get to bring us to ourselves, to help us hit bottom and experience a spiritually and culturally transformative humility. I don't know if Stage One fundamentalists will stage a temporary resurgence, dragging us all back into authoritarian religious or political regimes. And I don't know, if we regress into patriarchal authoritarianism, whether we will ever leave it, because over the last five hundred years, we have exploited the earth's resources so drastically that we won't get a simple second chance.

I don't know if Stage Two pragmatists will manage to desperately hang on, promising us techno-optimist salvation plans or shortcutting our need for spiritual growth with some clever engineering—whether of the planet, our own genome, or both.* I don't know if those shortcuts will simply forestall our moral and spiritual reckoning, or if they will prove dead ends that leave us dead in the end.

I don't know if Stage Three relativists will succeed in undermining confidence in traditional institutions but then leave us stranded, paralyzed, polarized, jaded, and incapable of coming together in concerted, constructive action.

I don't know if we will get another chance if we fail the test of this moment and collapse at the crossroads. Once more, recalling Dr. King, "We are now faced with the fact that tomorrow is today. We are confronted with the fierce urgency of now. In this unfolding conundrum of life and history, there *is* such a thing as being too late. This is no time for apathy or complacency. This is a time for vigorous and positive action."†

There's a lot that I don't know.

But I am confident of this: each time one of us leans through Perplexity and emerges into Harmony, our global civilization tips one human closer to having a habit of the heart that will help us survive and even thrive as never before. Each time one of us lets simple faith grow into complex faith, and then lets that complex faith die in perplexity and doubt, and then lets it be reborn as faith expressing itself in love, we are one human closer to a tipping point of hope for our species. Each time a faith community faces the chaos of letting go of faith expressing itself in beliefs and leans into, through, and beyond doubt into faith expressing itself in love, we are one community closer to avoiding self-destruction and surviving as a species.

Perhaps we are turning a corner. Perhaps we are coming to a place where we can see that faith may indeed be necessary for our survival. Not faith before doubt, of course. Not the faith that expresses itself in beliefs and stops there, the faith that is easily manipulated by demagogues and con artists, the competitive, winner-take-all faith that wants our in-group to triumph and says to hell with the losers and unbelievers.

---

* Although I am interested in all kinds of scientific advances, I am not a techno-optimist. I am suspicious of any shortcut intended to help us avoid our inner spiritual work.

† Dr. King used the phrase "fierce urgency of now" on at least two occasions: first, in his "I Have a Dream" speech on August 28, 1963, and second, in his "Beyond Vietnam" sermon on April 4, 1967. This quotation comes from that sermon, delivered at Riverside Church in New York City, and available here: http://inside.sfuhs.org/dept/history/US_History_reader/Chapter14 /MLKriverside.htm.

Perhaps we are coming to a place where we see the survival value and even the survival necessity of Stage Four faith. Faith after (and with) doubt. The faith of harmony, integration, connection, solidarity, wisdom, contemplative action, and moral intelligence. The faith whose fruits are not hostility but love, not anxiety but joy, not win-lose competition but peace, not panic or apathy but patience and persistence, not judgment but kindness, not greed but generosity and goodness, not betrayal but faithfulness, not self-centeredness but self-control. Faith that expresses itself in love.

I can't help but think that this message of faith expressing itself in love has been the goal toward which the Bible has been pointing all along. For example, I see it in the words of the Hebrew prophet Habakkuk, who said, in a time of terror and darkness, "The just shall live by faith" (or perhaps, better translated, "The just shall survive by faith").

I see this same message in the words of Jesus, when he said that with faith, we can move mountains, meaning that with faith, we can transform the most intractable elements of the human landscape from violence and fear toward wisdom and love. I see it in Jesus' words about having faith like a child—not the proud and rigid know-it-all arrogance of the religious gatekeepers but the flexible and humble faith of the curious and inquisitive.

I see the same theme when Jesus says we need faith like a grain of mustard seed, a faith that is measured not by its hefty belief content but by its amazing growth capacity. I see it in the miracle stories, when Jesus doesn't say, "I have saved (or healed or liberated) you," or even "My faith has saved (or healed or liberated) you," but rather "*your* faith has saved (or healed or liberated) you." I see it when Jesus teaches that we need, not a rigid wineskin of required beliefs, but an expansive, flexible, and dynamic faith, full of ferment and foment like new wine.

I see this theme unfolding in Paul's magnum opus, Epistle to the Romans, when he celebrated Abraham, not for the perfection of his beliefs, but for the compelling power of his deep faith, faith that persisted "against all hope," faith that resulted in new fertility, new birth, and new promise for all nations of the earth. I see it in 1 Corinthians 13, when Paul contrasted immaturity with maturity, and equated maturity with the realization that love matters most. Now that I've seen this theme of the primacy of love, I see it budding and blooming everywhere, and I can't unsee it.

Perhaps the dynamics of faith and doubt are only a personal matter, with great import to you and me as individuals. That would be enough. But perhaps whenever individuals like you and me move forward in love, the center of gravity of human civilization is shifted a little more toward love too. Then, each new child born into human culture has a slightly more loving starting point and they can throw the weight of their lives even farther in the direction of love. If that's a possibility, then perhaps Pierre Teilhard de Chardin was right when he said, "There is something afoot in the universe, something that looks like gestation and birth." "Above all," he said,

> trust in the slow work of God. We are quite naturally impatient in everything to reach the end without delay. We would like to skip the intermediate stages. We are impatient of being on the way to something unknown, something new. And yet, it is the law of all progress that it is made by passing through some stages of instability—and that it may take a very long time.

I fear that we don't have a very long time, given the dynamics that are in play in our world today.

But I trust, as we strain for what lies ahead, as we lean forward and press onward, through the basic work of Simplicity, through the dynamic work of Complexity, through the tumultuous but essential work of Perplexity, and into the unfolding work of Harmony, we will discover something unknown, something new (and profoundly original), something good and truly fine, indeed.

Like Rob, we wake up each day in a world of wonders rather than a world of answers. Like Hannah, we wake up each day with a passionate mission to love what's left with the time we have left. With more of us experiencing this kind of awakening, our civilization in doubt may stumble its way into Harmony, three steps forward and two steps back, and discover that it was lured, led, beckoned, and guided all along . . . not by the invisible hand of the market, which values all things by the measure of money, but by the invisible hand of love.

For several years, I've been following an online community called La Conversación en Curso, a space for Latin American Christians to process doubt and rethink faith in their context.* The community is led

---

* See https://laconversacionencurso.org/. See also my discussion of silence, music, and faith in *Naked Spirituality* (HarperOne, 2011), Chapter 26.

by Dani Aramayo and Roberto Sanchez Valin. Dani is a musician, and he frequently says, *"La duda es a la fe lo que el silencio es a la música,"* or "Doubt is to faith what silence is to music." What would music be without the pregnant silence before the first note and after the last, as the stage upon which all music dances? What would music be without the rest, without syncopated rhythm, without time to take a breath between melodic lines—all of which require an interruption of silence? Without the space created by silence, there could be no music, and especially no new music, because it's only when the old songs fade that new songs can be imagined and sung. As a musician, Dani understands: what seems like a negation is actually a necessity.

For a new song of faith to sing in you and in us, the silence of doubt is golden.

Reflection and Action

1. How did you relate to Rob's and Hannah's stories?
2. Why do you think I included at some length Hannah's thoughts on the destructive power of money?
3. Describe the idea of *ontogeny recapitulates phylogeny* (or the development of the individual mirrors the development of the whole).
4. Connect pre-modern, modern, and postmodern as civilizational descriptors to Simplicity, Complexity, and Perplexity.
5. I describe how the biblical prophets combine protest or critique with imagination. In that spirit, use your imagination to describe what a civilization in Harmony might look like.
6. What do you take away from my description of the friendship between Thomas Merton and the Dalai Lama?
7. What line, image, or idea from Howard Thurman most strikes you?
8. I suggest that Harmony has been core to the biblical message all along. Reflect further on one of the passages I mention, or bring in one of your own.

You're Not Crazy
and You're Not Alone

> Those who believe they believe in God, but without passion in the
> heart, without anguish of mind, without uncertainty, without doubt,
> and even at times without despair, believe only in the idea of God, and
> not in God himself.
>
> —Miguel de Unamuno

Before doubt, I thought that faith was a matter of correct beliefs. My
religious teachers taught me so: that if I didn't hold the right beliefs, or
at least say that I held them, I would be excommunicated from my community, and perhaps, after death, from God's presence. They taught me
this not to be cruel but because they themselves had been taught the same
thing, and they were working hard, sometimes desperately, to be faithful
to the rules as they understood them. I tried to do the same, and I would
still be doing so today if not for doubt.

Doubt chipped away at those beliefs, one agonizing blow at a time,
revealing that what actually mattered wasn't the paint of beliefs but the
clear window of faith, faith as a life orientation, faith as a framework of
values and spirituality, faith as a commitment to live into a deep vision of
what life can be, faith as a way of life, faith expressing itself in love.

For all those years, when I said, "I believe," I thought I understood
what I was doing. But more was going on, so much more.

Cradled in the snug nest of my faith community, inside the brittle
shell of beliefs, faith was quietly incubating. The cracking open of my
beliefs was not the destruction of faith but its liberation into a new tender
stage, a new fledgling consciousness, a new freedom to stretch my wings

and fly. Looking back, I now see that underneath arguments about what I believed to be true *factually*, something deeper and truer was happening *actually*.

For example, whether or not the creation story happened *factually* as described in Genesis, I was committing myself to live in the world as if it *actually* were a precious, beautiful, meaningful creation, and as if I were too.

Whether or not there was a *factual* tree in a *factual* garden with a *factual* talking snake, I was committing myself to *actually* live in the world aware that I have good and just limits that I should not exceed, no matter how tempting the fruit of power, pleasure, profit, or pride.

Whether or not the Exodus story *factually* happened in history, I was committing to live in the world as if I, and all my fellow humans, were *actually* on a journey from oppression to liberation.

Whether or not Jesus was *factually* born of a literal virgin, or walked on literal water, or multiplied literal bread, I was committing myself to live in the world as if what seems humanly impossible may *actually* become possible if we dare to live generously, against all odds.

What mattered most was not that I *believed* the stories in a factual sense, but that I *believed in* the meaning they carried so I could act upon that meaning and embody it in my life, to let that meaning breathe in me, animate me, fill me. The meaning was the hidden treasure, the hidden pearl, the spirit of the story hidden in its letters and words and punctuation.* Whether I considered the stories factually accurate was never the point; what actually mattered all along was whether I lived a life pregnant with the meaning those stories contained. To my surprise, when I was given permission to doubt the factuality of my beliefs, I discovered their actual life-giving purpose.

Looking back on my dance with belief and doubt, I do have regrets,

---

* This is a likely meaning of John 6:63, where Jesus says, "It is the spirit that gives life; the flesh is useless. The words that I have spoken to you are spirit and life." Paul makes a similar statement in 2 Corinthians 3:6, where he identifies himself as a minister "of a new covenant, not of letter but of spirit; for the letter kills, but the spirit gives life." In both of these passages, Christian translators often capitalize *spirit* to indicate the Holy Spirit. However, I think *spirit* most naturally refers here to *breath* (*pneuma* in Greek, *ruach* in Hebrew). In this sense, life-giving meaning inhabits or indwells a text or story just as life-breath inhabits a body, and without it, the story is at best useless, and at worst deadly. What matters is the literary meaning that enlivens the message, not its literal factuality.

at least a few. I regret all the energy I invested in perfecting beliefs, promoting them, defending them, and imposing them on others. I regret how I used my beliefs as a yardstick to measure, judge, accept, and reject others, and myself. I regret how much deference I showed to belief-police and doctrinal gatekeepers who were more like prison guards than good shepherds. My regrets fuel this hope: that future generations will learn to guide people beyond obsession with beliefs and into faith, faith that breathes meaning into life.

In spite of these regrets, I do not regret my journey of faith and doubt, because I do not regret who I have become. Faith and doubt together have made me who I am. I wouldn't want to live without either.

When I began my descent into doubt nearly fifty years ago, I felt utterly alone. Almost nobody talked about doubt; it was like confessing to a crime. Books on the subject aimed to lay doubts to rest as quickly and decisively as possible. Good Christians (and, I'm sure, good people of other religions) were expected, quickly and privately, to mend their doubts like an embarrassing tear in their pants and, failing that, to silence and suppress their doubts, to fake confidence and certainty in desperate hope that the next sermon, hymn, praise song, conference, book, or prayer would be the silver bullet that would vanquish doubt forever.

We doubters learned that it's hard enough to go through doubt, and even harder to do so in secret and alone, and harder still to do so while having to pretend you're not doubting at all.

But thankfully, the times are changing. First, a few pioneers "came out of the closet" as questioners and doubters.* Then a few more. Their courage created space for others.

One of those pioneers was my friend and colleague Rachel Held Evans. When I was first writing about her in the Preface, she was vital, alive, full of plans. When I was working on an early draft of the previous chapter, she died suddenly of complications from the flu and infection. She was only thirty-seven, the same age as my oldest daughter of the same first name, and she died on the morning of my sixty-third birthday. Rachel was widely known and deeply loved as a writer whose work explored "faith, doubt, and life in the Bible Belt."†

---

* See Appendix IV for some recommended resources on doubt.
† See https://rachelheldevans.com/about.

As I grieved, I went through my email archives and re-lived our interactions. I hadn't yet heard of her when she emailed me for the first time
in 2009:

> Hi, Brian. I'm a fellow author and a big fan of your writing. Just wanted
> to let you know that I'll be at the conference next week in Chattanooga
> and will probably flag you down at some point to get you to sign a book
> or two! :-) It's exciting to have such a progressive conference in this part
> of the country, and I appreciate you stopping by the Bible Belt. I'll be
> driving down each day from my hometown of Dayton, Tennessee—
> home of the Scopes Monkey Trial of 1925! Looking forward to your
> presentation in the Scenic City. Let me know if you need any restaurant
> recommendations, or if you want to take a tour of Monkey Town!

We met at the conference, got lunch at a local taco place, and immediately became friends. After the conference, she sent me an encouraging
note.* In the years that followed, more and more of our communication
involved me sending her encouraging notes, because Rachel dared to
speak freely and without apology to a new generation about her questions and doubts, always with piercing clarity and resilient grace. Her
reputation and influence quickly and deservedly grew, in large part because of her courageous vulnerability, which she conveyed with bold yet
tender honesty, as in this 2014 blog post entitled "I Don't Always Tell
You":

> I don't always tell you about the mornings I wake up and feel the
> absence of God as though it were a presence—thick and certain, re-
> membered all over again the way you remember in the morning that
> someone you love has died.

---

* Her note read, in part, "It was a real pleasure spending time with you this week, Brian. Thank
you so much for your interest and encouragement regarding my book; it really meant a lot to
me. I can't tell you how often I hear your name when people are describing major turning points
in their faith journey. Many of us were ready to give up on Christianity altogether when we first
encountered your work, and you helped us re-imagine our faith in a way that not only preserved
it, but enlivened it. I think that's why so many of us feel like we already know you. You have
been like a pastor to us . . . when we needed one the most. Enjoyed our talk at Taco Mac. I left
thinking about how it seems like people who believe that God himself loves his enemies are
remarkably prone to loving theirs too."

. . . I don't always tell you about how sometimes I'm not sure I want to bring kids into a world like this one, a world so full of suffering.

. . . What do you do when the religion that is supposed to give you comfort and direction is the cause of your pain and confusion?

What do you do when religious people respond to your questions by calling you names? By mocking you? By casting you out?

I don't always tell you about the depth of my doubt.

I don't always tell you about how the cynicism settles in, like a diaphanous fog.

Or about how sometimes, just the thought of reading one more Christian book I only half believe exhausts and bores me.

. . . Sometimes it frightens me, how effortlessly I can move from belief to unbelief as one would move from room to room.

. . . I don't always tell you, because when a reader says, "I love it when you write something VULNERABLE!" I wonder if she really means it, if she really wants to know that the demon whose voice she thinks she's quieted in her own heart is screaming like hell in mine, and that the scariest thing about being VULNERABLE, about exposing myself to the world without a religion or a platform or a "brand" for protection, is that I might lose them for good . . . or, perhaps, learn that I can breathe without them.

And that's not exactly the sort of born again experience the publishers pay for.*

Once, when a well-known preacher tried to reduce doubt to a cover-up for sexual shame ("You're doubting because you slept with someone you shouldn't have"), Rachel firmly but graciously took him to task:

As I've written before, the doubts I wrestled with most profoundly as a young adult were doubts related to salvation and religious pluralism. Those doubts often took the form of a single question in my mind: "Did Anne Frank go to hell?"

I cannot think of a more trite, inappropriate response to that question than, "Tell me who you're sleeping with." . . . As I've said on

---

* See "I Don't Always Tell You," rachelheldevans.com, July 28, 2014, https://rachelheldevans.com /blog/i-dont-always-tell-you?rq=doubt.

multiple occasions, most young adults I know aren't looking for a religion that answers all of their questions, but rather a community of faith in which they feel safe to ask them. A good place to start in creating such a community is to treat young adults like the complex human beings they are, and to take their questions about faith seriously.*

Rachel had a knack for capturing the heart of an issue in a simple sentence, like this one, for example: "I remain convinced that serious doubt, the kind that leads to despair, does not begin when we start asking God questions, but when out of fear, we stop."† Or this one (echoing another gifted writer on the topic of faith and doubt, Kathy Escobar): "[F]or all the people who come up to me at book signings with tears streaming down their faces because they feel so isolated in their journey through questions and doubt, I am thrilled that I can say . . . 'you're not crazy, and you're not alone.'"‡

Rachel was hailed in the *New York Times* as "the voice of the wandering Evangelical," a woman who evolved "to a faith that left room for doubt" and helped "thousands to question, find safety in their doubts and learn to believe in new ways."§ Elsewhere she was described as a "doubt-filled prophet," and although I think she may have quarreled with the word "prophet," she was not ashamed of her doubts.¶

Many of us noted that Rachel's last blog post addressed the subject of death and concluded with the words, "you are not alone. Ashes to ashes, dust to dust."

---

* "Is Doubt an STD?," rachelheldevans.com, April 12, 2013, https://rachelheldevans.com/blog/doubt-std-keller/. When readers felt she had been too hard on this well-known preacher, she responded with characteristic clarity, graciousness, and humility: "Some Helpful Critiques of Friday's Post ('Is Doubt an STD?'), rachelheldevans.com, April 14, 2013, https://rachelheldevans.com/blog/some-helpful-critiques-of-yesterdays-post-is-doubt-an-std/.

† See "Embracing Doubt," rachelheldevans.com, January 29, 2010, https://rachelheldevans.com/blog/embracing-doubt/.

‡ From Rachel's review of *Faith Shift* (Convergent, 2014) by Kathy Escobar, "You're Not Crazy, and You're Not Alone," rachelheldevans.com, November 12, 2014, https://rachelheldevans.com/blog/faith-shift-review/. Also of interest to people in Perplexity and Harmony, see Kathy Escobar's helpful *Practicing: Changing Yourself to Change the World* (Knox, 2020).

§ See Elizabeth Dias and Sam Roberts, "Rachel Held Evans, Voice of the Wandering Evangelical, Dies at 37," *New York Times*, May 4, 2019, https://www.nytimes.com/2019/05/04/us/rachel-held-evans.html.

¶ See Megan Briggs, "Rachel Held Evans, the Doubt-Filled Prophet, Has Died," churchleaders.com, May 5, 2019, https://churchleaders.com/news/349949-rachel-held-evans-doubt-filled-prophet-died.html/2.

Doubt, many of us know, can feel a lot like death.

I imagine a baby who has been comfortably protected in a mother's womb for nine months. I imagine how that first contraction interrupts her world. The pressure must be terrifying. Then, more and more waves of pressure come, and then, the fresh, fragile life feels she is being torn from life itself. She finds herself unable to resist as she is squeezed with agonizing pressure through a suffocatingly tight passage that feels like the end, like annihilation. Then, when it seems like her situation couldn't get any worse, she finds herself expelled into cold, dry, foreign emptiness rather than warm, familiar waters. She feels terrified by unintelligible lights that pierce the comforting, all-enveloping darkness she has always known. Noise surrounds her, harsh and uninterpretable sounds that are so different from the gentle pulse of her mother's heartbeat. She feels the need to do something she has never done before, to breathe. No wonder her first breath becomes a cry.

Birth to an infant surely feels like a cruel end to life as she has known it. It is surely the worst thing that has ever happened in her entire nine-month gestation.

But the worst things can be the doorway to the best things. Milk. A tender kiss. A warm blanket in even warmer arms. A smiling face full of bottomless acceptance and adoration. Outside the window, a robin sings and the wind whispers of a whole new world to explore, and beyond that, uncountable stars.

Doubt need not be the death of faith. It can be, instead, the birth of a new kind of faith, a faith beyond beliefs, a faith that expresses itself in love, a deepening and expanding faith that can save your life and save the world.

I cannot prove it. I do not know it with bombproof certainty. But this is my faith, for you, for me, for all creatures great and small. Like Rob in the previous chapter, I find myself saying, "Well, I'm still alive now. And right now. And right now. That's a pretty wonderful thing. A gift. A wonder. A surprise." And like Hannah, I find myself loving what's left with all the time I have left. Like Rachel and growing numbers of "faith after doubters" every day, I feel I can exhale and breathe free because I don't have to hide my doubts or fear them.

As I wrote this book, not only did I grieve the unexpected death of

Rachel Held Evans, a sister in faith after doubt, but I also accompanied my mother through her last months of life on earth. She was ninety-two and lived a good, long life, full of faith and, to all appearances, virtually untouched by doubt.

For the last five years, she was a widow, and in her last few years of widowhood, dementia slowly but surely stole her capacities. For a while, she took pride in using her computer and staying in touch with others through email, until one day, she forgot how to use her computer and never seemed to miss it. Later, the same thing happened with her phone. For a few months, she lost interest in eating; she just forgot how to feel hungry. Near the end, she became too frail to walk but couldn't remember that she couldn't walk, and so she suffered a series of falls. Her frailty and dependence created a new tenderness between us, reversing roles from my childhood when she fed me, changed me, bathed me, combed my hair, read to me, and helped me feel safe in a vast, fast, and scary world. Through it all, her simple faith remained sincere, pure, unwavering.

In some of my very earliest childhood memories, I am sitting in a classroom in a chair too big for me, my legs swinging far from the floor. My mom is teaching a Bible class to a group of older children using a felt board and flannel-backed figures. In one scene, Jesus sits under a tree, surrounded by children who are, in the terms of an old Sunday school song, "red and yellow, black and white." In another scene, Jesus holds a single stray sheep he has just retrieved, surrounded by the flock of ninety-nine to which it is being returned. In another scene, Jesus sits on a rock on a hillside, his disciples standing around him, listening to him teach. In scene after scene, Jesus is the central figure: calling Lazarus out of the tomb, standing between a woman and some men who want to kill her by stoning, healing a paralytic who has just been lowered through a deconstructed roof, hanging on a cross with Roman soldiers gathered around him, talking to Mary Magdalene outside an empty tomb.

In the terms I use here, my mother seldom ventured into Complexity and, as far as I could tell, never into Perplexity. Simplicity was her lifelong spiritual home, and since the perimeter of that space was not terribly broad or wide, she went deep, not necessarily through intellect but through intuition and emotion. Because Jesus and his love were so central to her, in the deepest heart of her Simplicity, she discovered a bottomless well of love. That love became for her the "sound of the genuine," and as a result, she developed a spirituality that transcended her stated theology.

When dementia drained away her desire to attend the church service offered at her assisted living facility, love remained. When dementia sapped her enjoyment of reading—including reading her beloved leather-bound large-print Bible—love remained. When dementia erased a few more of her memories every day until my brother and I held more of her story than she did, even then, love remained. It was a simple love, a pure, deep love, and in the end, it revealed itself as the realest, most durable, and most striking thing about her beautiful, long, generous life.

One of her sisters also experienced dementia in her final years. I remember visiting my aunt about a year before her death. Her companion/caretaker welcomed me in and then my aunt showed me around her home, stopping to tell me one by one about the people in photographs above her fireplace. She pointed to my mother, having no idea that I already knew who she was. "That's my sister. I can't remember her name, but she was married to a doctor and she had two cute little boys." A few minutes later, we sat on her couch and she looked at me with the warmest smile and said, "I am so glad you have come to visit me, dear, but I just can't remember who you are!"

I saw that same primal love in my mother's eyes in her final months. It was love that didn't depend on who *the other* was, because it reflected who *she* was. (I know that dementia is much more vicious to many people than it was to my mother and her sister, taking the parts of their brains that make love even possible, and this is no fault of theirs.)

Age, frailty, and dementia took one capacity after another from my mother, until eventually, love was all she had left. Could that be her final message to the world, her final gift to her son, a doubting believer?

People often ask me what my parents thought of my books. I know they read some of them cover to cover, but others, I don't think so. Because their faith remained largely in the zones of Simplicity and Complexity, I think they felt I was prescribing medicine for conditions they didn't suffer from. (My dad was a doctor, so the metaphor seems apt.) They winced whenever my work (or my character) was the target of a hostile review or editorial in a religious magazine they subscribed to, but they never once asked me to back down. And I think I know why: they understood that even if doubt wasn't a problem for them personally, it was a problem for others. That made it a problem they cared about because they cared for others. I think more and more people who do not struggle with doubt are coming to realize this, as their congregations "shrink and wrinkle." If they keep driving doubters away, especially young doubters, they will soon be sitting in an otherwise empty building. The reality of doubt is a problem that directly or indirectly affects all of us, doubters and non-doubters, so the gains and losses of doubt touch everyone.

As I re-read a late draft of this manuscript, a new realization came to me. I came to see that the greatest loss I experienced through doubt was the loss of supremacy, and that loss was one of my greatest gains. (By *greatest* I mean the loss that was deepest, most significant, most subtle, and most wonderful.) The beliefs I held so piously had, for all my life, without my consent or even awareness, contributed to a sense of religious privilege, superiority, and supremacy. Those beliefs deserved to be doubted, and if I had not doubted them, that supremacy would still reign as a covert monarch in my psyche.

The process of doubt not only dethroned that sense of religious supremacy; it took away the taste for supremacy of any kind. On this side of Perplexity, I don't want to be better than anyone. I don't want to win in any way that makes others lose. I even wince a little whenever I speak of the four stages, because I know that some people will interpret them in a way that makes Stage Four supreme, and that thought repulses me. Harmony is, at its heart, a state and stage that loves solidarity, not supremacy. If it took the agony of doubt to bring me to this place, then thanks be to God, and blessed be doubt.

I imagine you feel the same way. The more we hear the sound of the genuine, the more the deepest habits of our hearts are renovated and remodeled in the way of love, and the more supremacy loses its appeal. Faith after doubt is faith after supremacy. Instead of standing over others as judges or ruling over others as commanders, we want to join with one another in the circle dance of love and joy. Instead of winning over others and using them in our schemes for profit and prestige, we want to feast with them at a round table as siblings. Instead of analyzing others, showing their logical inconsistencies and exposing their hidden agendas, we want to join with them as co-creators of a better world and a new day, as part of the community of all creation. We gladly trade supremacy for solidarity.

The road to faith after doubt is often lonely. But beyond the loneliness, you discover a place of solidarity where everything is sacred and everything belongs, including your doubts and including you. This replacement of supremacy with solidarity, I imagine, involves an actual rewiring or re-patterning of our brains.

You'll remember that way back in Chapter 2, I offered a simple description of the human brain, using the metaphor of a three-member committee. We begin life with our instinctive brain, our oldest, fastest, and most highly developed committee member, geared toward survival, safety, and pleasure. Then we emerge into our intuitive brain, that great facilitator of relationships and belonging. Then, our intellectual brain comes online, specializing in independent analytical thought, in forming beliefs and opinions, and in discerning meaning. As we grow, to one degree or another, we learn to integrate these three modules or members of the brain committee into one whole person.

In some of us, survival and pleasure predominate. In some, relationships and belonging predominate. In some, beliefs and opinions predominate. But as we mature, some of us, like Rachel, like my mother, create a whole-brained, whole-hearted, whole-self integration in which love infuses the whole, integrating instinct, intuition, and intellect in the service of the common good. You might say we lean into Harmony or we practice Harmony, even though we may be currently centered in Simplicity, Complexity, or Perplexity. And how do we do it? We let our supremacy wiring be deconstructed, and we rewire our brains for solidarity.

We surrender the supremacy of our ego, our self-centered demands for power, pleasure, prestige, prominence. We surrender the supremacy of our group, whether that group is defined by religion, race, politics, nationality, economic class, social status, or whatever. We even surrender the supremacy of our species, realizing that humans can't survive and thrive unless the plankton and trees, the soil and bees, and the climate and seas thrive too. We gladly shed supremacy to make room for solidarity. That gain, we discover, is worth every cost.

Faith after doubt, we might say, means living beyond supremacy. For all of the problems with traditional beliefs, at least they told us that there is a supreme being, and we are not It. In other words, at their best, those beliefs humbled us and tried to dethrone us from our individual supremacy, teaching us that life isn't about *me* and life is bigger than my little personal agenda. Sadly, though, those same beliefs too often kept supremacy alive for us on a bigger scale. Our religious communities began speaking humbly to God, and then they spoke boldly about God, and then they spoke proudly for God, until too often they spoke arrogantly as if they were God. Our gods became our mascots and symbolized the supremacy of our race, nation, tribe, or religion.

Doubt, we might say, can liberate us from these supremacist projections. It is our way of deconstructing a foolish, ego-driven faith and preparing the way for a meaningful life—and a life-giving faith—beyond supremacy.

As we release our desperate grasp on supremacy, as the desire to dominate slips through our fingers, something in us dies. Much is lost or forgotten, deemed not worth remembering. But in the letting go, something new comes, is born, begins, grows: a sense of connection, of not-aloneness, of communion and union and belonging. We descend from the ladders and pedestals we have erected, and we rejoin the community of creation, the network of shalom, the ecosystem of harmony. The loss is no small thing, ah, but the gain is incomparably greater.

In that spirit of solidarity, I conclude this book with three benedictions to you, wherever you are on your journey through faith and doubt into deeper, wider, wilder faith. The first is adapted slightly from a poem by Rainer Maria Rilke.*

> *God speaks to each of us as God makes us,*
> *then walks with us silently out of the night.*
> *These are the words we dimly hear:*
> *You, sent out beyond your recall,*
> *go to the limits of your longing.*
> *Embody me.*
> *Flare up like a flame*
> *and make big shadows I can move in.*

---

* From Rilke's *Book of Hours: Love Poems to God*, translated from the German by Anita Barrows and Joanna Macy (Riverhead, 2005), Poem I 59. I replaced the male pronoun "he" with "God."

Let everything happen to you: beauty and terror.
Just keep going. No feeling is final.
Don't let yourself lose me.
Nearby is the country they call life.
You will know it by its seriousness.
Give me your hand.

The second benediction comes from my friend Rev. Kathi McShane, an exceptional Methodist minister in California. In these words adapted from William Sloane Coffin, she invites us to bring all of ourselves, all our capacities of mind, heart, and body, and instead of selling ourselves (and God) short, to risk "something big for something good." Whatever faith after doubt is, it is not simply a set of disembodied opinions or beliefs (or denials of opinions and beliefs). In dangerous times on a small planet, faith after doubt is an embodied, whole-self commitment to "flare up like a flame" (as Rilke said), to let our hearts be set on fire by the truth and love of a Mystery bigger than we can ever fully grasp.*

May God bless you, keep you, be gracious to you.
May God give you grace never to sell yourself—or God—short.
Grace to risk something big for something good.
Grace to remember that the world is now too dangerous for anything
    but truth,
And too small for anything but love.
So may God take your mind and think through it.
May God take your lips and speak through them.
May God take your hands and do good with them.
May God take your heart and set it on fire.

Finally, I offer this simple benediction, modeled on the beatitudes, to remind you that your honest doubts are not a curse but, rather, a blessing indeed:

Blessed are the curious, for their curiosity honors reality.

---

* For Coffin's original benediction, see https://www.baptiststandard.com/opinion/editorials/editorial-risk-something-big-for-something-good/.

Blessed are the uncertain and those with second thoughts, for their
minds are still open.

Blessed are the wonderers, for they shall find what is wonderful.

Blessed are those who question their answers, for their horizons will
expand forever.

Blessed are those who often feel foolish, for they are wiser than those
who always think themselves wise.

Blessed are those who are scolded, suspected, and labeled as heretics
by the gatekeepers, for the prophets and mystics were treated in the
same way by the gatekeepers of their day.

Blessed are those who know their unknowing, for they shall have the
last laugh.

Blessed are the perplexed, for they have reached the frontiers of
contemplation.

Blessed are they who become cynical about their cynicism and suspi-
cious of their suspicion, for they will enter the second innocence.

Blessed are the doubters, for they shall see through false gods.

Blessed are the lovers, for they shall see God everywhere.

Reflection and Action

1. In this chapter, I recall the lives of two people I loved who died as this book was being written. Reflect on key people who have positively influenced your journey of faith and doubt.

2. Discuss the role of supremacy and solidarity in your life and in our civilization at large.

3. Respond to this sentence: "We doubters learned that it's hard enough to go through doubt, and even harder to do so in secret and alone, and harder still to do so while having to pretend you're not doubting at all."

4. Respond to this sentence as well: "I came to see that the greatest loss I experienced through doubt was the loss of supremacy."

5. How do you feel about the choice of the Rilke poem as the first of three benedictions that end this book? What lines or images from the poem most speak to you now, and why? Respond from your heart to the final line of the poem: "Give me your hand."

6. Similarly, respond to the McShane/Coffin benediction and the "doubters' beatitudes." Feel free to acknowledge anything that is problematic for you. Then affirm what you most need to hear.
7. Briefly skim back over this whole book. What is one big (or small) idea and one deep (or simple) feeling that you will take with you from this book? What ideas or insights might you want to share with others? To whom might you recommend this book, and why?

Acknowledgments

As always, I am deeply grateful to my life partner, friend, and co-parent/grandparent, Grace (Gagliardo) McLaren. For over forty of our sixty-four years, we have been companions on these paths of faith after (and with) doubt. I am also deeply grateful to our children, Rachel, Brett, Trevor, and Jodi, and to their partners and children. It has been said that we raise our children for eighteen years, and they raise us for the rest of our lives, and my experience bears that out. My faith journey has been enriched beyond words by their experiences, questions, challenges, and insights.

Special thanks to my literary agent Roger Freet for introducing me to Elisabeth Dyssegaard, my editor at St. Martin's Essentials. I am so grateful to be working with you both!

Finally, thanks to all the people whose stories are reflected in these pages, directly and indirectly. Your conversations over coffee, a walk, phone, or email have led me into insights I never would have had sitting alone at my desk, and your openness about your doubts has helped me to engage my own. We are in this together.

Appendix I. The Four Stages of Faith

	SIMPLICITY	COMPLEXITY	PERPLEXITY	HARMONY
PERCEPTION	Dualistic	Pragmatic	Critical/ Relativistic	Integral/ Holistic
FOCUS	Right or wrong	Success or failure	Honest/ authentic experience or dishonest/ inauthentic experience	Inclusion and transcendence
MOTIVE	Pleasing authority figures, being right (or considered right)	Achieving goals, being successful (or considered successful)	Seeing through appearances to reality, being honest, authentic, true to myself	Finding connec- tion, seeing things whole, making contribution
KEY VALUES	Being right/ clean/good, obeying authorities, staying faithful to tradition, re- maining loyal to in-group	Being free and independent, winning, succeeding, achieving goals	Being fair, acknowledg- ing bias and mistakes, facing inconvenient truths	Being compassion- ate, seeking common good
ASSUMPTION	Everything is known or knowable	Everything is doable or possible	Everyone has an opinion; every view- point is a view from a point	We are all connected, part of a greater whole
AUTHORITY FIGURES	Leaders who know and teach the right answers, God-like	Coaches who can help me succeed	Manipulators who control the naive and trusting	Fallible people like you and me
US/THEM	Good/Evil	Winners/ Losers	Honest/ Dishonest	Part of a Bigger Us

	SIMPLICITY	COMPLEXITY	PERPLEXITY	HARMONY
LIFE IS . . .	A war	A game	A joke, a quest, and/or a deception	A mysterious gift
IDENTITY	Dependent or co-dependent	Increasingly independent	Counter-dependent	Interdependent
BELONGING	I am part of the good, right, and true group	I am part of the success-ful, effective, and winning team	I am one of the honest, thoughtful, and independent individuals	I am seeking understand-ing, connection, and the common good, even with opponents and enemies
GOD IS . . .	Supreme Be-ing, almighty protector, warrior, law-giver, patron, patriarch	Encourager and guide who can help me prosper and succeed	Myth or a mystery	Loving presence, creative wis-dom, known through experience and metaphor
CORE QUESTION	What do our authority figures say?	What are the steps to success?	What is the hidden agenda or bias I need to be suspicious of?	What part can I play for the common good?
MISTAKES ARE . . .	Legal infrac-tions, moral failures, disobedience to authorities, ignorance of the rules	Lack of com-mitment, preparedness, effort, or positive attitude	Failure to question, challenge, think critically	Inevitable, part of learning and growth
STRENGTHS	Highly committed, willingness to sacrifice	Enthusiasm, eagerness to learn, ideal-ism, action	Honesty, curiosity, critical thinking	Integrates previous strengths, with greater depth and wider circle of compassion

	SIMPLICITY	COMPLEXITY	PERPLEXITY	HARMONY
WEAKNESSES	Narrow-minded, judgmental, combative, willing to inflict suffering, false certainty	Superficial, naive, overly pragmatic, excessive confidence	Aloof, uncommitted, cynical, suspicious, elitist, depressed	Susceptible to previous weaknesses
GOOD NEWS	Wrongs can be forgiven	Help is available	You are encouraged to question and challenge the status quo	Everything belongs, all are connected, all life is sacred
ATTITUDE TOWARD DOUBT	Doubt is a failure, weakness, defection, betrayal, or sin	Doubt is a problem to be solved or sickness to be cured	Doubt is a virtue to be cultivated	Doubt is a necessary part of life, a portal from one stage to another
FAITH IS . . .	Assent to required beliefs	Means to desired ends	An obstacle to critical thinking	A humble, reverent openness to mystery that expresses itself in non-discriminatory love

Appendix II.
Before Simplicity: Stage Zero

For people in later stages, what appears as Stage One arrogance can be annoying. But in that apparent arrogance, there is, I think, a grain of truth. Stage One truly is important because all of us are born into Stage Zero. In infancy, we experience life as unconscious and all-controlling egocentricity. Our needs, our problems, our desires are all-consuming for us. We are incapable of caring about the needs of others because we are, for some weeks or months, unaware of our own individual existence, much less theirs. We can't remember it, so it's hard to describe it, but as infants, we are our dirty diaper, our empty belly, our gas pain, our tickle, our chill. This isn't a fault or character flaw; this is simply what it means to be a newborn.

Stage One feels so important because graduating from infancy to Simplicity is so absolutely necessary for every human born. It could be said that our addictions and other dysfunctions sometimes return us as adults to a condition of infancy, where we lose concern for others, where we lose a sense of right and wrong, where our needs or fears or cravings or reactions take over our identity. It may also be that some children are so poorly parented that they grow in age without leaving this stage, perhaps even reaching adulthood with the characteristics described in the following table:

	INFANCY/ EGOCENTRICITY	SIMPLICITY
PERCEPTION	Narcissistic	Dualistic
FOCUS	Survival/comfort	Right or wrong
MOTIVE	Feeling safe, comfortable, happy	Pleasing authority figures
KEY VALUES	Surviving, staying safe, being comfortable	Being right/clean/good, obeying authorities, staying faithful to tradition, remaining loyal to in-group

	INFANCY/ EGOCENTRICITY	SIMPLICITY
ASSUMPTION	I would be happy if others would cooperate	Everything is known or knowable
AUTHORITY FIGURES	My protectors, caregivers, providers	Leaders who know and teach the right answers, God-like
US/THEM	Those who please me/ Those who don't	Good/Evil
LIFE IS . . .	Family, a party	A war
IDENTITY	Undifferentiated/ Presumptive	Dependent or Co-dependent
BELONGING	My mother or parental figure is my universe	I am part of the good, right, and true group
GOD IS . . .	Undifferentiated from parents or caregivers, Candyman, Magic Genie	Supreme Being, almighty protector, warrior, law-giver, patron, patriarch
CORE QUESTION	Am I safe and comfortable? Do I like this? Does this make me feel good or bad?	What do our authority figures say?
MISTAKES ARE . . .	Punishable behaviors	Legal infractions, moral failures, disobedience to authorities, ignorance of the rules
STRENGTHS	Emotionally transparent, aware of my needs and desires, uninhibited, spontaneous	Highly committed, willing to sacrifice
WEAKNESSES	Largely oblivious to the needs and desires of others	Narrow-minded, judgmental, combative, willing to inflict suffering, full of false certainty
GOOD NEWS	I am loved/I am safe	Wrongs can be forgiven
ATTITUDE TOWARD DOUBT	Doubt is inconceivable at this stage	Doubt is a failure, weakness, defection, betrayal, or sin
FAITH IS . . .	Trust in my caregivers (or in my own ability to get what I need by any means necessary)	Assent to required beliefs

In this light, we can see why people centered in Stage One Simplicity feel they are so important. They're right. They are. All newborn children need Stage One people to raise them from infantile egocentricity to Stage One Simplicity. In fact, that's what we mean by *raising* a child. Their mistake, of course, is failing to realize that people in Stages Two, Three, and Four have as much to offer them as they have to offer those in Stage Zero.

We would be wise to remind ourselves that there are better and worse forms of Stage One. Some rules, beliefs, and authority figures are genuinely helpful and others are less helpful or even harmful, abusive, or deadly. Children, of course, have no choice about which form of Simplicity their parents hold, and as they come of age and emerge into later stages, they have the right—and we might even say the responsibility—to think critically about the Stage One framework in which they were raised, even as they are grateful to have been raised out of Stage Zero.

Appendix III.
Integration of Stage Theories

	SIMPLICITY	COMPLEXITY	PERPLEXITY	HARMONY
WILLIAM BLAKE	Innocence	Innocence/Experience	Experience	Higher Innocence
SØREN KIERKEGAARD	Aesthetic	Ethical	Ethical	Religious
WILLIAM PERRY	Dualism a, b	Multiplicity a, b	Relativism a, b	Commitment a, b, and c
MARY BELENKY, BLYTHE CLINCHY, NANCY GOLDBERGER, JILL TARULE	Silence, Received knowledge	Subjective knowledge	Procedural knowledge	Constructed knowledge
JAMES FOWLER	Primal, Mythical/Literal	Synthetic/Conventional	Individual/Reflective	Conjunctive/Universalizing
NICOLA SLEE			Paralysis, awakenings, relationality	Apophatic faithing
JAMES KOHLBERG	Blind egoism, Instrumental egoism	Social relations	Social systems	Contractual, mutual respect
CAROL GILLIGAN	Preconventional, Conventional	Conventional	Postconventional	Postconventional
KEN BLANCHARD	Enthusiastic beginner	Enthusiastic beginner, disillusioned learner	Disillusioned learner, capable but cautious performer	Self-reliant achiever

	SIMPLICITY	COMPLEXITY	PERPLEXITY	HARMONY
PAUL RICOEUR	Precritical/ First naivete	Precritical/ First naivete	Critical	Post-critical/ Second naivete
BAILEY W. JACKSON, III	Naive	Acceptance (active, passive)	Resistance (active, passive)	Redefinition, Internaliza- tion
JEAN KIM	Ethnic awareness	White identification (active, passive)	Awakening to social political consciousness	Redirection, Incorporation
CLAIRE GRAVES, DON BECK, KEN WILBER	Archaic/ Instinctive, Animist/ Tribal, Egocentric/ Exploitive, Absolutist/ Authoritarian	Scientific/ Strategic	Relativistic/ Personalistic/ Communi- tarian	Systemic/ Integral, Holistic
RICHARD ROHR	First half of life	First half of life	Transition/ Crisis/ Midlife/ Great suffering or great love	Second half of life
HINDU ASHRAMA	Student	Householder	Forest Dweller	Wandering Sage
SCOTT PECK	Stage I, Stage II	Stage II	Stage III	Stage IV

APPENDIX IV.
RESOURCES FOR DOUBTERS

Although it's not often celebrated this way, the Protestant Reformation was an adventure in doubt. Before the Protestant faith could be articulated and embraced, Luther, Calvin, Zwingli, Bucer, Simons, and the other reformers had to demonstrate the audacity to doubt the pope, the cardinals, and the Magisterium, standing against the current of Western church tradition and biblical interpretation that had been building for 1,500 years. What the Wittenberg door and the newly invented printing press were to the audacious doubters of the Protestant Reformation, podcasts, websites, books, and events are to the "great emergence" happening today.

PODCASTS

A quick online search will lead to a wide array of resources. (Note: podcasts, like blogs, come and go. These are podcasts I have spoken on or know of personally, and new ones are popping up as old ones go inactive.)

> *Homebrewed Christianity* (and other Tripp Fuller productions), *The Bible for Normal People*, *The Liturgists*, *Ask Science Mike*, *The Zeitcast*, *For the Love!*, *The RobCast*, *Nomad Podcast*, *Another Name for Every Thing*, *Irenicast*, Peter Rollins podcasts (various), *The Growing Edge*, Doug Pagitt podcasts (various), *Prophetic Resistance*, *Progressive Christian Voice*, GracePointe Church, *That's What She Said*, Sermons from St. Gregory of Nyssa in San Francisco, *Thanks Be to Pod*, *Can I Say This at Church?*, Vinings Lake Church, *Parenting Forward*, *Theology Doesn't Suck*, *BadChristian*, *Changing Faith*, *Tamed Cynic*, *Christian Humanist*, *Thinking God*, *Enneagram Journey*, Center for Open and Relational Theology, *Patchwork Podcast*, *EcoCiv*, Living the Questions (DVD resources), FutureChurch, *Eternal Current*

AUTHORS

Here is a sampling (far from complete) of contemporary and recent authors who are helping people navigate toward faith after doubt in a broadly Christian context, presented in random order:

Diana Butler Bass, Doug Pagitt, Kathy Escobar, Rachel Held Evans, Fr. Richard Rohr, Sarah Bessey, Rob Bell, Phyllis Tickle, John Dominic Crossan, Ilia Delio, Paul Smith, Cynthia Bourgeault, Peter Rollins, Nadia Bolz-Weber, Michael Dowd, Barbara Brown Taylor, John Pavlovitz, Enuma Okoro, Thomas J. Oord, Cindy Wang Brandt, Thomas Merton, Walter Brueggemann, Howard Thurman, Marcus Borg, Kate Bowler, John Shelby Spong, Barbara Holmes, Robb Ryerse, Jacqui Lewis, Mark Karris, Jim Finley, Frank Schaeffer, Sr. Joan Chittister, Otis Moss III, Kaitlin Curtice, Philip Clayton, Sr. Simone Campbell, Carlos Rodriguez, Adam Hamilton, Wil Gafney, Frederick Buechner, Colby Martin, Aaron Niequist, Pete Enns, Mike McHargue, D. L. Mayfield, Gareth Higgins, Steve Chalke, Danielle Shroyer, Dave Tomlinson

Resources in Spanish

See *La Conversación en Curso* for great resources and links to other resources for Spanish speakers: https://laconversacionencurso.org/.

Events

A more thorough and more global list of events needs to be compiled to help people in search of faith after doubt. Thankfully, Compassionate Christianity.org is providing an up-to-date list of U.S. events on their website. Here are a few that are annual (usually) and easily searchable online: Wild Goose Festival, January Adventure, Evolving Faith, Conspire (Center for Action and Contemplation), Awakening Soul, Gladdening Light, Revolutionary Love, Progressive Youth Ministry, New Story Festival, Companions on the Inner Way, Greenbelt Festival (UK).

Four-Stage Congregations

Thankfully, there are more and more congregations that welcome and support people in the work of all four stages. Unfortunately, there is no single comprehensive list to help you find a four-stage faith community. But here are some practical suggestions:

1. This website helps people find just and generous Christian congregations: https://convergenceus.org/churches. For people from

Evangelical backgrounds, here is a helpful network: https:// withcollective.org/. Roman Catholics can find connections to forward-leaning Catholics through the Franciscan Action Network, https://franciscanaction.org/. You can find links to Jewish and Muslim faith communities here: http://www.jewishemergentnetwork .org/, and http://www.mpvusa.org/.

2. Often, trained spiritual directors can help you find a supportive faith community, so a first step might be to consult with a spiritual director: https://www.sdiworld.org/.

3. Often, congregations that have learned to welcome LGBTQ persons have done so by embracing faith after doubt. Here's a resource in this regard: http://www.welcomingresources.org/usa.htm.

4. Sometimes, doing an online search with a cross-reference can help. So you might search for the name of a favorite author or organization, your city or state, and *church*.

RECENT BOOKS FOR DOUBTERS

Any online search will generate a long list of books on faith and doubt, nearly all of which will be helpful in some way. But here are several of my favorites, along with descriptions of some of my own books that may be of additional interest.

Rachel Held Evans, *Searching for Sunday* (Nelson, 2015). All of Rachel's books come from a heart that doubt had broken open . . . open to mystery, open to wonder, open to human pain, open to the *other*. Her last book went deepest, both into doubt and into faith.

Sarah Bessey, *Out of Sorts* (Howard, 2015). Sarah's work, like Rachel's, rings especially true with people from conservative Christian backgrounds whose faith runs so deep that doubt is especially disruptive.

Kathy Escobar, *Faith Shift* (Convergent, 2014) and *Practicing* (Westminster John Knox, 2020). In the terms used in this book, *Faith Shift* is a perfect guide for people entering Stage Three, and *Practicing* is a guide out of Stage Three into Stage Four.

Kaitlin Curtice, *Native* (Brazos, 2020). Kaitlin's dual identity as a Christian and as a member of the Potawatomi tribe positions her to feel the social as well as the personal dimensions of doubt. She's a gifted writer who simultaneously brings comfort, challenge, and inspiration.

Colby Martin, *The Shift* (Fortress, 2020). This is one of the most practical and helpful short books to help people on their way out of conservative Christian faith and into a more progressive or expansive expression.

Mark Karris, *Religious Refugees* (Quoir, 2020). Mark brings theological, pastoral, and psychological training to his mission of helping people grapple with what he calls the D/R (deconstruction and reconstruction) journey. You'll feel his pastoral presence on every page.

Peter Enns, *The Sin of Certainty* (HarperOne, 2016). Voltaire is credited with saying, "Doubt may be uncomfortable, but certainty is ridiculous." This book, along with Peter's podcast, *The Bible for Normal People*, can be a lifeline for people who are seeking to survive in the discomfort of honest uncertainty.

Kate Bowler, *Everything Happens for a Reason: And Other Lies I've Loved* (Random House, 2018). Kate's personal encounter with cancer intersects with her scholarly research into a religious phenomenon called the Prosperity Gospel, and she models an honest faith in that crucible.

Frank Schaeffer, *Why I Am an Atheist Who Believes in God* (Frank Schaeffer, 2014), captures the agony and insight of a passionate human being seeking faith after doubt. Many of my generation will remember that Frank's father was a famous theologian, which adds intensity to Frank's own search to embody an honest faith of his own.

Among my own books, the *A New Kind of Christian* (Fortress, 2019) trilogy should be of special interest to readers of this book. *A New Kind of Christian* introduces the reader to a fictional character named Dan Poole, a pastor who is entering a period of doubt. *The Story We Find Ourselves In* continues the story and explores a fresh way of approaching the Bible. In *The Last Word and the Word After That,* Dan and his fellow characters grapple with the conventional doctrine of hell. My nonfiction counterpart to the trilogy, *A New Kind of Christianity* (HarperOne, 2010), explores ten questions that are at the core of many doubters' struggles with Christian faith.

Appendix V.
Spirituality Through the Stages

In my book *Naked Spirituality* (HarperOne, 2010), I share three postures of prayer or contemplation for each of the four stages. These one-word prayers suggest a general attitude of the heart, summarized as follows:

Simplicity

Here. By simply entering the moment, resting, and opening ourselves to God (the mystery beyond our understanding), we render ourselves receptive to the love, joy, peace, and wisdom that we need. We enter the present and open ourselves to the Presence that surrounds us and accompanies and inhabits us at our deepest core of being.

Thanks. By cultivating gratitude, we resist greed and become attentive to the blessings that already are with us. We realize that it is not having but appreciating that brings happiness. Rather than being defined and dominated by our complaints, we celebrate the blessings that are already ours, for free.

O! By holding our hearts open to wonder that is beyond words, we resist shrinking God to the size of human concepts and notions and experience humble reverence and worship in a spirit of awe and devotion.

Complexity

Sorry. As we face, name, and lament our failures, weaknesses, and wrongs, we train ourselves to see ourselves through God's eyes of truth, mercy, compassion, grace, forgiveness, and full acceptance. We come to accept our acceptance, just as we are, and we are set free from denial and self-defense.

Help! We face our limitations in strength, ability, understanding, and wisdom, and we open ourselves to resources beyond our current capacities. We translate our vague anxieties into specific needs and desires and we name and focus our desires in the presence of God.

Please! We take the sensitivity we have gained in facing our own failures, weaknesses, and limitations, and we extend this sensitivity to others, joining our compassion with God's compassion in holding the needs and pain of others and of the world.

PERPLEXITY

When? In times of uncertainty, grief, and fear, we acknowledge the pain we feel, and even as we hope for it to end, we recognize that there may be lessons, virtues, and capacities to gain while it persists. We pour out our emotions, simultaneously hoping for relief and preparing ourselves to endure.

No! We refuse to deny our pain, we refuse easy answers that seek to explain our pain away, and we refuse to give up on finding meaning in the madness. We assert our freedom to be angry, at God, with God, at our conceptions of God, at life, at others, at ourselves. And we refuse to let our anger consume us.

Why? Rather than give up all hope, we hold open the questions for which we can find no satisfying answer. We acknowledge our feelings of forsakenness and abandonment. By asking why, we don't demand an answer, but we refuse to foreclose upon a possible answer. We acknowledge our unknowing.

HARMONY

Behold. We see what is here, without judgment and without needing to explain or comprehend. Humbled and broken open by perplexity, we find ourselves able to see with a non-dual mind, beyond our old habits of assessing everything in terms of us/them, like/dislike, good/bad, convenient/inconvenient, and so on. In a sense, we seek to join God in seeing everything with eyes of maturing compassion and non-discriminatory love.

Yes. We consciously say *yes* to God and love. We yield ourselves to be instruments of love and peace.

(Silence). We discover that apart from all our words, we can simply be . . . with God, with ourselves, with our neighbors, and with all creation, in harmony, in love.

Appendix VI.
Guidelines for Groups and Classes

The simplest way to use this book in a group or class is to invite everyone to read a chapter (or a few chapters) with a pen or pencil in hand, underlining sentences and paragraphs that most strike them. (Most e-readers have underline functions too.) Then, participants come to the meeting with two or three passages to share. Each person reads their first passage and answers this question: *Why did you choose this passage and why is it meaningful to you?* Others can then ask clarifying questions within an agreed-upon time frame. After everyone has shared one passage, you can go around the circle a second and third time if time permits. Then, you may want to close your time together reading one of the benedictions in the Afterword.

This approach works best if you want to discuss the book in one to five sessions. Five sessions, for example, could be organized as follows:

Session 1: Get acquainted, set group guidelines, discuss Preface and Introduction
Session 2: Review group guidelines, discuss Part I
Session 3: Discuss Part II
Session 4: Discuss Part III
Session 5: Discuss Afterword and have a party

If possible, you'll get more out of this book if you discuss it chapter by chapter, using the *Reflection and Action* questions included in the book. This could naturally be done in thirteen to sixteen weeks, but it could be done in a shorter time frame as well if the group covers two to four chapters at each gathering. One person can be assigned to lead each chapter discussion, choosing only one or two of the questions for the sake of time.

It makes sense to set ground rules for your group. Here are some you can use, adapt, and add to:

1. Come prepared. If you aren't prepared, still come, but please tell your conversation partners at the beginning of the meeting so you don't feel pressure to pretend.
2. Assign a timekeeper. Decide, for example, to give each person three to five minutes to speak without interruption. That gives everyone a chance to speak. Allow people to pass if they would rather not speak.
3. Participate, but don't dominate. In general, don't speak twice until you have invited quieter members to speak once, and if you're normally quiet, encourage yourself to open up.
4. Be curious, but don't engage in cross-talk. Ask questions of one another to gain greater understanding, but don't correct, disagree, fix, diagnose, teach, and so on.
5. Be grateful and respect confidentiality. Thank people for courage and vulnerability. Thank people for honesty. Thank people for showing up. And respect their privacy by sharing information only with permission.

You may also find the Six Commitments of Common Good Communication to be helpful as group guidelines. They're based on these values: example, curiosity, clarity, decency, fairness, and persistence. Details are here: https://www.votecommongood.com/the-six-commitments-of-common-good-communication/.

If your group is enjoying the study and wants to "go public," you can share photographs and insights from your group on social media, using the hashtag #faithafterdoubt and @brianmclaren. By doing so, you let your example invite others into meaningful conversations of their own.

Turn the page for a sneak peek at
Brian D. McLaren's new book

Do I Stay Christian?

A GUIDE FOR THE DOUBTERS, THE DISAPPOINTED, AND THE DISILLUSIONED

BRIAN D. McLAREN

Author of *Faith After Doubt*

Available Spring 2022

❧

CHAPTER 14

BECAUSE IT WOULD BE A SHAME TO LEAVE A RELIGION IN ITS INFANCY

The form of Christianity that has any chance of retaining my commitment is not a regressive Christianity, rushing headlong into the sixteenth or nineteenth century. Nor is it a conservative Christianity, change resistant and defensive. It is rather an *anticipatory Christianity*, leaning into the future. Echoing Paul's radical aspiration (Philippians 3:7 ff.), we count everything we have already attained as loss. We write it off. We leave it behind. We forget about it. (I would hesitate to put it this bluntly if Paul didn't use this same stark language himself.) Then, we strain forward to what lies ahead, pressing on toward the goal, responding to the call to love, justice, joy, and peace, as taught by and embodied in Jesus.

Ilia Delio, a brilliant Franciscan nun and scholar, speaks powerfully of anticipatory Christian faith. The Christianity we have known until now emerged in what has been called the first axial period, a time of great intellectual foment that began around 800 BCE and continued until about 200 BCE. In the first axial age, our species had a kind of internal, individual subjective awakening. As individual thinkers, we began to take both our individual inner life and also a shared understanding of the cosmos more seriously. We wouldn't be where we are if not for the first axial age. But now, like people halfway through a doorway, we are moving beyond it. We are entering a second axial age.

Unlike residents of the first axial age who woke up each day as independent individuals in a fixed and static cosmos, more and more of us today have moved into a new conceptual cosmos. We wake up in an ongoing cosmic story of interdependence and constant dynamic change. Delio explains:

> This new universe story is *radically new* compared to the cosmos of the axial period because our universe is dynamic and unfinished. Since the axial religions, including Christianity and Judaism, emerged in a fixed static cosmos, our new cosmology invites a new story of religion. This new story of religion demands a new theological method . . . one based . . . on anticipation of the future. The cosmic narrative is still unfolding and thus the story is not yet complete. In this respect, we live in an anticipatory universe . . . which means the future is our truest and deepest reality.

The first axial age had remarkable staying power. But step-by-step over the last few centuries, data accumulated like snow on a winter roof. Our fixed and static cosmos collapsed under its weight. When spring came, builders of a new paradigm worked in the ruins to create a new vision of the cosmos. Thanks to innovators like Sir Isaac Newton in physics and James Hutton in geology, thanks to Charles Darwin in biology and Einstein and Hubble in quantum physics and astrophysics, thanks to Adam Smith and Karl Marx in economics, thanks to Sigmund Freud and Jean Piaget in psychiatry, thanks to Alfred North Whitehead and Isabelle Stengers in philosophy, thanks to Ken Wilber and Thomas Berry and Michael Dowd in macrohistory, along with many, many others, we have been thrust into a new universe where everything is in motion.[1]

Subatomic particles and waves spin in indeterminacy. Stars and their planets come and go. Continents shift, rise, and fall, as do oceans. Species are not fixed but in the making, some diminishing toward extinction, others emerging to thrive in new forms. And religions are part of this dynamic process, too, as theologians like Monica Coleman, Barbara Holmes, Wil Gafney, Sally McFague, John Cobb, Rosemary Radford Ruether, Tim Burnette, Tripp Fuller, Philip Clayton, Rosemary Hewitt Suchocki, Thomas Oord, and many others affirm.

As a result, most of us woke up this morning in a universe that was

---

1. White men dominated in the modern period. You'll notice more diversity in the list of postmodern leaders at the end of this paragraph.

not at its best at the beginning. Nor is it at its best now. It is en route, becoming, in process, always presented with the possibility of evolving into something more beautiful, diverse, alive, and conscious—or stagnating and decaying toward extinction. We do not know what the universe can become, given enough time and enough opportunity, aided by our own faith, hope, courage, and love.

If the Christian faith is to have a creative and constructive future, it will have to undergo its own metamorphosis from a first to a second axial age religion, from a regressive/conservative religion to a progressive/anticipatory one. Like conscious caterpillars in a cocoon, we must imagine life with wings. We must inhabit and tell a new cosmic story.

Here's one attempt: Our adventure begins some 13.7 billion years ago with an expansion, blast, or silent bang of unimaginably hot matter/energy and space/time. From that genesis moment, what we call the universe begins to unfold in all directions and dimensions, known and unknown. As this expanse slows and cools, simple atoms form and converge, creating the components of the first generation of stars. Those original stars burn and burn until they burn themselves out, collapsing in on themselves. Then they explode as supernovas, their unimaginable heat fusing simple atoms into more complex atoms that form new generations of stars and planets, resulting in the physical universe we know today.

About 4.5 billion years ago, around one of those stars, space dust and debris congeal into our little planet. Roughly half a billion years later, some complex chemicals come together and develop the ability to take in energy, first from other chemicals and later from sunlight. Stage by stage, these complex chemicals come together as single-cell life forms. Starting about 3.4 billion years ago, some of these simple life forms start producing oxygen as a byproduct of their existence, and with more oxygen, the planet slowly becomes more hospitable to more kinds of organisms.

Eventually, some of these simple one-celled organisms begin living together cooperatively and reproducing, gradually becoming more complex organisms with diversified parts working together. By 1.2 billion years ago, some of these organisms are identifiable as primitive plants. About 800 million years ago, early sponges become the first examples of what we would call animals. Over the next 250 million years, both plants and animals further diversify.

Then, around 540 million years ago, conditions suddenly change (for reasons we do not yet understand). These changes wipe out many of the first generation of living things. But in the aftermath of this extinction event, a wide array of new organisms develop in what we call the Cambrian Explosion. Over the next 65 million years or so, life diversifies and expands at an unprecedented rate, with sea worms burrowing in the ocean floor, armored trilobites moving across the sand and silt, and primitive arthropods and even finless, jawless fish swimming through the water above them.

As life teems in the oceans, some plants develop the ability to survive on land, first mosses, then ferns, then more complex plants. Meanwhile, as bony fishes develop and diversify, some develop the ability to breathe air through primitive lungs, and soon, amphibians begin living at least part of their lives on land. From there, terrestrial reptiles develop, so that by 300 million years ago, reptiles are spreading across the continents. More extinction events occur around 250 million years ago, leading to the age of the dinosaurs. As the dinosaurs diversify and spread around the earth, birds and mammals also develop.

Yet another mass extinction event occurs around 60 million years ago, wiping out the dinosaurs and leaving mammals and birds space to diversify and expand. Among the evolving mammals, primates evolve, and among the primates, the first hominins emerge about 2.5 million years ago. They soon develop the ability to craft and use tools. Several hominin species diversify—including lineages known to us as *Ardipithecus, Australopithecus,* and *Homo.* Among our genus, *Homo habilis, Homo erectus, Homo neanderthalis,* and others develop as distinct species.

Then, about 200,000 years ago, a scrappy new species emerges in Africa. Around 150,000 years ago, they develop language. These talking hominins, known to us as *Homo sapiens,* spread north through Europe and Asia, gradually displacing or assimilating the other remaining hominins. Between 33,000 and 13,000 years ago, modern humans reach the Americas, completing their planetary dispersion. Only about 5,500 years ago, humans invent writing, making it possible for you to read (or hear) these words I am now arranging.

Obviously, I've constructed this brief history from available data, and as more data emerges, this overview will be improved upon. But whatever the details, in this universe, three things are abundantly clear: first, the earliest form of something is not its pure or original or best or permanent or ideal form. In fact, there really is no pure, original, best, or ideal form. Every form is in process, adapting, evolving, mutating, changing.

Second, over time, the universe becomes more complex, more diverse, more alive, more interdependent, more conscious, and, we might say, more beautiful and good. From simple physics to complex physics, we advance to simple and more complex life, and from more complex life we advance to simple and more complex consciousness. And in the context of whatever degree of complex consciousness we currently possess, more beauty and moral goodness continue to emerge and mature, along with more curiosity to know and articulate what is true . . . and more imagination to envision and create what could be true in the future.

And third, extinction happens on the path of evolution. When conditions change, life forms must either evolve to cope with them or go extinct. When some life forms prove incapable of adaptation, new life forms evolve to fill their niches. That means that no species, including our own, is absolute, invincible, supreme, or ultimate.

So, this is the evolving universe in which I wake up every morning, and when I look to the future, I see two abiding options: evolution and extinction.

But again, as I noted in Chapter 7, Christianity in all its conventional, first-axial-age forms does not allow me to live in this universe, because the first axial age constricted it within a change-averse set of boundary conditions. Since the original form was the highest and best form, diversity is rebellion from that original expression. Creative or progressive change is heresy, apostasy, or corruption. Since a first-axial-age God created and rules this first-axial-age universe, any who dare to evolve and diversify face damnation.

I ask myself: how can a universe like this be anything but regressive and authoritarian? If patriarchy was the earliest form of life we can remember, then patriarchy must be the highest and best form of human society. It is the job of authority figures to clamp down on diversity and change as a threat to their very way of life. Their determination to remain in control is backed by a cosmic Supreme Patriarch behind or above human patriarchy. The Supreme Patriarch will punish all who evolve and reward all who resist change.

Building on the work of Teilhard de Chardin, Karl Jaspers, Ewert Cousins, and many others, Sr. Ilia Delio's diagnosis is helping many of us understand why we are so frustrated with Christianity as it currently stands. Peppier music isn't enough to fix a religion anchored in the first axial age, especially when the only future hope it offers means complete destruction of the existing universe so we can be evacuated to a new heavenly creation where everything is forever and finally fixed (in multiple senses of that word).

It's not that you and I are rebellious infidels who *won't* accept first-axial-age Christianity as it is; rather, we are honest human beings who *can't*. The best we can do is *pretend* to accept it, but that kind of pretense corrupts our conscience and turns good faith into bad faith.

So, where does that leave us? Clearly: the jig is up. Christianity's days are numbered. A growing proportion of smart and honest Christians of each new generation will abandon the sinking ship, just as they have been doing for centuries in Europe and decades in the United States. In the not too distant future, Christianity will only exist in those enclaves where authoritarian leaders rule over submissive flocks who enfold their religious lives within the assumptions of the first axial age.

Or is it that simple? If we are right, if the universe is actually evolving in a very different story, and if, on our planet at least, human consciousness is still in its early infancy, then wouldn't that mean that Christianity is also in its infancy, and it has another possible option alongside extinction, namely evolution?

And wouldn't an evolving Christianity have an option beyond being forever ruled by authoritarian patriarchs who demand adherence to an outdated conceptual universe? Wouldn't our very understandings of evolution and extinction mean that those gatekeepers and company men who have the futile mission of keeping change at bay are actually one asteroid or climate catastrophe away from an extinction event? Rather than being the faithful stand-ins for our radical founder, might they be blind guides (lacking foresight, however well-meaning) who are leading Christianity toward a ditch of extinction?

And if that's true, might we, far from being disloyal heretics, actually have the opportunity to become the evolutionary descendants of Jesus who are called to carry on his radically progressive vision in our brief time on this earth?

In framing our situation this way, I'm not suggesting that these conservative gatekeepers need to be vilified and scapegoated. They are part of the story, too, doing the best they can, and most of them sincerely believe in what they're doing. Of course, it would be nearly impossible for people in the first axial age to immediately accept the radical insights of a visionary leader like Jesus. Of course, there would be two steps back after every three steps forward. Of course, there would be evolutionary dead ends before some part of the spiritual gene pool would find a way forward. Of course, old paradigms would need to be preserved until the new paradigms evolved sufficiently to be worthy of trust. And of course, even in their misguided resistance to change, conservative leaders would be preserving some treasures that deserved to be preserved.

This way of thinking allows me to view the authoritarian gatekeepers and religious company men with compassion and empathy. Each in their own way, they all have a part in the story, but nobody has the last word. I must see myself and my colleagues in the same way, with humility, because unless we proceed wisely, our branch on the evolutionary tree of life will also be short. There is more than one way to go extinct.

We are not defined exclusively by whom we came from in the past. We can also be defined by what we can become in the future. This is an anticipatory Christianity, and it changes everything, as Sr. Ilia Delio concludes:

> If we take the future as our starting point for thinking about God, creation, and humanity—then *everything* we know must . . . be realigned to an evolving universe, including our theologies, philosophies, economic and political systems, cultural matrices—in short, our planetary life.

In this light, Christianity looks very different to me. Instead of an old, mature, fully formed, maybe even worn-out religion, I see it as a religion still in its earliest infancy. And that raises a new question for me: If I leave the Christian community and conversation, will I be abandoning an infant, speaking in terms of deep evolutionary time?

I remind myself: The universe isn't in a hurry by human standards. It has been unfolding and expanding, diversifying and beautifying in its current form for 13.7 billion years. I remind myself: If we compressed the universe's whole existence into one year, our planet doesn't even form until September 11.[2] The first forms of life don't emerge on Earth until around September 30, but no multicellular organisms evolve until December 14. The dinosaurs rule the earth from December 27 to 30, and the first humans don't appear until December 31 at 11:39 p.m. Jesus comes on the scene at 11:59:56, which means that all of Christianity has existed for a mere four seconds. Four seconds!

Or to frame it differently, if we say that modern humans have been around for 200,000 years, Christianity has been around for 1 percent of our species' history. Yes, for better and for worse (as we've seen), the religion made a big splash in a relatively short time. But imagine two scenarios. First, imagine that human civilization, led by its largest living religion, destroys itself in the next century or two. Wouldn't you have to be suspicious, at least, that a species that survived for 198,000 years without Christianity could only last 2,000 years with it? That's not a great reflection on Christianity!

But conversely, imagine that somehow, we reverse our accelerating slide into catastrophic climate change and environmental overshoot. Then imagine that we reverse the accelerating concentration of money, power, and weapons in a tiny group of hyper-elite oligarchs. And then imagine that we manage to keep those superrich oligarchs from using their growing cache of weapons to plunge us into a mushroom cloud of mutually assured destruction. In that light, imagine that the human race lives for another 200,000 years.

Looking back from that vantage point in the 2020s, the first 2,000 years of Christian history will be to our descendants only 1 percent of Christian history, proportional to what the first twenty years of Christianity are to us. If you're familiar with Christian history, you already know that we know next to nothing about those first twenty years after

2. For more on this overview, see *The Cosmic Timeline*, available here: http://visav.phys.uvic.ca/~babul/AstroCourses/P303/BB-slide.htm.

Jesus' crucifixion, except this: It was very unlike what we call Christianity today. There were no churches, no denominations or celibate clergy (and really, no clergy at all as we know it), no formal creeds or systematic theologies, no organs or Sunday school programs, no annual celebration of Christmas or Easter. It was a twenty-year-old movement, younger to me as I write than the Civil Rights movement and the environmental movement, just twice as old as the Black Lives Matter movement, and a bit older than the #MeToo movement.

So I ask myself again: Why should I leave a religion in its infancy? Wouldn't that be like giving up on a baby because after ten months, she still can't walk, talk in complete sentences, read, do basic algebra, or even poop in the potty?

Wouldn't I be wiser to redouble my efforts to help this fledgling religion learn to walk, stop biting its playmates, and feed itself?

Perhaps, then, we should see this tantrum-prone baby's current regressive behavior and temper tantrums as signs of developmental frustration. Perhaps our terrible two-year-old religion is on the verge of a breakthrough.

That's what Sr. Ilia Delio dares us to believe, and I stand with her. She concludes her majestic book *Making All Things New* by offering us six challenges to seize this opportunity. We must *know the earth and our own bodies,* because we have become so obsessed with concepts that we have lost touch with our creatureliness. Second, we need to *see our world religions as sources of energy* that can mature and guide us forward. Third, we need to *understand that thought is a physical reality*: it exists as an emergent phenomenon in brains and can be replicated in other brains, and like any other evolving expression of life, it can lead us forward. Fourth, we need to fully *embrace the idea that something big and beautiful and alive is evolving in the universe,* something that includes individual humans but is bigger than the sum of its parts. Fifth, to thrive in this dynamic universe, we need to *cultivate a zest for living and a spirit of adventure,* to "wildly fling ourselves into the arms of divine Love." And finally, we need to *dare to trust in the process,* the process of evolving life, the process of birth and growth of which we are a small part.[3] Doing so will help us become

---

3. *Making All Things New: Catholicity, Cosmology, Consciousness* (Orbis, 2015), pp. 197–200.

"artisans of a new future," a "new catholicity," and a "new religion of the world," grasping this moment as "the kiss of God."

If we see our situation in this light, doesn't the earth need at least a few people like you and me to stay Christian—especially in this pregnant, anticipatory moment?

Hannah Davis

A former college English teacher, BRIAN D. McLAREN was a pastor for twenty-four years. Now, he's an author, activist, public theologian, and frequent guest lecturer for gatherings in the U.S. and internationally. His work has been covered in *Time, Newsweek, USA Today, The New York Times, The Washington Post*, CNN, and many other media outlets. The author of more than fifteen books, including *Do I Stay Christian?* and *A New Kind of Christian*, he is a faculty member of the Living School at the Center for Action and Contemplation. McLaren lives in Florida.